Managing Special and Inclusive Education

BELMAS

British Educational Leadership, Management & Administration Society

Published in Association with the British Educational Leadership, Management and Administration Society. This series of books published for BELMAS aims to be directly relevant to the concerns and professional development needs of emergent leaders and experienced leaders in schools.

Titles include:

How Very Effective Primary Schools Work (2006)
By Chris James, Michael Connolly and Gerald Dunning

Educational Leadership: Personal Growth for Professional Development (2004)
By Harry Tomlinson

Developing Educational Leadership: Using Evidence for Policy and Practice (2003)

By Lesley Anderson and Nigel Bennett

Performance Management in Education: Improving Practice (2002)
By Jenny Reeves, Pauline Smith, Harry Tomlinson and Christine Ford

Strategic Management for School Development: Leading Your School's Improvement Strategy (2002)
By Brian Fidler

Subject Leadership and School Improvement (2000)
By Hugh Busher and Alma Harris with Christine Wise

Managing Special and Inclusive Education

Steve Rayner

SAGE Publications
Los Angeles ▪ London ▪ New Delhi ▪ Singapore

SAGE Publications Ltd
1 Oliver's Yard
55 City Road
London EC1Y 1SP

SAGE Publications Inc.
2455 Teller Road
Thousand Oaks, California 91320

SAGE Publications India Pvt Ltd
B 1/I 1 Mohan Cooperative Industrial Area
Mathura Road, New Delhi 110 044
India

SAGE Publications Asia-Pacific Pte Ltd
33 Pekin Street #02-01
Far East Square
Singapore 048763

Library of Congress Control Number: 2007924714

British Library Cataloguing in Publication data

A catalogue record for this book is available from the British Library

ISBN 978-1-4129-1888-6
ISBN 978-1-4129-1889-3 (pbk)

Typeset by C&M Digitals (P) Ltd, Chennai, India
Printed in Great Britain by T.J. International, Padstow, Cornwall
Printed on paper from sustainable resources

Contents

About the author

Steve Rayner (PhD) is Director of Postgraduate Research Degree Studies in the School of Education at the University of Birmingham, UK. Research interests include the study of individual differences in learning, pedagogy and special educational management. He has more than 70 publications across this field, including key texts such as Riding and Rayner (1998) *Cognitive Styles and Learning Strategies,* and Rayner and Ribbins (1999) *Headteachers and Leadership in Special Education.*

Glossary

ADD – Attention Deficit Disorder
ADHD – Attention Deficit Hyperactivity Disorder
AERA – American Education Research Association
ASD – Austistic Spectrum Disorder
AST – Advanced Skills Teacher
BELMAS – British Educational Leadership, Management and Administration Society
BERA – British Education Research Association
BSP – Behaviour Support Plan
CA – Change Agent
CMT – Change Management Team
CPD – Continuing Professional Development
CAF – Common Assessment Framework
CAMHS – Child and Adolescent Mental Health Services
BEST – Behaviour and Education Support Team
CSIE – Centre for the Study of Inclusive Education
DES – Department of Education and Science
DfE – Department for Education
DfEE - Department of Education Employment
DfES – Department of Education and Skills
DH – Department of Health
EBD – Emotional Behavioural and Disorders/Difficulties
EBSD – Emotional, Behavioural and Social Difficulties
ECM – Every Child Matters
EP – Educational Psychologist
EFA - Education for All
ESRA – Extended Schools Remodelling Adviser
ERA – Education Reform Act
ESL – English as a Second Language
EWO – Education Welfare Officer
FAS – Funding Agency for Schools
FINE – For Inclusion North East (SEN Regional Partnership – North East England)
HLTA – Higher Level Teaching Assistant
HMI – Her Majesty's Inspector (Schools Inspectorate)
HOC – House of Commons

ICT – Information Communication Technology
IEP – Individual Education Plan
IQEA – Improving Quality of Education for All
ITE – Initial Teacher Education
LA – Local Authority
LEA – Local Education Authority
LSA – Learning Support Assistant
MI – Multiple Intelligences
MISE – Managing Inclusion and Special Education
MDA – Multi Disciplinary Assessment
MLD – Moderate Learning Difficulties
NAHT – National Association of Headteachers
NASEN – National Association of Special Education Needs
NCIE – National Center of Inclusion and Education
NCSL – National College of School Leadership
NGA – National Governors Association
NSPCC – National Society for the Protection of Children against Cruelty
NUT – National Union of Teachers
OECD – Organization for Economic Co-operation and Development
Ofsted – Office for Standards in Education
PAT – Pupil Achievement Tracker
PPA – Planning, Preparation and Assessment
PMLD – Profound and Multiple Learning Difficulties
PSE – Personal and Social Education
PSLD – Profound and Severe Learning Difficulties
QA – Quality Assurance
SAI – Schools Access Initiative
SEF – School Evaluation Form
SEN – Special Educational Needs
SENCo – Special Educational Needs Co-ordinator
SENDA – Special Educational Needs Disability Act (2001)
SIP – School Inspection Partner
SLD – Severe Learning Difficulties
SMT - Senior Management Team
SW – Social Worker
SSD – Social Services Department
SSE – School Self-Evaluation
TA – Teaching Assistant
TDA – Teaching and Development Agency for Schools
TQM – Total Quality Management
UNICEF – United Nations International Children's Education Fund
UNESCO – United Nations Educational, Scientific and Cultural Organization
VfM – Value for Money

Acknowledgements

I want to thank Eileen for her patience, understanding and support during the writing of this book. I am also grateful to Michael, James and Helen for critical friendship and proof reading.

A note of thanks should also go to countless colleagues, but especially Helen Gunter and Steve Armstrong, who have each in their own way influenced so much of my thinking over the past few years. The responsibility for the perspective in this book, however, is entirely mine.

A final word of thanks should go to Kevin Rowland, Dave Traxson, Ann Scarsdale and many other colleagues for their work in partnership running the Birmingham University MISE Course (2000–2005). Its demise is yet further evidence that we are now moving beyond the 'special or inclusion' debate toward a new era of a personalized and integrative provision for SEN policy.

Steve Rayner

Foreword

The topic of this book is the management of special and inclusive education. It is written for all those who are interested in leadership and the management of personal diversity in education.

To be effective, a manager requires an understanding of context, a clarity of purpose and an appropriate application of knowledge. Educational leadership requires an integrative aspect that by default involves the management of change, learning and growth. Managing inclusive or special education is further complicated by an evolving definition and understanding of special educational needs (SEN), as well as an awareness of the contested debate surrounding a system of special or inclusive education. Understanding and developing educational leadership or management is also in itself far from straightforward. It is, however, an even more complex subject when reapplied to the SEN context.

The prospect of writing this book has therefore been both a daunting challenge and an almost impossible task. By definition, inclusive education seems quite literally all embracing and at many levels of policy statement, simply a call for humanity in sound educational provision. In an ideal world very few would defend discrimination, exclusion, alienation or restrictive practice based upon individual differences. In education, the irony of such practices existing in deeply embedded social and professional cultures, and reflected in personal attitudes or educational systems, is profound. The irony deepens, if we accept that educationists are motivated by a desire to make a difference, help pupils grow, succeed, or develop and most of all learn.

The school workforce, similarly, is by and large engaged in and motivated to making this *educative process* happen. To be concerned with inclusive and special education, therefore, is to continuously work with the fundamental issues surrounding the management of learning and teaching, and the core purposes of schooling (Ainscow, 1991; Croll and Moses, 1998; Rosenholtz, 1989). It is a deep-seated concern for the learning needs of every child that drives an endeavour to 'seek to leave no child behind'. In the English educational context, this core professionalism reflects many of the ideas underpinning the agenda of *Every Child Matters* (DfES, 2003d) and the future of an inclusive and special education.

THE BOOK

The book is organized into three major parts with three chapters in each and a conclusion in the final section. While the immediate focus is education in the

UK, much of the content will contain ideas and argument relevant to the international setting. Case examples of policy management and special educational provision are drawn from international contexts as well as the UK.

Part I is a critical review of SEN policy and the present inclusion imperative with its implications for an evolving model of strategic leadership, planning and provision. The book, finally, offers a re-casting of theory to present the notion of *inclusive leadership* fuelling an approach and operation of a model for managing special and inclusive education (MISE). The MISE model is deliberately used as a conceptual framework for the structure of this book.

Part II is an exploration of managing inclusive education and SEN provision in the educational organization and the wider setting of a local community. The focal point for this discussion is knowledge associated with an inclusive form of leadership, implementing change management, workforce remodelling and integrating policy in provision. It offers a way forward for managing the *Every Child Matters* policy agenda in the UK which is reflected in similar initiatives in other countries (for example, *No Child Left Behind* in the USA).

Part III is a discussion of how to approach managing SEN provision, inclusive learning and teaching in institutional contexts. The focal point for this discussion is professional learning and leadership knowledge applied to the practice of managing educational inclusion. This will include a consideration of learning, teaching, behaviour management, pedagogy and the curriculum. It examines the ideas behind personalized education and the tensions inherent in managing diversity and differences in the school community.

CONTINUING PROFESSIONAL DEVELOPMENT MATERIAL

At the beginning of each chapter is a summary outline of its contents. This generally includes a brief thematic précis of content and a set of key concepts or implications for leadership and management. The reader, depending upon their own motivation and purposes, may well wish to look at this before deciding what parts of the book should be first read.

At the beginning of each part of the book is a brief discussion of key themes found within that section and a set of materials (for presentation/ workshops) devoted to developing an agenda for MISE in the institutional context. This is offered as (CPD) Continuing Professional Development material, the powerpoint material can be downloaded from: http://www. sagepub.co.uk/steverayner. It may be photocopied and is intended as a prompt for planning and organizing work. The conceptual framework used in this material is one of inclusive leadership and an integrative management of SEN policy. The material is structured in the form of a presentation or handouts, intended for individual or group activity, or workforce teams focusing upon leadership, management and SEN/inclusion policy planning and development.

Series Editor's Preface

For ten years BELMAS has been collaborating with Sage Publications to produce new books in educational leadership and management that are both informed by innovative, recent research, and inspired by a profoundly critical understanding and commitment to best practice. Hugh Busher and the late Harry Tomlinson have been distinguished Series Editors during that period and have produced and helped others to contribute to a series of books that inspire teachers and all engaged in educational work to identify the best that can be achieved in a particular field – as a basis for developing their own work in support of learners. Readers of the series owe each of them a debt, though it must be recorded with great regret that Harry Tomlinson died in 2005, before this latest new work could appear. Hugh Busher recently resigned as editor and so, as Publications Coordinator for BELMAS, I find myself with the privilege of introducing this latest addition to the series.

I have been very fortunate – as any reader of this new book will soon discover. Steve Rayner is surely right to identify his topic as a 'complex' and 'daunting' task – that of enabling readers to understand, apply and develop leadership and management in the context of making the 'educative process' happen for children and young people, in all their limitless diversity. This important new contribution to the field of inclusive and special education will not only benefit practitioners, but should also be read carefully by providers and policy makers in the recently enlarged arena of Children's Services. The author summarises the most significant antecedents to current provision, and exposes often irresolvable conflicts and dilemmas which persist in their train. In mapping the links between managing and learning, he challenges and sets out an alternative to the influential, often taken to be inevitable, implications of working with learners in a managerialist culture that mistakes conviction for justification, expediency for reason and justice, and too often advocates narrowly instrumental strategies based on 'short-term utility and kite-marking'.

Steve Rayner never loses sight of the need for deep commitment to 'making something worthwhile happen' in the lives of learners, which he proposes as the overriding purpose of educational leadership and management. His conception of how such an aspiration can be achieved for those young people whose diverse particularities are too often unrecognized or overlooked, is indeed complex. Drawing upon Aristotelian constructs of knowledge and ethics, he provides a key-stone foundation for re-constructing and utilizing *praxis* as a way of making the 'learning community' part of the 'learning leadership' endeavour. His central model, successfully tested and applied over five years in the West Midlands, becomes operational through realizing the full implications of what it is to learn and work in a 'learning community'. Practitioners are shown how clarifying intentions and identifying tasks can be carried out systematically, within a multi-disciplinary setting, through an integrated and reflective process of learning and managing, in which meaning and purpose are never allowed to drift apart. The educational goal here is termed 'transformative learning', a practice emphatically distinguished from the rhetorical flourish known as transformational leadership.

This book is richly imbued with insight and knowledge, and organized so that it can readily be used as CPD material. It is warmly recommended – a valuable addition to the literature and a welcome and overdue enlargement of the series' professional and educational range.

Michael Strain

Introduction

The content of this book draws upon the fields of educational management and leadership, special educational needs and educational inclusion. It blends this theory with material from work in research and continuing professional development for school leadership and SEN education. Such an approach requires a re-appraisal of developments in the field of educational policy, management and leadership. Emphasis, most recently, has focused principally upon leadership and the management of change as the pre-requisite qualities in organizational effectiveness both in the public services and the educational system. A popular distinction, for example, is to separate leadership from management as a distinct and independent function or role-activity. Leaders may or may not be formally accredited as a manager or occupy a position of authority in an institution. I agree on the one hand with Bush and Bell (2002: 4), when they write that:

> Assuming a difference between leadership and management is dangerous … because it can lead to allegations of 'managerialism', an emphasis upon implementation or the technical aspects of management with little regard for the values and purposes of education.

Furthermore, an artificial separation of the roles, actions and practices associated with strategic and operational aspects of leading professional practitioners or managing provision is simply unhelpful. I agree with Glatter, who concludes:

> Erecting this kind of dichotomy between something 'pure' called 'leadership' and something 'dirty' called 'management', or between values and purposes on the one hand and methods and skills on the other, would be disastrous. (Glatter, 1997: 189)

The idea of leaders exercising good management is tied to managers presenting effective leadership. I suggest any reader of this book who is working in education is by definition and necessity a leader and is managing some aspect of professional provision. The nature of this leadership is largely determined by a specific context. The role will change, maybe formal, informal, recognized, rewarded or simply taken for granted.

The approach proposed in this book is one that presumes a practitioner immersed in learning who should contribute to shaping their own professional development. I hope this will encourage the reader as a potential or practising leader to reflect on their own place and time, as well as involvement with policy, to work with practice, and seek to improve provision. I want this book to encourage leaders to think about their work and I invite the reader to engage with theory and generate new ideas and knowledge that will in turn inform how to work with children, young people and adults, thereby providing and strengthening the opportunity to learn. In Aristotelian terms, this is how the idea (*eidos*) shapes the learner's action (*phronesis*) to produce practical wisdom (*telos*). The formation and product of this synthesis of professional learning and knowledge is *praxis*. As Bernstein argued, in *praxis* there can be no prior knowledge of the right means by which we realize the end in a particular situation as this is only finally specified in deliberating about the means appropriate to a particular situation (Bernstein, 1983: 147). As we think about what we want to achieve, we alter the way we might achieve it. There is a continual interplay between ends and means, between thought and action. There is no easy solution or template even if one is claimed, and then conveniently called best practice. While we can and should avoid 're-creating the wheel', and learning from other practice is extremely useful, we cannot avoid the necessary work of making 'the wheel run for us'.

In doing this work, a learning process can be construed as producing new knowledge as well as contributing to a personal *praxis* forming part of an individual's educational professionality. I recall a powerful example by way of illustration. I was fortunate to witness the exchange and interpretation of ideas and knowledge unfolding in the work of a Comenius 3 EU Research Project (1999–2003) involving collaborative team work between three different, national partners (Italy, England, Sweden). The project generated new and interesting knowledge comprising a shared if sometimes uneasy agreement to a set of values and structures and applied commitment to an inclusive leadership ideal (Lucietto, 2003). My expectation, therefore, is to replicate this kind of approach. For the professional managing SEN provision, this *praxis* is as much about pedagogy as it is policy, and it is as much about individual differences as it is social justice. Beyond this, the same practitioner must remain equally concerned for efficiency and efficacy in developing what Aristotle called the work of the artisan (*techne*). Importantly, however, they will always remain exercised by a concern for equity in social provision and empathy for the individual. This concern is to be focused upon what is right and the development of *phronesis*.

A learning community

The term 'learning community' is used in this book. It is also a term now widely used in education and as is often the case has come to mean different things to different people. The term as used in this book is understood to describe an educational organization that is characterized by the following principles:

- Learning is positioned as a core activity. This means seeing the workforce, pupils, parents and other members of the wider community involved in school work as life-long learners creating, sharing and using knowledge.

- A corporate mind-set that formally values critical reflection and organizational reflexiveness as principles in a collective notion of a learning organization engaged in knowledge production (Senge, 1993).

- A construction of strategic management that reflects an emphasis upon learning with a readiness to continuously invest resources in a cycle of problem posing, decision making, problem solving, and decision-taking activity (see MISE model, Level 5, Chapter 3).

The learning community can be developed in a school or service in such a way that it is recognized as possessing the following features:

- Stakeholder representatives in the wider community are actively engaged in the work of learning (this involves professionals, parents, pupils and other members of the wider community who can contribute to the educational purpose of the organization).

- The structured learning activities of the learning community deliberately and actively engage a full diversity of stakeholders in participation and access to the institution (curriculum, management, governance, social life).

- An inclusive ethos is cultivated that positions the learning community as a hub for a distributed engagement in education for citizenship and political literacy.

Finally, a school functioning as a learning community will aim as an organization to nurture a life-long commitment to learning in its members as well as a shared notion of human dignity, social identity and a positive sense of self. Members of the education workforce, including the student body, need to share in the opportunity to lead and contribute to the educational community. Managing inclusion and special education is in large measure an exercise in enabling and contributing to this opportunity. It is this aspiration we should not forget as practitioners in the day-to-day churn of pressure and problems, success and failures, or intention and outcome, as we tackle the task of preparing our children as learning citizens for the so-called knowledge society. In such a world, however, people should matter, will be different and will always have their part to play. To aspire to building such a community in and beyond the school setting may mean bringing a new and positive meaning to being special and a genuine sense of belonging to the community. For those students marked by their differences, which in the past have too easily resulted in stigma and separation as they are pushed or simply drift to the margins of provision, access and support for learning are imperatives.

Implicit in this work, however, remains the need to integrate and function. It is a tough call. Education, special education, and inclusion will invariably entail uncertainty and complexity, as context, contest and circumstances present dilemma and contradiction. This will dictate hard decisions and necessary actions as part of every day life. As the manager of an SEN unit in a comprehensive school once quipped as we chatted,

> Special education is a ceaseless compromise in an attempt to resolve the dilemma of infinite need and finite resource. There is never an end in sight.

Learning to manage is completely embedded in the content and process of managing to learn and is in itself a career-long journey. It is easy to forget this as demands for instant success litter the pathway. It is human – but also a necessary aspect of the process of learning – to experience difficulty and such challenges need to be framed in a way wherby we understand that to fail is in part to learn rather than to err.

Beyond transformational leadership and managerialism

In a busy time where a work/life balance is typically threatened by over-load; burn-out is increasing amongst professionals; short-term utility and quality kite-marking are so often the name of the game; when the stretching of human capacity with performance prescriptions, as well as change management and target-led improvement, is prevalent in all service sectors (as well as the classroom) and is now dominating a management agenda; and while the practice of installing a growing bureaucracy for quality assurance laced with accountability is found everywhere – and all this is endlessly combined in a managerialist mantra based on distrust and blame that is apparently as vital for leadership in the educational setting as is water for life – we need to reclaim ground in the wake of a deluge of externalised accountability and better influence a world in which there is an increasing effort at imposing a new identity for the educational professional.

The endeavour remains one of encouraging the educational professional to 'interpret' and 're-structure reform' as part of the task of implementing policy and making provision. To lead in managing SEN policy and inclusive provision begins and ends with the task of nurturing human growth in an educative process. The management of diversity in education is about accepting differences, working with the strengths of individuals and participating in the process of learning how to learn. It is a formidable challenge. But it is a pursuit steeped with intrinsic reward. The satisfaction of knowing and making a difference in the education of people both managing and learning to manage their own journey is often a teacher's first and final motivation. This reward is even more intense when the learning is restorative as well as empowering and is what makes special the work of enabling choice and change in the lives of the 'hard to teach'.

Conclusion

My argument, then, is that leadership contributes to management – a continuing process of learning in which practitioners are engaged in change and personal growth associated with professional development (see Gunter, 2001; Rayner and Ribbins, 1999). Research and scholarship form important aspects of this integrative process: as do the inter-relational aspects of critical theory and empowerment as applied to an organizational culture.

Crucially, all of this should be measured in terms of its relevance to functional and pragmatic considerations tied to the work-place context. I am at this point reminded of the futility of teaching children to hunt sabre-toothed tigers in a post-Ice Age, as described in a wonderful satire written many years ago for the benefit of educators interested in curriculum design (Benjamin, 1939). Purpose and function should not be lost in the day-to-day work of management nor in a complex abstraction of theory or the political contest of vested interests impacting upon provision for individual differences in our educational system. All of these elements, however, need to be acknowledged and should be integrated into a management of educational provision.

Part I

Understanding Special Education and Inclusion Policy?

Part I lays the foundation for an understanding of SEN leadership and management in education. It involves the identification of a key skill-making sense – as it is applied to a continuing inter-play between context and persons, structure and agency, or culture and attitude; this in turn moves on to a second series of contextual interactions creating a mix of policy, provision and practice in the organizational setting. Management is essentially practical. Determining intention, executing aims and purpose, organizing resources and people, evaluating outcomes and result, all require strategic and operational action. In an educational setting, however, this action is shaped and formed by educational values and the core functions of learning and teaching. These values are in turn linked to and reflect epistemological and pedagogic principles, beliefs and theory.

Practitioners may or may not be aware of some of the ideas or assumptions underpinning much of the framework taken for granted when following policy guidelines or statutory guidance. These nonetheless exist and understanding as well as knowledge can help to further improve practitioner performance. The process of contributing to informed decision making is enhanced and empowered by knowledge and research. Bolman and Deal (1984: 4) state that:

> Managers in all organizations … can increase their effectiveness and their freedom through the use of multiple vantage points. To be locked into a single path is likely to produce error and self-imprisonment.

At its most immediate, such theory is personal and amounts to thinking through a position, perspective, or policy leading to reflection upon decisions, actions and practice. As a team leader and a school manager, I recall the need and the benefit of trawling the perceptions and perspectives of colleagues. Similarly, there is clearly value in developing and sharing professional knowledge to improve provision. Such an approach involves considerable investment over time in the continuing acquisition and production of knowledge. This kind of career-long professional development is typically associated with organizational learning. It is, furthermore, also somehow apt to presume that educational institutions such as schools, colleges and universities engaged in the business of education will literally all be operating as genuine learning organizations.

In approaching the topic of managing inclusion and special education, a first consideration for the practitioner is context. The first chapter in this section presents one such context in an historical review of special education in the UK. This provides a critical appraisal of the development of a national framework for SEN provision. It identifies key issues and themes underpinning the logic of policy making. It explains some of the thinking, beliefs and attitudes shaping national policy. The origins of special educational needs, integration and inclusion (social and educational) are described and linked to the pattern of provision laid down as a basis for better meeting the individual needs of children of school age. Deepening appreciation of context in the area of SEN leads to the questioning of principles and policy and a continuing inclusion imperative with its implications for planning and provision.

Chapter 2 provides a critical global account of this policy imperative, useful to readers interested in current and future developments in SEN policy. and those engaged in the planning and implementing of such policy.

The final chapter introduces the MISE model. This describes an integrative management that embraces an inclusive form of special educational leadership and a conceptual basis for understanding and developing practice in managing special and inclusive education. A recently emerging approach to evaluating and developing SEN policy and provision has been described as 'transformative', drawing upon research, critical perspective and evaluation to enable learning (Mertens and McLaughlin, 2004). It is not to be confused with a contemporary model of management known as 'transformational leadership'. The latter is vulnerable to the excesses of a 'charismatic tyranny' very often associated with an approach that deliberately creates intense uncertainty in an early stage of new management. It is characterized by a deliberate shaking down of structures and a visionary-led transforming of cultures and practice. The by-product of such management is often a high dependency in so-called subordinate followers or workforce. It is also a form of managerialism that results in a huge systemic implosion or even total collapse in performance after that person has left the organization. Transformational leadership of this sort does not lead to sustainability or growth but can produce a quick win and make-over that looks good for the short term. This chapter will be particularly relevant to those readers interested in a discourse and basis for developing the leadership and management of special and inclusive education.

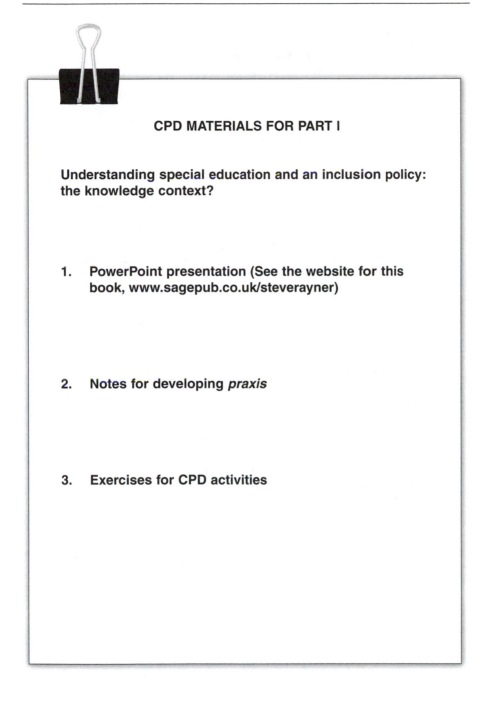

CPD MATERIALS FOR PART I

Understanding special education and an inclusion policy: the knowledge context?

1. **PowerPoint presentation (See the website for this book, www.sagepub.co.uk/steverayner)**

2. **Notes for developing *praxis***

3. **Exercises for CPD activities**

2. NOTES FOR DEVELOPING
***PRAXIS* [1]**

KEY ISSUES/QUESTIONS

Try answering the following questions as a workforce or small group exercise:

1. What is educational inclusion and what is special education? Do we need both types of provision? What is a fit-for-purpose policy for managing diversity in the school and educational inclusion?
2. How do we know and then meet the additional needs of pupils when planning and making provision?
3. Is there a way to develop policy taking us beyond the inclusion debate?
4. How can educational provision satisfy the requirements of the government standards agenda, Every Child Matters and school improvement?
5. How do the issues of inclusion feature in school life? Identify an inclusion touchstone theme and explore staff perceptions, attitudes and values in their first response to how they would manage the situation or people.
6. What provision should be developed to ensure successful and effective provision for meeting individual differences?
7. How should you be applying inclusion to the school workforce remodelling exercise?
8. How does the school development process engage with each level of the MISE model?
9. How can you develop an integrative management described in the MISE model in your own work and in the school organization?

2. NOTES FOR DEVELOPING *PRAXIS* [2]

CORE THEMES/CONCEPTS

Managing inclusion and special education effectively involves encouraging a discourse in the community aimed at generating a knowledge and an understanding of the following concepts in forming a policy for managing diversity and difference:

- Antecedents to inclusive education (models of disability, SEN, personal deficits and educational disadvantage).
- Medical disorders and psychophysical dysfunction.
- Multiple definitions of inclusion (integration, assimilation and accommodation).
- Global trends and inclusion ideology, principles and features in provision.
- Implications of inclusion for policy, provision and praxis.
- Individual needs – SEN, disability and learning difficulties.
- Human rights, social justice and discrimination.
- Diversity and difference in the school population (personal and social differences).
- Culture, values and attitudes in the organizational community.
- Educational equity, access and entitlement.
- Resource management and support for learning infrastructure.
- Community practice, participation, enablement and voice.
- Belonging and well-being in the learning community.

2. NOTES FOR DEVELOPING *PRAXIS* [3]

KNOWLEDGE SOURCES – KEY READING

Armstrong, F., Armstrong, D. and Barton, L. (eds) (2000) *Inclusive Education: Policy, Contexts and Comparative Perspectives*. London: David Fulton.

Booth, T. and Ainscow, M. (2002) *Index for Inclusion: Developing Learning and Participation in Schools* (2nd Edition). Bristol: Centre for Studies in Inclusive Education.

Burnett, N. (2005) *Leadership and SEN: Meeting the Challenge in Special and Mainstream Settings*. London: David Fulton.

Cheminais, R. (2006) *Every Child Matters*. London: David Fulton.

Cole, T. (1989) *Apart or A Part? Integration and the Growth of British Special Education*. Milton Keynes: Open University Press.

Daniels, H. and Garner, P. (eds) (2000) *Inclusive Education: Supporting Inclusion in Education Systems*. London: Kogan Page.

Florian, L. (ed.) (2006) *The Sage Handbook of Special Education*. London: Sage.

Gibson, S. and Blandford, S. (2005) Managing Special Educational Needs. London: Paul Chapman.

MacBeath, J., Galton, M., Steward, S., MacBeath, A. and Page, C. (2006) *The Costs of Inclusion*. Cambridge: University of Cambridge, Faculty of Education.

Thomas, G. and Vaughan, M. (2004) *Inclusive Education: Readings and Reflections*. Maidenhead: Open University Press.

Web-sites at: www.teachernet.gov.uk/wholeschool/sen
www.teachernet.gov.uk/wholeschool/sen/regional/contacts

2. NOTES FOR DEVELOPING
PRAXIS [4]

ACTION PROMPTS

1. The question of SEN policy and provision reflects fundamental issues related to professional values, attitudes and knowledge associated with core purposes of learning and teaching. A new knowledge of the history of SEN policy and provision can open up greater understanding of what and why provision exists in its present form. Revisit a vision for what your own institution represents and ask member groups of the community how this reflects key issues or features of national and regional SEN policy. Consider how you fit in with existing provision.

2. The following suggestions form a basis for revisiting and developing purposes and practice in relation to existing leadership practices and the management of SEN provision in the organizational setting:

   - Review and record a shared understanding of the meaning of management and leadership in your own institutional context/workforce team.
   - Review key approaches to problem posing and decision making as part of strategic/operational management across the school community (check how these link to different groups in the educational community).
   - Work towards restating a policy for the management of time and change, and/or place and space, as part of a leadership project for enabling equity in the academic curriculum.
   - Select a level and or dimension of the MISE model and explore the way in which it applies to an inclusion or diversity policy and provision (for example, use the model to review arrangements in place for managing bullying in the work-place).

3. DEVELOPING THE LEARNING GROUP AND PRACTITIONER ENQUIRY IN ORGANIZATIONAL LEARNING

Reflect on the nature, purpose and conduct of meetings, team-work and action groups in your organization. Aim to develop and publish a policy statement together with guidance for the school workforce on how to lead collaborative approaches to managing the learning group. Include:

- Revisiting theory explaining the way in which groups, teams and meetings should be organized to work effectively.
- Organizing meetings and/or groups/teams that are fit for purpose – this requires clearly stating the nature and function of these groups to include a variety of tasks such as:

  - Peer support and problem solving.
  - Professional learning for identified tasks (action research/practitioner enquiry/mentoring).
  - Self-evaluation, audit and accountability.
  - Partnership/learning community activity.
  - Community governance.

- Convene a CPD learning group to produce a set of guidance for the structure and management of an action/working group.
- Organize a provisional schedule/time commitment for CPD learning groups in the school year.

3. DEVELOPING SEN POLICY IN THE LEARNING ORGANIZATION

Complete these tasks utilizing the approach of distributed leadership/CPD teams and/or working groups.

- Agree and articulate the place and purpose of special education in an inclusive policy context.
- Record a shared understanding of the meaning of SEN and inclusion policies and/or provision.
- Create a policy for CPD, change management and project leadership in the academic year.
- Develop the role of the special school or support service for children with SEN.
- Form a policy for developing data management and evidence-based practice for service improvement.
- Make a strategic plan for inter-facing with a Common Assessment Framework and building inter-agency action.
- Investigate the kind of knowledge production or management required for improving SEN expertise and the implications for CPD.
- Create a strategy document briefing the SMT/governing body on the personalizing learning agenda, ECM Every Child Matters and the extended school initiative.
- Set up a forum or council for stakeholder groups in the school/learning community.

3. PERSONAL AGENDA FOR PROFESSIONAL ACTION

Managing policy involves securing potential contributions at a national, regional and local level. This can involve an interactive form of policy management resulting in the SEN leader/expert both interpreting and shaping the development of new policy and related provision. The following are examples of how a leader (this could be a teaching assistant, class teacher, SENCo, school leader, service manager) can engage at all three levels in forming policy:

- Contribute to a consultation exercise with the government (DfES; Ofsted; QCA) or a professional association (for example, UNISON; NUT; NASEN; NAHT).
- Approach the SEN Regional Partnership to work with an existing or proposed project in the area of policy and provision for the LA (local authority) or attempt to develop SEN provision in collaboration with local schools (cluster, federation or pyramid).
- Identify an aspect of local provision that might be improved (apply one of the touchstone themes described in Chapter 1).
- Conduct action research into one or more aspects of community life/inclusion (a touchstone theme forms different stakeholder perspectives).

3. STRATEGIC LEADERSHIP FOR MANAGING DIVERSITY AND SEN PROVISION

The following suggestion forms a basis for developing inclusive policies and provision in the learning community. Create and task a working group made up of representative members of the school community to review the inclusion policy. They should report to the Governing Body:

- School ethos – what values and attitudes officially and informally make up the organizational climate and culture in the school community?
- School provision – explore the current status of procedures, protocols and practices relating to SEN and learning disability (admissions, assessment, environment, support for learning infrastructure, curriculum design, CPD).
- School policy planning for the ECM agenda and issues surrounding future development (specialist status, extended school, inter-agency collaboration)?
- School resources – audit and estimate levels of resource involved in improving the inclusion policy to encompass a policy for managing diversity and difference in the school community.

Recommendations from this group should seek to include a strategic direction and set of proposals for updating the inclusion policy. Particular issues or problems emerging from this activity should be addressed as part of a process of managing a 'learning organization'.

1

Understanding SEN Policy Since Warnock (1978)

This chapter presents a critical summary of SEN policy and provision, providing a historical context for SEN leadership and the management of special and inclusive education. It aims to establish a foundation for relevant knowledge and offer a framework for an understanding of some of the key issues and ideas that have shaped this policy and provision during the past thirty years in the UK. It explains:

- The nature of special education and SEN provision in the UK.

- The impact of an inclusion imperative in special education.

- The modernizing imperative introduced by the Labour government in the UK (DfEE, 1997).

- Future roles for the special school in the educational system.

POLICY AND CONTEXT: KNOWING, THINKING AND CRITICAL ACTION

A first step in exploring an area of educational policy is to consider the influence and history of knowledge relevant to the context to inform a critical engagement with contemporary issues and practices relating to the management of provision. There is, in present national and international SEN educational policy, an interesting and sometimes volatile mix of contradictory ideas and legislative dissonance. One recurring example is an intense political debate surrounding the closure of special schools and the development of inclusive provision. This is continuing to pose a significant political challenge, particularly at a local level. It is linked to the wider challenge of strategic direction, resource management, quality assurance and social justice, as well as responding to pressure for revision of specialized forms of pedagogy and curricula. It is the case, however, that history does not always involve improvement or tell a story of resolution or progress.

National policy for SEN: past, present and future?

A natural threshold in the history of special education in the UK is the work and report of the Warnock Committee (1974–1977). In 1973, Margaret Thatcher, then Secretary of State for Education, announced the Warnock Enquiry. In 1974, this enquiry started its ground-breaking review of the state of British special education, which was set against increasing worldwide pressure for comprehensive integration. The Warnock Report (DES, 1978), taking its formal title and many other ideas from a contemporary publication (Gulliford, 1971), introduced a new concept in the area of special education – special educational needs. The special help proposed was aimed at a broad range of children experiencing learning difficulty, and the Warnock Report suggested 20 per cent of the school population would need such special help at some time during their school careers. A child with disability, it was emphasized, should be seen as an individual with full human rights and particular special educational needs rather than a patient with a medical illness or disorder. A focus was drawn to the idea of provision resolving learning difficulties. It also stressed the necessity for professionals to work closely with parents as partners in the process of helping the child.

The Report made a number of far reaching recommendations. It also made an early reference to the necessity for a 'whole school policy' in making provision for SEN, and the need to move toward greater levels of integration within the mainstream school. Three types of integration were identified and included:

- Location: where children attended separate special units but on the same site as mainstream schools.

- Social: where children went to separate special classes but mixed with 'ordinary' children at mealtimes, playtimes, assemblies and so on.

- Functional: where children attended the same classes as the non-handicapped and shared the same curriculum.

A subsequent policy directive in education was toward supporting new forms of integration. For pupils experiencing Emotional Behavioural Disorders/Difficulties (EBD), or presenting Profound and Severe Learning Difficulties (PSLD), this proved more problematic, although the notion of re-integrating such pupils gathered momentum, encouraging those working with these young people to think in terms of support for learning and re-integration in a mainstream school.

The Report (DES, 1978: 123, 8.8) concluded that there were three groups of pupils who would need special schools:

- Children with severe or complex physical, sensory or intellectual disabilities who require special facilities, teaching methods or expertise that it would be impracticable to provide in ordinary schools.

- Children with severe emotional or behavioural disorders who have very great difficulty in forming relationships with others or whose behaviour is so extreme or unpredictable that it causes severe disruption in an ordinary school or inhibits the educational progress of other children.

- Children with less severe disabilities, often in combination, who despite special help do not perform well in an ordinary school and are more likely to thrive in the more intimate communal and educational setting of a special school.

The Warnock Committee, therefore, while it recognized a continuing but reduced role for special schools also cautiously encouraged integration. It stressed that Section 10 of the 1976 Education Act had 'confirmed the direction' of much of the report's content. The report's wide-ranging recommendations were at the time welcomed by most professionals. Among many recommendations, Warnock hoped that close links would be forged between special and ordinary schools, exploiting the expertise of the former for the benefit of latter.

Developing SEN provision: the Education Act 1981

Margaret Thatcher's first Conservative government enacted the 1981 Education Act, adopting much of the philosophy of the Warnock Report. The proposals for reform, however, were resource neutral. The government did not prompt free additional money even for the Warnock priority areas (although contrary to widespread allegations of 'cuts' many LAs were to find additional funds for special education in the 1980s). Important implications of the 1981 Education Act were that from 1 April 1983:

- It repealed all previous Education Acts relating to special educational treatment needs.

- It brought into law the concept of 'special educational needs'.

- It abolished the categories of handicap brought into being by the 1944 Act.

- It required that the LA maintain a 'statement' on each child, outlining his/her individual special educational needs, and that this be reviewed annually (with parents involved in compiling this statement).

- The LA had a duty to provide special education for children as young as two years old and from birth on parental request.

- It required the provision of special education within ordinary schools wherever possible.

The Act defined special educational needs and this definition was to prove crucial to policy development throughout the next two decades. A similar version was used in an extension of statutory guidance with publication of the SEN Code of Practice (DfE, 1994). The definition was subsequently reinforced in the 1996 Education Act, Section 312, and stated that:

> A child has special educational needs ... if he has a learning difficulty which calls for special educational provision.

The 1996 Act continues by defining a child with learning difficulty when:

(a) He has a significantly greater difficulty in learning than the majority of children of his own age.
(b) He has a disability which either prevents or hinders him from making use of educational facilities of a kind generally provided for children of his own age in schools within the area of the local educational authority.
(c) He is under the age of five and is, or would be if special educational provision were not made for him, likely to fall within paragraph (a) and (b) when of, or over, that age. (Educational Act 1996; Section 312.2)

For children best served by placement in a special school or class, or preferably provided with the necessary support and educated alongside other children in ordinary classes, a 'statement of needs' was required, drawn up by teachers, psychologists, other professionals and at least in theory with the active involvement of parents (the practice was often misleading rhetoric rather than reality). Appeal procedures were also described.

The 1981 Act also required every LA to educate all children in ordinary school – but only if this was compatible with:

- parental wishes;

- the efficient education of other children;

- the efficient use of resources.

The implication was that only those children with the most severe difficulties or presenting the most disruptive behaviour would need separate special schooling. The expectation was that this would particularly include children with EBD. Parental lobby groups for children with dyslexia and autistic spectrum disorder began to emerge during this decade. While the implementation of the Act was to be hampered by lack of resources and a need in schools for extra money from the LEAs (Local Education Authorities), an administrative focus upon the SEN statement reflected its importance as an entitlement statement for parents wishing to place their child in a special school.

It was not surprising therefore that movement towards the 'whole school' policies identified by the Warnock Committee and later also in the Fish Report (ILEA, 1985) did not halt the growth, even in the late 1980s, of children placed in special schools, classes or non-designated special units. A fervent supporter of 'schools for all', Sayer (1983: 16) talked at the time of 'the constant pressure to revert to a closed circle of special educators'.

Generally, these trends in SEN provision did not reflect a successful drive toward integration. For example, during this period, the proportion of the nation's children in special provision did not significantly fall, dropping marginally from 1.52 per cent in 1988 to 1.47 per cent in 1991 and remaining at a higher level than in 1977 (Cole, 1989).

Promoting diversity, choice and change

The Education Reform Act (ERA) (DES, 1988), after the 1944 Education Act, was perhaps the most far reaching piece of UK education legislation enacted during the last century. It represented a revolution within education, replacing a philosophy grounded in notions of professionalism, vocation and public service with an approach centred on consumerism, accountability, enterprise and resource. It also marked a significant switch from local to national political administration, controlling both policy making and implementation, and bringing with it a dramatic increase in the number of non-elected government agencies (for example, the Office for Standards in Education [Ofsted] to carry out school inspection). It also established the basis for subsequent waves of government policy-implementation aimed at modernizing public services in health and education in the UK.

An insight into this dramatic shift of control from local to national policy management and more centrally managed implementation of policy is offered by simply counting statutory and non-statutory guidance issued to schools in England and Wales in the period immediately following the ERA. In a seven year period from 1987–1994, for example, over 90 statutory instruments affecting education were issued by central government; this in striking contrast to the 31 issued during the entire forty three year period between 1944 and 1987 (Walters, 1994). Together with the Education Act 1986, and the Education Act 1993, this legislation reflected a programme of continuing change presented as a root and branch reform of the educational system. Key policy features in this legislation included:

- school site-based management (local management of schools);
- introduction of the Funding Agency for Schools (FAS) and grant maintained schools;
- establishing The Office for Standards in Education (Ofsted);
- introduction of the National Curriculum.

Major themes for all involved in education in this package of reform continue to underpin contemporary policy making in spite of changes in government throughout the past fifteen years. Rayner (1994) described these themes as being focused upon:

- the individual needs of the 'client' as a 'consumer and producer' in education;
- learner (and curriculum) entitlement;
- parental rights and responsibilities;
- professional accountability.

Reflected in these themes is an over-arching policy commitment by the UK government (and more recently the devolved regional assemblies in Scotland, Wales and Northern Ireland) to reform an educational system predicated upon consumer choice and accountability. Schools operating in a quasi market-place have been subjected to a 'retail trade ideology' and are expected to generate choice and diversity via competition, offering an increasing choice of provision for parents and producing value for money. Underpinning this policy commitment is a practice of government-sponsored managerialism that in the same period progressively became a dominant feature of policy implementation.

The impact of these changes upon the 'educational landscape' included developments such as the appearance of league tables detailing school performance; the Ofsted School Inspection System; National Curriculum tests; teacher appraisal; local school finance; and site-based management. Headteachers became managers responsible for budgets, resources and spending, as well as the repair and upkeep of the whole school (from toilets to drainage, playing fields to classrooms, curriculum examinations to light bulbs). The way schools were funded changed. A formula was introduced based on pupil numbers, resulting in a much less certain revenue stream from year to year and involving schools in total financial management. Pupils with Emotional Behavioural and Social Difficulties (EBSD) or SEN who posted challenging behaviours (for example ASD or ADHD) were quickly perceived by many school managers to be an educational and financial liability. Children with Severe Learning Difficulties (SLD) were largely perceived as special and requiring alternative provision. A greater degree of integration was achieved for children with physical disabilities or sensory impairment (principally those identified with hearing or visual impairment). Compounding the effects of this change in resourcing was the introduction of a prescribed, common (national) curriculum, an increased pressure upon teachers and schools to raise levels of academic achievement, and a continuing call to accountability in the form of Ofsted, government non-statutory guidance, a parental lobby and the national media.

The child, school, care and welfare

The Children Act (DOH, 1989) was intended to provide protection for children at risk, reflecting a separate but related dimension to the care and education of young people. The key clause stated that '... the needs of the child are paramount'. In a salutary example of unintended consequences in policy implementation as a process, many social service departments and LEAs in the UK interpreted this legislation as a requirement for tough, restrictive codes of practice for adults, which were to be ruthlessly applied. It is difficult to imagine the climate which resulted. In some parts of the country, the effect of the Children Act was the creation of a 'McCarthy-like witch-hunt'. Among residential workers and many teachers, there was a feeling of increasing powerlessness. The fall-out from this activity affected all special school provision but particularly residential schooling for children with social, emotional and behavioural difficulties.

The injustice of the new climate and the additional stress on staff working with children presenting challenging behaviour were reflected in contemporary press articles. A selection, by way of example, included the following headlines: 'Unions Warn Teachers Over Threat of False Abuse Claims' (*The Times*, 1993), 'Staff Concerned About Rise in Allegations' (Whiteley, 1993) and 'Guilty Until Proved Innocent' (Marchant, 1993). The less certain ethos of contemporary school settings perhaps masks a continuing situation in which management of children's rights and protection contribute to a 'goldfish bowl' scenario capturing how concern for accountability and regulation is continuing to impact upon practitioners. I am, for example, today aware of several headteachers suspended for unproven allegations of physical abuse. This is a continuing story that now (in contrast to ten years ago) receives very little attention.

There is a pattern of recurring key questions in policy development for special education during this period. These include asking to what extent SEN provision:

- Should reflect nurturing and caring rather than educational attainment?

- Should be shaped by theories of welfare and social justice, education or health?

- Should be located in a special school and segregated, rather than inclusive and in a mainstream school?

- Be structured in the future – how should placement be determined (is an assessment bureaucracy typified by the Statement of Special Educational Need actually required)?

Whether in the light of history a degree of segregation is seen as a necessity for SEN provision, and that there will always be a need for a special or alternative option for some young people, is still at the heart of a continuing policy debate. Certainly, study of the past suggests that despite the limitations of a restricted curriculum and isolation, many special schools, classes and units have opened up new educational and social opportunities for their pupils, have reversed patterns of hopelessness, failure and behaviour – and continue to be popular with many parents and children.

MAINSTREAMING SEN PROVISION (1990–1999)

An infra-structure for special education and SEN introduced during the post-Warnock period was the multi-disciplinary system of identification and assessment of pupils with SEN. The SEN Code of Practice (DfE, 1994) reflected a development of this system and was non-statutory government advice for which schools were obliged to have regard. It marked the beginning of an approach to educational policy that saw a controlled yet devolved responsibility to schools for SEN policy management. It included, for example, guidance on the conduct of statutory assessment, the statementing procedure, the requirement for an annual review, an emphasis on the idea of partnership with parents and the operation of SEN tribunals, (DfEE, 1993b; DfEE, 1996).

Excellence for all: inclusion and SEN

The new Labour government, soon after taking power in the UK, published a Green Paper entitled 'Excellence for All Children' in late 1997, setting out a statement of policy and intention in respect to pupils with SEN (DfEE, 1997; 1997a). The key principles of this approach included:

- setting high expectations for children with SEN;
- supporting parents;
- increasing the number of children with SEN in mainstream schools, whenever possible;
- emphasis on practical support and not on procedures;
- providing better opportunities for the professional development of teachers and other staff;
- promoting partnership in SEN provision, locally, regionally and nationally.

A central theme throughout the Green Paper was the issue of inclusion. It was not defined but rather described as a process, and an emphasis was placed on developing an infra-structure to support this goal. A whole chapter was devoted to issues related to EBD. The following key issues were identified:

- early identification and intervention;
- effective behaviour policies which support inclusion;
- reinforcing staff skills and enhancing specialist support;
- dissemination of best practice;
- developing 'fresh approaches' in the secondary phase of education.

The Paper stated that by the year 2000, a national programme would be in place to help primary schools better manage early intervention with pupils at risk of developing EBD; to give greater opportunity for teachers to develop their skills in working with pupils experiencing EBD; to provide a national programme to offer support to EBD special schools experiencing difficulty; and to supply resources for schemes designed to renew the motivation of young people with EBD at Key Stage 4 in secondary schooling (13–16 year old students).

Social inclusion: guidance for schools

A sensitive issue for government during this same period was the continuing rise in the number of pupils excluded from school. The government (DfEE, 1999) issued draft guidance to all LAs and social service departments entitled 'Social Inclusion: Pupil Support', prepared by several departments responsible for education, health and justice, reflecting a new emphasis upon multi-agency approaches to young people in difficulty. The intention of this document was to 'bring together ... advice on improving school attendance, managing pupil behaviour and discipline, the use of exclusion and education out of school' (p. 1) The guidance was deliberately intended to emphasize the importance of early intervention and multi-agency working to prevent disaffection and reduce the numbers of pupils being excluded from school.

A series of annexes was attached providing more detailed instruction for schools in respect of recently enacted law. For example, the procedures for exclusion and school attendance were set out in detail, describing powers given to the police in the Crime and Disorder Act 1998 to return truants to school or another place designated by the LA if they believed the child to be of school age and absent without authority.

Meeting SEN: a programme of action

At around the same time as promoting attention to the issue of social exclusion, the DfEE (1998b) announced a new programme of action for SEN provision. This policy statement laid out the government's plans in the light of responses during the consultation period for the Green Paper on SEN (DfEE, 1997). Leading priorities identified were

- working with parents;

- improving the SEN framework;

- developing a more inclusive education system;

- developing the knowledge and skills of staff;

- working in partnership to meet SEN.

The action programme highlighted the importance of early intervention, and multi-agency support for pupils and their parents. From 1999, every LA was expected to have in place a parent partnership scheme, with a responsibility for supporting parents in the legal process of statementing pupils with SEN or in an SEN tribunal.

The SEN framework was to be improved with the introduction of a revised SEN Code of Practice (DfES, 2001b). This was intended as a safeguard for pupils' interests, with a focus on preventative work, school-based support, procedures for SEN tribunals and the reduction of bureaucracy. Further guidance detailed advice on improving work related to the early stages of the code, involving 'school support' and 'support plus' for pupils. The role of the SEN Co-ordinator (SENCo), as a 'middle manager' in main-stream schools in the UK, was formally recognized.

A significant feature in the Code was the re-categorization of SEN. Areas of need were defined to include children presenting learning difficulty associated with Cognition and Learning Needs; Behavioural, Emotional and Social Development Needs; Communication and Interaction Needs; Sensory and/or Physical Needs; and 'Other'. The new emphasis upon developmental needs was supported by the Government publication of a tool-kit for learning and teaching children with SEN (DfES, 2003a). Further guidance describing how to use data in evidence-based approaches to managing the Code and SEN provi-sion reflected an increasing official demand for information related to per-formance management in the school system (DfES, 2003b). These reflected parallel trends in the USA, as the federal government there responded to the standards agenda by enacting new legislation aimed at enforcing pupil progress and leaving no child behind (see Rouse and McLaughlin, 2006, for a useful comparative appraisal of this policy enactment).

MODERNIZING POLICY (2001–2006): EVERY CHILD MATTERS

A leading piece of legislation in the period following the re-election of the Labour party included the 2001 SEN and Disability Act (SENDA). The SENDA made it unlawful to discriminate against pupils on the basis of dis-ability. This had immediate implications for issues surrounding access to education. Since 1996, the Schools Access Initiative (SAI) has provided the funding to make mainstream schools more accessible to children with dis-abilities and special educational needs. So far, over 6,000 schools have bene-fited from the initiative (NUT, 2006).

One noticeable effect of this legislation lay in the area of site management with the installation of ramps to paved areas, facilitating access to school campuses for the physically disabled. A sum of £100m was made available for this scheme to allow bids from LAs in England in the periods of 2005–06, 2006–07 and 2007–08. The SENDA (DfES, 2001a) required that by law all schools had to take reasonable steps to ensure disabled pupils were not placed at a substantial disadvantage, either in relation to admission arrange-ments to a school, or associated services provided by, or on behalf of, a school. The powers of the SEN tribunal were increased and it was renamed the SEN and Disability Tribunal.

Further influential official publications on special education during this period included reports on SEN provision compiled by the Audit Commission (2002; Audit Commision and Ofsted, 2002) and on the future of the special school (DfES, 2003c). The Audit Commission found that statutory assessment was costly and bureaucratic, stressful for parents and added little value in meeting a child's needs. It also stated that SEN statements cre-ated an inequitable distribution of resources, and in general administration of SEN assessment together with the placement of children failed to support early intervention and inclusive practice. The Special School Report (DfES,

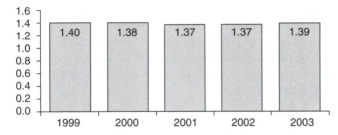

Figure 1.1   Number of pupils in all special schools as a percentage of the number in mainstream schools (1999–2003) (Source: Ofsted, 2004: 7)

2003c) published by the UK's government, however, argued for continuing support of special schools but recommended a programme of change in which the role of the special school would be transformed. In many ways, the report merely repeated post-Warnock commentary, typified in an article written some twenty years earlier by Brennan (1983). Nonetheless, a continuing pressure for inclusion, reinforced by the practice of Ofsted inspection of LEAs in England and Wales, resulted in many LEAs closing special schools during the 1990s – although there had never been a government instruction for LEAs to carry out this action.

The uncertainty, variation and conflict in approach to maintaining the special school and special education during this period should not be under-estimated. Porter and Lacey (2002) reported special school numbers remaining constant but the nature of provision changing as inclusion of children with SEN in mainstream schools gathered pace (confirmed in Figure 1.1). The trend lay towards mainstream provision for particular groups of pupils – research evidence revealed that 70–80 per cent of children with Down syndrome were to begin their education in the mainstream during the early part of the 1990s (Cunningham et al., 1998), with special schools for children with severe or moderate learning difficulties experiencing marked changes in their population with children presenting more complex difficulties and disabilities (Male, 1996a; 1996b). A growing number of special schools for pupils with EBSD were replaced by special units in mainstream schools (Cole et al., 1998).

According to official statistics, the total number of pupils in special schools fell slightly from 98,100 in 1996 to 95,600 in 2001, as did the number of schools, from 1763 to 1175. Pupils with statements of SEN do not automatically attend special schools, but a greater proportion (60.4 per cent) of those with statements are placed in mainstream schools (DfES, 2002a). The age profile for special school populations reveals a consistent increase in numbers for children up to fifteen years of age (DfES, 2001c). Comparatively, these age and gender characteristics relate to data across Europe (OECD, 2000). The UK lies fifth out of 16 European countries in the number of special schools per 100,000 of the school population.

Finally, Ofsted published figures drawn from school inspection data presented in Figure 1.1, reflecting the continuing use of special school placement in educational provision for children with SEN (Ofsted, 2004: 7). To some extent this may be interpreted as a consequence of uncertain policy and a resulting mixed array of provision. On the other hand, it might be seen as a residual need or demand for particular special school provision that is distinctive and different, mirroring the continuing complexities of special and inclusive education.

A new framework for schools and services

An emphasis upon modernizing schools and developing inclusion resurfaced in official policy during the period from 2000–2005. Cheminais (2006) describes a projected new world of education reflected in this policy, in which a school became a networked gateway for learning rather than its sole provider (as has been the traditional role of the school). The policy directive for modernizing reform was linked to the document, *Every Child Matters* (DfES, 2003d). The language used in this document shifted markedly to reflect a focus upon child development rather than one traditionally used to describe educational policy. Government guidance in the form of a strategy for this policy agenda described the need to develop and strengthen a children's workforce:

> The children's workforce stretches across many professional and organizational boundaries. The workforce of the future will work better across those boundaries, in multi-disciplinary teams. More coherent career pathways will allow for progress across as well as within those boundaries. And all professionals will be able to focus more on early identification and prevention of problems, while strengthening protection for the most vulnerable. (DfES, 2005a: 1)

Social and personal considerations were given first priority in an educational approach that was holistic and very deliberately 'wrapped around the individual child'. Service provision, including education, however, was also construed as a provider commodity located in a quasi market-place. The assurance of high standards and user choice reflected values and economics associated with consumerism (with parent and child identified as client, customer and consumer). Policy centred on the notion of inter-agency structure and a focus was drawn to the following five key outcomes for a child's development.

Professionals would be further required in an evidence-based approach to ensure monitoring and accountability that bench-marked and showed that children:

- are healthy;
- stay safe;
- enjoy and achieve;
- make a positive contribution;
- achieve economic and social well-being.

The Children Act 2004 reinforced this movement toward integrating children's services. The individual rights of young people resurfaced as a bigger political idea in this legislation, partly as a continuing theme of 'child protection', but also as a response to an increasing focus on social justice and equity in education. The SEN Strategy (DfES, 2004c: 3.9) further reinforced a policy of inclusive education. The document stated 'every teacher should expect to teach children with SEN', and four key aspects to the strategy included:

1. Improving provision for intervention in the early years phase of education.

2. Removing barriers to learning through the improvement of access and support for learning in and beyond the mainstream school setting.

3. Raising expectations and achievement for pupils with SEN by developing where appropriate targeted support for transition points, alternative curricula and differentiated pedagogy.

4. Improved partnerships via school workforce remodelling, professional networking, extended schools, home–school partnership, local community activity and inter-agency action.

Cheminais (2006) identified the following implications in this policy agenda for local development:

- Personalization in learning, care and support (see for example, an integrated inspection of children's services).

- A developing 'wraparound' care and multi-disciplinary service delivery in and around schools and in Children's Centres.

- An early intervention and integrated and effective child protection provision (see for example, National Service Framework standards for children, young people and maternity services).

- Improved information sharing between agencies and a common assessment framework across services.

- A School Self-Evaluation SEN Policy and Provision (2006 – Ofsted Framework).

- Local authority SEN funding formula for service provision (including schools).

Any practitioner wishing to stay abreast of the 'establishment policy agenda' in England and Wales should find Cheminais' recent work very useful (Cheminais, 2002; 2004; 2005; 2006). The following adapted checklist (Cheminais, 2005) of a 'five-year strategy for children and Learners' gives substance to Cheminais' account of the policy agenda and the intended provision for a future in which every child matters. This involves restructuring provision and the school workforce on a big (perhaps overwhelming) scale and describes the following developments in SEN provision:

- **Children's Centres** – in schools or on school sites; one-stop shops open from 8.00 am–6.00 pm providing a range of services, including outreach.

- **Extended full service schools** – integrating health, social service and education.

- **Every School a Healthy School** – curriculum content reflecting the five outcomes described in *Every Child Matters*.

- **Widening of the primary curriculum** – to include PE/sport, playing music, learning an additional language for all children.

- **Networks of primary schools** – supporting and challenging each other in a collaborative process of renewal.

- **Building schools for the future** – refurbished or new build secondary schools as part of a government modernizing policy.

- **Academies/specialist schools expanding** – with some to have second specialisms, for example SEN, Gifted and Talented.

- **Foundation partnerships** – schools having collective responsibilities for targetted aspects, for example SEN, 14–19 curriculum, school improvement, excluded pupils.

- **New relationship with schools** – changes to the school self-evaluation and inspection framework, with an emphasis upon evidence-based practice, data analysis, a school improvement partner.

- **New school profiles** – information for parents about services offered and an increased opportunity to participate in the school community.

- **Three-year budgets** – for schools as part of a new LA formula.

A second useful example of a special school/service leadership response to this so called 'modernizing' policy agenda is provided in the case examples found in Burnett's account of a research project for the then recently established National College of School Leadership (Burnett, 2003; 2005). This research reported leading edge work in SEN policy development and provision in several LEAs, documenting the restructuring and development of special schools/services in an inclusive setting.

Counting equity and moving beyond inclusion

Two recent publications reflect a growing concern for counting the cost of an inclusive policy in mainstream education in England. An influential research project funded by the NUT in 2004–05 evaluated SEN policy in 20 schools (ten first and/or middle-primary; nine secondary; and two special) from seven different LEAs in England. The sample was selected to represent a range of policies on inclusion (MacBeath et al., 2006). The study, perhaps unsurprisingly, reported a mixed picture of success and failure in terms of inclusive provision but more importantly, a worrying trend for unintended outcomes associated with inclusive approaches negatively impacting upon children with SEN or learning difficulties. Two key findings were that school leadership was critical but relatively powerless without systemic reform; and that a destructive contradiction in government policy existed (collaborative practice in conflict with market-place competition). The researchers concluded that:

> The most striking aspect of this study is the good will of teachers who believe in inclusion and try to make it work but do not find their good will repaid by the level of professional support they deserve. It is time for a thorough review of policy and practice. (MacBeath et al., 2006: 67)

The question of continuing management in a joint approach to inclusion and special education is a key factor in both developing as well as implementing policy and provision. The NUT-sponsored research pointed to a need for a careful appraisal of the education cost involved in current arrangements aimed at the delivery of SEN and inclusion policy. The Education and Skills Committee of the House of Commons very recently published their SEN Report (House of Commons, 2006). It gave a detailed summary of its review of SEN policy in England, drawing upon a considerable breadth of testimony from various representative groups and individual practitioners. Eight specific issues emerged from the review including:

1. Improving levels of resource and forms of provision for pupils with SEN in mainstream schools.

2. Continuing and stated policy support of special school provision for some pupils.

3. An initiative aimed at raising the standards of achievement for pupils with SEN.

4. Reforming the SEN statementing procedure.

5. Enhancing the role of parents in decisions about SEN placement.

6. Clarification of the definition of SEN in national policy.

7. Differentiated provision to match different types of SEN (including EBSD).

8. Revision of the legislative framework for SEN policy that would clarify the need to have regard to issues of discrimination and the Disability Act 2001.

The report suggested that policy should be developed for the specific purpose of establishing a new national framework built around the principle of flexibility, and ensuring an arrangement for child-centred provision. It is interesting to note when looking back at the history of SEN policy and provision that Cole (1989) can identify these self-same principles in the work of policy makers in Victorian England, in the 1945 Education Act, and again more recently in policy planning and legislation since the Warnock Report (DES, 1978).

While this interpretation might seem somewhat discouraging, suggesting a lack of progress, it actually points to the recurring significance of key principles and core values that form the basis of SEN policy, provision and practice. It is possible, furthermore, that we are now actually at a threshold, comparable to the Warnock Report in the latter part of the last century, in the development of SEN policy in England. In this sense, educational leaders and policy makers face an interesting and perhaps exciting opportunity to develop new forms of policy and provision that are required to meet learning differences and additional needs in all children. The ideas that have shaped this development of SEN policy, particularly those surrounding the desire for inclusive provision, will be more closely examined in the next chapter.

2

The Ideal of Inclusion

The policy context for educating children with SEN has been dominated in recent years by the pursuit of social and educational inclusion. Some educationists refer to inclusion as a quality of provision, others an educative process, an ideal, or a political and social issue related to human rights. In the alternative view of a sceptic, it is a monument to political correctness. This chapter sets out to address the complexities of definition and planning associated with the inclusion ideal and its implications for managing special education policy and provision. It examines:

- The impact of an inclusive imperative in education;

- The meaning of an inclusive policy and provision;

- Implications for managing SEN policy and practice.

IS EDUCATIONAL INCLUSION SEN POLICY?

What is educational inclusion? There are many definitions of inclusion found in the literature: some writers emphasize social inclusion (Gerschel, 2005b; Walker and Walker, 1997), others educational inclusion (Tilstone et al., 1998; Wolger, 2005), while many more describe an approach that encompasses a values-based approach to provision (Cheminais, 2005; 2006; Clough and Corbett, 2000; O'Brien, 2001). The challenge presented by this pursuit of equity in terms of opportunity and support is also captured in a definition published by the National Association of Special Educational Needs (NASEN) in the UK:

> ... inclusion is not a simple concept, restricted to issues of placement. Its definition has to encompass broad notions of educational access and recognise the importance of catering for diverse needs. Increasing mainstream access is an important goal. However, it will not develop spontaneously and needs to be actively planned for and promoted. (NASEN, 1998)

Topping and Maloney (2005) introduce the topic of inclusion by stating that 'like learning, inclusion is a dynamic process, not a static condition – a journey not a destination'. Much like learning – when described as a continuing process in the introduction to the Inclusion Index (Booth, 2000). Inclusion is aligned to continuing school improvement. In this way, it is deliberately presented as a relevant and positive principle for schools engaged in the standards policy agenda, reflecting a presumption that an inclusive school will by definition be a good school (Stainback and Stainback, 1996; Zemelman, 1998). To sum up, inclusion is an ideal that for several years has been universally accepted by many as an inalienable right and a necessary condition for any fair and equitable social or educational system (Slee, 1998). For some, inclusion is a quality of provision, for others it is a process, an educational ideal, or yet more importantly a matter of human rights for all children. Alternatively, it is criticized by many as a monument to political correctness. For busy practitioners, it is sometimes simply just a messy confusion of contradictory or idealistic thinking and discourse (see Farrell, 2001; Hornby, 1999; 2001). For a school or service manager, and for leadership in the area of SEN policy and provision, it is without doubt an imperative that continues to shape theory and impact upon practice.

CONSTRUCTING EDUCATIONAL INCLUSION

For the practitioner engaged in leadership and managing provision, an exercise in defining inclusion is perhaps best thought of as a continuing process of constructing and reconstructing meaning and making sense of their own approach to SEN policy. An example of the range of differing perspectives adopted by educationists is presented in the following checklist. Representing a selected sample spanning a decade or more of educational literature, the first set of definitions is a concerted effort on the part of researchers to answer the question of what exactly is meant by inclusion (Table 2.1).

The second set of definitions reflects a similar effort but focuses more specifically on what inclusion looks like as part of the answer (Table 2.2). This interestingly ends with the articulation of what is involved in belonging to an inclusive school (the Langdon School, Newham LEA, London), as described by a group of students to an audience of educationists at a Centre for the Study of Inclusive Education (CSIE) conference.

Table 2.1 Inclusion explained as policy

- **Clark et al.** (1995: v) … inclusion can be understood as a move towards extending the scope of 'ordinary' schools so they can include a greater diversity of children.
- **Florian** (1998: 15) … within special education, the term inclusive education has come to refer to a philosophy of education that promotes the education of all pupils in mainstream schools.
- **Slee** (2000: 195) … inclusive education refers to education for all comers. It is a reaction to discourses that exclude on the basis of a range of student characteristics, including class, race, ethnicity, sexuality, perceived level of ability or disability, or age.
- **Lorenz** (2002: 1) … the successful mainstreaming of pupils with special educational needs (SEN) who would traditionally have been placed in special schools.

The context for understanding most of these definitions is an ideology of social justice. A cornerstone of this model is the principle of equity in education. It is used as an organizing theme in the collection of papers to be found in a very useful edited reader produced by Thomas and Vaughan (2004). The commitment to equity and social justice has been further explored in recent educational research employing critical theory and post-modern perspectives for explaining the political processes embedded in schooling and education.

Table 2.2   Inclusion explained as provision

- **Ballard** (1995: 1–2) Inclusive schools deliver a curriculum to students through organisational arrangements that are different from those used in schools to exclude some students from their regular classrooms...
- **Stainback and Stainback** (1996: xi) An inclusive school is a place where everyone belongs, is accepted, supports and is supported by his or her peers and other members of the school community in the course of having his or her educational needs met.
- **Shaw** (1999: 11) Our school is well known as an inclusive school. Our school reflects our community. We have male and female students from all cultures, races and religions with all abilities and disabilities. There are many languages spoken in our school.

Antecedents to inclusion: understanding an inclusive SEN policy

In an effort to better understand some of the ideas and principles underpinning inclusion as a policy, it is useful to consider a number of antecedents in special education. These can influence beliefs, attitudes and values and are evident in the tacit knowledge of practitioners in mainstream and special schools. A category-based model of SEN, for example, has been identified as bound up in a widespread reluctance by teachers to embrace inclusion as a practice. Practitioners acknowledge inclusion but regard it as an ideal and therefore an unrealizable policy.

Research reported by Adams et al. (2000) revealed that categorization of SEN as stated in the original SEN Code of Practice (DfE, 1994), and broadly similar to the Warnock Report's definitions of SEN, remains intact twenty years later in teachers' informal theories of SEN and their tacit knowledge of learning and teaching. They conclude that teachers' understanding of disability in their research reflected an informal and pervasive categorization of students. 'Special' was constructed and 'rationalized' by teachers through the articulation of informal theory and practice. A marked distinction between MLD and SLD was not only evident in teachers' understandings, it was expressed in the design of differing provision and teaching practices in a range of settings.

Understanding and promoting an appropriate model of disability or learning difference are central to planning policy and managing the intended, or more importantly, experienced provision for learning and teaching in the SEN context. The dominant paradigms or models in special education that provide a set of antecedents for the policy of inclusion comprise the following three explanations for disability and special needs.

1. The Medical Model is often described as a 'deficit model', and presumes that pathology or disorder is the basis for defining disability or learning difficulty. Put simply, the student with SEN is conceived as a medical problem and having an illness. The medical difficulty is also conceived in terms of cause and effect. Assessment, diagnosis, and intervention are deemed correct approaches in this model and are completed to enable an intervention aimed at a cure for the problem. Skrtic (1991) suggests that special educational knowledge and practice are based on this clinical model, and within it are two confounding principles; the pathological and the statistical theory. Both are seen to logically reduce to a normative model for explaining human behaviour.

At its most blatant, this model led to widespread take-up of individual treatment plans in special schools in the UK during the period 1960–1985. More recently, it has been evident in the massive rise of identifying and labelling of children with Attention Deficit Disorder (ADD) or Attention Deficit Hyperactivity Disorder (ADHD). This is combined in a clinical and prescriptive framework with an expectation of access to drug-based therapy. In a less direct but nonetheless pervasive fashion, it continues to influence an individualized approach to SEN provision (reflected in the IEP (Individual Education Plan) and SEN Code of Practice), albeit the latter is grounded in an educational needs model of disability.

An important implication of the medical model is that it creates an expectation that specialist expertise is required for an exceptional group of special children. Adams et al. (2000) claimed that this model is typically applied in the special education of children with severe learning difficulties, reinforced by a theory of learning that legitimizes special labelling of the child, the special provision made for the child, and a professional expertise associated with the special education of that child. It describes 'sickness' as the explanation for failure to progress, or the presenting of challenging behaviour, which is more readily 'excused' by the teacher or parent as a manifestation of something organically 'wrong' with the child. Any fault or problem is located within the child, and not because of the adult or social setting. Therapy lies at the heart of provision dominated by this model. Special school and specialist expertise are valued as essential resources in a placement-led provision. It is in such provision that a restorative but possibly palliative function in the education and care of individual children is attempted.

2. The Educational Needs Model   constructs disability or difficulty in relation to perceived norms of individual capability, achievement and behaviour. A special educational need is defined as an age-related indicator of under-development. SEN are also conceived to exist on a spectrum of severity and scope (Norwich, 1990). The model is immediately more relevant but challenging for teachers, as, by definition, children with SEN are located within every teacher's purview. The very essence of 'special' in this model, then, when applied to teachers' skills, techniques and expertise is a presumption of an opportunity and responsibility for teaching all children. It is, however, evident that the medical model has continued to influence the educational needs model. The identification and assessment of children with special educational needs, in particular, reflect a diagnostic approach to disability that employs the idea of a psychological deficit and a needs assessment, leading to an appropriate specialist intervention or placement. This approach is usually completed with an exercise in matching special needs to existing educational provision.

The SEN framework was developed around the core construct of need as a cornerstone for planning the educational provision for children with SEN. The view that special needs are an educational issue continued to be refined in developments of policy and provision throughout the latter decades of the last century. In the UK, the Education Reform Act 1988 legislated for entitlement and the requirement that all children follow a national curriculum. While the Act allowed for dis-application, this was generally ignored. The framework for placement of children with SEN continued to grow in an expanding bureaucracy for multi-disciplinary assessment, as well as in the development of an innovatory provision in the form of support services for SEN children in mainstream settings.

The regulating mechanism for SEN provision was the SEN Statement, which to all intents and purposes became a school voucher for entitlement and resources. Unsurprisingly, as the ERA Act also strengthened the powers of parental choice, so advocacy and an appeal to rights and entitlement accompanied these developments. A tribunal system was organized to provide for disputed assessments and any legal challenge to provision for SEN children (see Gersch and Gersch, 2003). The legal responsibility for the administration of what might be described as the labelling machinery of identification and provision lay with the LEAs, and more recently, in a move towards a unified service structure for children, the LAs.

3. The Social Disability Model emerged in parallel to the special education needs model. From an intellectual perspective, a new sociology of education was hugely instrumental in offering an alternative paradigm for interpreting special education. Tomlinson (1982), for instance, suggested a difference between the two key terms – 'socially constructed' and the then widely accepted 'normative' disability – which had been thought of as an intrinsic feature of the child. For Tomlinson, the concept of 'learning difficulties' was socially constructed, arising from the values, beliefs and interests of the actors in that field, defined as largely middle-class professionals. Significantly, the majority of students labelled SEN were of working-class origin. Tomlinson (1982: 5) argued that:

> Professionals and practitioners have vested interests in the expansion and development of special education. They also have very real power to define and affect the lives and futures of the children they deal with …

She concluded that previously held assumptions about disability and segregated education could be challenged as part of problematizing existing SEN provision. The political movement associated with disability groups was described by Thomas (1997) as part of a wider reaction to traditional theories of learning difficulty, diagnostic assessment and special needs associated with utilizing models of medicine or behavioural psychology and a segregated special provision.

A literature emphasizing social justice, equal opportunities and human rights emerged as a strong lobby in the political arena in the UK (Oliver, 1998). Its application in the school context was joined with a discourse focusing upon entitlement, enablement, access to learning and the common curriculum. This was reinforced by resistance to so-called exclusionary forces in society, and a talking-up of the task of building a transformative school culture. The movement was associated with educationists particularly interested in critical theory, curriculum innovation and inclusive education (see the work of Booth, 2000; Clark et al., 1997; Clough, 1998).

A consensus in much of this work rejects any possibility that inclusion can be achieved by means other than the total extinction of special education. In line with this perspective, Slee (1998) argues there is no room for compromise between aspirations of social justice and the use of deficit driven models of special needs. Inclusion, framed in this way, is by definition a political process. This position implies that working for inclusion in schools means rejecting any theory associated with models of disability that are not framed in a constructionist perspective of learning. Such work will also by definition and in turn connect with the politics of power, empowerment and importance of social identity. It is an approach that identifies culture and society as leading arbiters in any explanation of learning difficulty. This would mean, for example, that students with EBSD would be seen as presenting misbehaviour that is an effect of the organizational and environmental setting rather than a personal problem. The causes of learning difficulty in this model are systemic and are emphatically located in the school setting (see for example, Lawrence et al., 1984; Schostak, 1983).

THE IDEOLOGY OF INCLUSION: SOCIAL JUSTICE AND EQUITY

Lorenz (2002) commented in a manner not dissimilar to Thomas and Vaughan (2004) that inclusion might be understandably regarded as ' ... the buzz word of the decade'. She continues, 'Everywhere you turn there are policies and mission statements about services and organisations becoming even more inclusive' (p. 1). This imperative for inclusion was deeply embedded in educational policy during the 1990s, was intended to improve education and social inclusion in the community. The policy was most directly applied to SEN in the form of reducing barriers to access and learning in school for children with disability. It was widely perceived by most practitioners and managers in the UK as statutory policy. Furthermore, there has always been an actual ambivalence and lack of clarity in government SEN policy which has produced a number of uncertainties, contradictions and conflicts, not least, those surrounding the closure of special schools and the principle of mainstreaming all children with SEN. There is the possibility, however, that it is not simply government irresponsibility at play here. It is argued by some that SEN is a problematic term, and furthermore, the idea of inclusion is in itself too idealistic and as a consequence forms a contradictory and unrealistic policy (Hornby, 1999; MacBeath et al., 2006).

Nonetheless, the ideal of inclusion is generally described by educationists as representing an uncertain but dominant ideology in the world of education. In a survey of educational psychologists in the UK, Evans and Lunt (2002) reported a generally held opinion that full inclusion is problematic, and imposes limitations which should be carefully considered in any planning of policy and provision. Fuchs and Fuchs (1994) describe how an early division in the form of two opposing groups of special educationists quickly dominated the development of professional attitudes to educational inclusion. There emerged on the one hand 'abolitionists', challenging the 'status quo' while striving to de-construct and transform the field, and were 'demonized' as 'out of touch ideologues' by an opposing group of 'conservationists', who emphasized realistic and pragmatic issues as a justification for a special and separate special education. Florian (2006) suggests that this division has continued to 'polarize' the field. Attitudes to SEN policy will reflect the values and beliefs implicit in any of these positions adopted by professional staff. A useful exercise for CPD in school is a values clarification exercise linked to this question of policy review, focusing in particular on understanding inclusion and revealing practitioners' attitudes to managing diversity and individual difference.

The pressure to conform to inclusion as an educational ideal was very intense during the 1990s. Croll and Moses (1998) claim that a commitment to inclusion was typically regarded as a school staff or an institution having achieved the 'moral high ground'. The point is made forcibly that this 'imperative' was so intense that it might even be seen as reaching the status of an 'ideological hegemony'. Croll and Moses (2000: 181) go on to claim that:

> ... an inclusionist ideology can be regarded as dominant in the sense both of being the focus of most cutting edge, policy-relevant thinking in SEN, and as attracting at least some level of support from virtually all concerned with SEN provision.

They provide an interesting analysis of practitioner perspective that reveals an important insight and distinction in understanding policy and practice – that policy in the minds of teachers often represents an ideal and a template for a preferred state. In practice, policy is converted to a code or protocol for action that whilst reflecting the values and substance of the ideal will never actually be realized as a perfect match in the 'real world'. A policy on admissions may therefore not be implemented in exactly the way intended.

By necessity, interpretation plays a role in the implementation of policy, and the process is one of best fit rather then prescription. In this sense, policy is about direction and desirability, but not necessarily about actual practice. There is an expectation and anticipation in this approach therefore that not all parts of any given policy will ever be realized. The prevailing view of practitioners was that a commitment to inclusion did not contradict a belief that while more children should be in mainstream schools, some children will always need separate provision. This position was reinforced by a second and contrasting ideology related to SEN and a needs model of disability, which emphasized the primacy of meeting children's individual needs as overriding any ideological commitment to an inclusionist ideal.

The meaning of inclusive education

A crucial step in the generation and application of new knowledge for any organization when formulating or implementing institutional policy is the extrapolation of meaning. In terms of effective management, especially in an educational setting, this should mean ensuring a shared understanding and an agreement of principles with policy. While in reality this does not mean assuring total agreement or consensus, it must represent a collective commitment to a professional purpose, identity and endeavour.

In terms of educational inclusion, it is doubly important that exploring and sharing meaning are part of the planning process. This is applicable at all levels of policy management. The attribution of meaning is an essential part of managing this process. Interpretation, judgement and action are subjective and personal but also social and collective, and should therefore involve collaborative decision making and decision taking (see the MISE model, Level 1 in Chapter 3). It also demands team and group work founded on notions of practice that should be facilitated as a distinctive form of inclusive leadership (see Chapter 4). At school level, it is important that an agreed understanding of SEN is articulated in a policy document – a working document and not simply rhetoric. It is crucial too that all members of an organization have regard to this policy and can refer to protocols that guide procedures and practices found in the document. Such a policy statement will invariably cross-reference to other statements describing pastoral systems and a subject-based curriculum (including behaviour management, well-being and personal or social development).

There have been a number of studies investigating professional perspectives on the question of inclusion. Norwich (2000) completed a literature review investigating teachers' attitudes towards the integration and, more recently, inclusion of children with special educational needs in mainstream schools. The review revealed some evidence of positive attitudes, but none for the idea of total inclusion or as Norwich calls it, the 'zero reject' approach to special educational provision. Avramadis and Norwich (2002: 129) also reported on the attitudes and perspectives of teachers involved in making inclusive provision for children with SEN. The results confirmed research elsewhere (by Adams et al., 2000). Teachers' attitudes were strongly influenced by the nature and severity of the disabling condition presented by students (construed as a within-child causal factor). They were much less interested in teacher-related issues, educational factors and more generalized, environment-related variables that might explain SEN or impact upon inclusive provision. The researchers further reported finding a positive correlation between attitude to inclusion and the availability of resources in the form of physical and human support.

Grossman (2004) and Kugelmass (2003) have argued that inclusion is increasingly seen as a leading challenge for all school leaders, whether they are working in mainstream or special education. Others, for example, Leithwood et al. (1999) suggest that with a growing diversity of intake reinforced by the new demands of a knowledge society, schools will need to develop new forms of knowledge management suitable for operating in an arena of intensifying uncertainty. This will also imply organizations growing a greater capacity for collective problem solving, and ensuring a capacity for being able to cater for an increasingly wider range of students. In the USA, Riehl (2000) identifies three key tasks in a comprehensive approach to school management of diversity. These are:

- generating new meanings of diversity;
- promoting inclusive practices;
- building connections between schools and communities.

The role of a school leader is linked to the potential for inclusive, transformative development. To *transform* in this way should not be confused with other uses of the term transformation, linked to the business-orientated models of transformational leadership (see Simkins, 2005). In this context, Riehl (2000: 56) is referring to an approach in which it is claimed, there is the potential for school principals to engage in inclusive and enabling transformative developments. She concludes:

> When wedded to a relentless commitment to equity, voice, and social justice, administrators' efforts in the tasks of sense making, and promoting inclusive cultures or practices in schools, and building positive relationships outside of the school, may indeed foster a new form of practice.

Kugelmass's research (2003: 11) across three national contexts into inclusive leadership also reveals how a collaborative culture is the hallmark of an inclusive school culture. This has implications for SEN policy as well as education reform. A particular point here is the leaders' practice observed in Kugelmass's study, in which they are observed deliberately positioning and modelling collaborative practice in their everyday interactions with staff as well constructively developing formal and informal opportunities for staff to collaborate with one another. These collaborative processes are further explored in Chapter 5 and point to the importance of community growth, distributed leadership and participatory decision making.

Student voice offers an interesting and perhaps sometimes overlooked topic in this area of special and inclusive schooling. Allan and Brown (2001) report research that relates student accounts of their special school experiences. A broad notion of inclusion surfaces in this student perception of schooling, portraying time in special school as only part of the community to which they belong and often construed as largely instrumental in preparing them for life-long inclusion. The pupils' experiences were recounted as largely positive, reflecting personal achievements, progress and independence, rather than isolation and oppression (see also Cook et al., 2001). The researchers summarize key features of their findings by identifying four messages communicated by the 'disabled insiders'. These are:

1. Disabled people gain positive personal and social benefits from being with similarly disabled people.

2. The logic of inclusion in large part relates to a powerful psychological dimension of belonging. This means that authentic inclusion depends upon access and involvement reflected in the nature of the given specific context.

3. Moving pupils around the system of schooling, especially outside their own neighbourhoods, has dramatic and traumatic consequences for the lives of individuals. Young disabled people can tell us what inclusion means for them.

4. Inclusion cannot be realized through the denial of disability.

It is possible to argue that special schools bring immediate benefits for students, affirming self-regard and strengthening social identity. An homogeneous community can reinforce positive peer relations and self-reference for students presenting any of the various categories of SEN or disability. On the other hand, the same psychological processes might be interpreted as an exercise in reinforcing social stigma and pejorative labelling. The researchers (Cook et al., 2001: 309) concluded that the 'insider voices' of both disabled adults and young people need to be heard if 'inclusion' is not to 'perpetuate the subjugation of disabled people in other settings'. The policy debate in regard to SEN provision and inclusion is set to continue, albeit that recent developments in the UK suggest a sense of sliding shifts in the policy framework as a groundswell gathers to suggest a view that 'total inclusion' may not work.

Global trends in developing educational inclusion

The movement toward educational inclusion is a global trend. In recent years the inclusion imperative has led to a call for integration and the mainstreaming of children with SEN in many countries (O'Hanlon, 1995; Pijl and Meijor, 1991). In a survey of policies for integration in eight Western countries, Pijl and Meijor (1991) suggested that several early forms of integration (inclusion) took the form of actual integration in regular and special schools (or classes) to wider preventive measures for reducing placement in special education provision. The following examples of education research are selected from the literature to illustrate the varied pattern of inclusive education occurring across the globe (see Table 2.3). It is evident, when reading these accounts of research that commonalities exist in both an understanding and an approach to the policy of educational inclusion. It should be noted too that situated context is identified again and again as a determining factor in explaining the nature and success of SEN policy and practice.

Table 2.3   Global trends in managing inclusion

Country	Research Findings
ISRAEL Avissar et al. (2003)	• Principals perceived the expected social success of mainstreamed SEN students as higher than their expected educational success. • The severity of disability affected practitioner perception and the prediction of success. • Key environmental variables, namely age, level of education and in-service training, were related to principals' views and practices regarding inclusion.
NORWAY (Tangen, 2005)	• Developing an inclusive policy should reflect both a philosophy of inclusion and a distribution of disability-specific information. • For inclusion to succeed teachers and school administrators need to act as change agents in school improvement as a regular part of their work.
ENGLAND/PORTUGAL/USA Kugelmass (2003)	• Effective inclusion reveals a motivation for inclusion supported by external forces. • Commitment and belief in inclusion with differences among students and staff perceived as a resource. • Collaborative interaction style among staff and children and inclusion understood as a social/political issue.
CANADA Zaretsky (2005)	• Special education provision is a key leadership challenge within the context of diversity, efficiency and performance (it can be a countervailing force to school improvement efforts). • Attitudes about learning capacity limited promotion of instructional interventions in schools. • Teachers were reluctant to encourage or engage with politicized parental lobby groups and wished to preserve a professional identity and a traditional autonomy in decision making. • A prime need in managing inclusive policy is to create relational networks with many partners.
HONG KONG (Heung, 2006)	This research is an evaluation of a government initiative aimed at implementing an adapted version of the Inclusion Index (N=100 schools). • Schools were committed to developing inclusion allied to school improvement. • Inclusion is restricted by the emphasis upon academic results, league tables and intense competition. Inclusion is reinforced by a concern for individual student performance/issues of educational equity.
NEW ZEALAND (Kearney and Kane, 2006)	In an evaluation of The New Zealand Disability Strategy the researchers found that the strategy at the moment

(Continued)

TABLE 2.3   (Continued)

takes the form of a charter or mission statement, it is still recent, and the researchers conclude that an evaluation will be forthcoming in the near future. Key features of the strategy included:

- To ensure that no child is denied access to their local, regular school because of their impairment.
- To ensure that teachers and other educators understand the learning needs of disabled people.
- To ensure that disabled students, families, teachers and other educators have equitable access to the resources available to meet their needs.

The existence of well-established separate provision in special schools and classes from an early stage in the development of SEN provision has been repeatedly identified as a barrier to developing full inclusion, also creating a number of complex policy dilemmas and leading many countries to operate what Pijl and Meijor (1991) refer to as `two tracks' of provision. This was essentially a continuing arrangement of contradictory parallel but separate segregation and integration provision. Ainscow et al. (2000), nonetheless, optimistically identify a shortlist of several countries that have moved more emphatically toward a single-track inclusive provision (for example Australia, Canada, Denmark, Italy, New Zealand, Norway, Portugal, Spain and Sweden). In these countries, the mainstream neighbourhood school is seen as the appropriate placement for pupils with special needs, although even in these more inclusive contexts the situation often exhibits variation from place to place and is usually not an example of total or full inclusion.

RECONSTRUCTING INCLUSION: DIVERSITY
AND DIFFERENCE

I believe we may have reached a point in the policy development of educational inclusion and special education where there is a need to turn to a mixed perspectives paradigm for reconstructing inclusion (Rouse and McLaughlin, 2006) and special education (see Mertens and McLaughlin, 2004). Such a movement might additionally build upon an integration of theory and practice (more fully explored in Chapter 4). I recall the first special school headteacher for whom I worked, once suggesting that 'driving forward should always involve making full use of a rear-view mirror'. I suggest that direction is about utilizing the past, both in terms of history and knowledge, and synthesizing a new knowledge pool for drawing upon ideas and strategy for future purpose and action. For policy makers, this requires the kind of integrative leadership located in a framework of functional and integrative management more fully considered in Chapter 3. At a broader level, it also reasserts the need for a pragmatic base in theorizing difficulty and disability. Bayliss's suggestion when considering future SEN policy some time ago is that:

A rational model will need to have a clear understanding of 'special educational needs' as an emergent property of complex systems. This requires an analysis of how needs are determined and for us to be clear how this process is constituted. (1997: 75)

Bayliss continues this penetrating argument by asking us to think of individuals with disability interacting within a social and physical world, implying that we need in turn to conceptualize 'specialness' as an emergent behaviour within chaotic or complex systems. This requires a synthesis of theory. It also requires a pragmatic approach to learning and teaching if it is to lead at all to understanding the contextualized and interactive nature of knowledge generation.

Managing SEN policy and provision

The idea that an integrative synthesis of theory and practice is necessary in special education is not new (see Baker and Bovair, 1989; Carpenter et al., 1996). The problematic nature of SEN categories and a dilemma of difference associated with managing equity and diversity in an inclusive policy is yet more closely examined by Norwich (2006: 61). This approach seeks to achieve a balanced recognition of 'dilemmas of difference' more fully explained in earlier work (Norwich, 1993). It posits a need for the creative blending of multiple policy values and the acceptance of 'ideological impurity' (Norwich, 2000). It infers the need for a carefully redefined and balanced functional approach to managing policy and provision. It is reflected, too, in the idea of 'responsible inclusion' presented by Evans and Lunt (2002), in an effort to preserve and improve the utility of assessment-led intervention. This is presented in a different but complementary way with the idea of 'optimal placement' as a basis for an inclusive SEN education in what amounts to twin-track provision (Farrell, 2004). The attempt, again, is to offer a pragmatic mediation between the management of resources and a real-life situation and the ideal of education for all in an inclusive provision.

All of this, arguably, points to the position outlined by Bayliss (1997), in which he identifies an SEN policy imperative. He calls for the development of a rational model of intervention drawing upon a synthesis of context and the various competing models of SEN and disability. A similar conclusion is reached in the House of Commons Education and Skills Committee Report on SEN provision in England (HOC, 2006). The Report emphatically states, for example, that the Warnock SEN Framework is now a failing system and should be replaced with a new and clearly developed strategy for SEN provision in England (see HOC, 2006: 6). The report points to a need for a new and balanced approach, reflected in repeated allusions to a 'third way' in the reconstructing of SEN policy. The message from officials giving evidence to the committee is of ensuring a 'flexible continuum of provision for children with SEN'. As part of this dialogue, policy makers presenting evidence at the committee hearing made repeated reference to personalized education, inferring a new direction in SEN policy for England and Wales. (I will return to this idea in a later chapter.) For the present, it is important to realize that while inclusion is a policy imperative, it is one that as Armstrong (2005) recently acknowledged is very much steeped in a problematic and contested political arena.

Such a redirection of policy arguably involves a careful restating of a functional aspect to educational management. I should make it clear, however, that this is not to propose returning to the 'functional or behaviourist model of education or management', so intensely criticized by educationists such as Skrtic (1991) or Fulcher (1989). It points, instead, to developing new understandings of 'managing diversity', 'individual differences', 'learning leadership' and 'inclusion' that do not deny disability or the psychology of personal growth, on the one hand, in contrast to an awareness of discrimination and contrastive judgment on the other (see Cremin and Thomas, 2005).

In making this turn in direction, I am aware that many educationists and policy makers who adopt the social justice model of disability will regard any alternative to full inclusion a contradiction in terms. In this perspective, an inclusive policy is one that will re-orientate the normalizing tendency associated with our history of defining knowledge in education. As Skrtic (1991: 105) stated, accepting this means rejecting a structure that is driven by a functional imperative. It involves a wholesale jettisoning of a history and knowledge that encompass both the medical and disability models of individual need. This means losing a useful and pertinent perspective on the question of learning difficulty and making provision for learning differences in the school classroom. Put simply, we should be cautious that the baby is not thrown out with the bath water.

The immediate challenge for those managing inclusion and special education is one of ensuring efficacy and efficiency, but always and firstly achieving equity. Managing inclusion should therefore reflect an inclusive leadership characterized by an enduring concern for diversity, access and achievement. Such work is self-evidently about managing change and increasingly dealing in multi-level, interactive contexts involving a continuing series of contradictions, dilemmas and shifting functions within a dynamic system. This day-to-day reality is volatile, it is uncertain and it often feels like an overwhelming mix and churn of constant change.

To manage well in this context reflects a pragmatic need to deal with anxiety and stress and assert control. A deeper need is to assert leadership and regain lost ground or renew an approach to public service, professionalism, and an inclusive leadership or policy that positions the educative process and a moral *praxis* at the heart of the school system (see Chapters 1 and 4). This is made all the more clear as the excesses of a decade or more of managerialism, fixated on the seemingly easy metrics of performance-related target-setting that are imported from the world of business and accountancy, erode teacher professionality and most alarmingly a sustained sense of vocation. The model of management (MISE) presented in the next chapter is intended as a template which can be used to facilitate the thinking, action and function of those engaged in managing special and inclusive education.

3

The MISE Model: Managing Inclusion and Special Education

Managing inclusion and Special Educational Needs (SEN) is a continuing challenge for the educational community irrespective of location (Special, Primary, Secondary, Tertiary, Further and Higher Education). The task identified in this chapter is to integrate professional knowledge and mapping of an intellectual terrain in the management of inclusive learning and SEN provision.

Mapping as an exercise reveals the topography or relief of the conceptual domain describing existing policy and provision. It is a tactic and tool to be used for the purposes of exploration and charting routes in the journey of knowledge creation. The major implications emerging from this chapter are to do with *how* to manage in order to enable learning and teaching for all pupils and students regardless of individual differences or social diversity. Using the trigger questions of why, what, when, and for whom, a review of SEN practice and provision using the MISE model as a framework is a first step toward frameworking inclusive leadership and renewal of SEN policy. Management issues emerge that involve interrogating structures and agency in the learning organization and wider local community.

LEADERSHIP AND MANAGEMENT FOR LEARNING

A core function of educational policy is the effective organization of knowledge management and learning. Managers and leaders in education are people who take on a particular role in making all of this happen. It is worth noting that this work is done by people, with people and for people. The personal and social context of educational leadership and learning is its *sine qua non* and in part captured by the two fires and goblet symbol from Gestalt psychology on the cover of this book. The interaction of learners, learning and teacher is captured in the perceptual shift of form and a new meaning emerging in the shape of the goblet. The creation of new knowledge might well be portrayed by the goblet in this caption yet it is entirely a product of the process of learning, perception and understanding. In the task of managing inclusion and special education, integrating the educative process (learning and teaching) within a specific context is the entire basis for realizing success, achieving quality, producing knowledge in learning leadership.

Yet, just as in the Gestalt, the final outcome of management is greater than the sum of its many constituent parts, including social structure, agency, culture, values, knowledge, self and the situated context.

The work of an educational leader or manager in the contemporary context of the knowledge society has been typically presented as an individual determining strategic direction, performance focused and acting as an agent of transformational change. This sits uneasily alongside the notion of a head-teacher engaged in facilitating professional learning and knowledge creation. It is also a description of leadership in which making sense and educative endeavour are not emphasized. Bush and Bell (2002: 4) state that:

> ... three levels of management, strategic, organisational and operational must work in harmony towards a common purpose ... Each level of management depends upon the other two. Organisational and operational management can be aimless without clear values and purposes but even the most inspiring leadership will fail if it does not lead to effective implementation. Combining these three levels is the prime function of management.

This function when working well produces knowledge, facilitates personal growth, professional development, celebrates achievement, values the individual person and is set against the backdrop of life-long learning. It is by definition about educating and providing an education for all.

Mapping leadership and management knowledge

I still recall today reading with interest a slim publication of non-statutory advice published by the DfE in 1993, towards the end of my period of special school headship. Much of the content was aimed at preparing the incumbent for finance and site management. It was prepared by Coopers and Lybrand, the accountancy firm based in the UK, and heralded what has become a string of such publications by the UK government (the most recent is the PricewaterhouseCoopers study into school leadership, 2007). While a great deal of the advice was useful, the reason why this booklet is still on my shelf is for its summary of establishing a working framework or map in preparation for local management (DfE, 1993a: 8).

The mapping of a metaphoric 'terrain' related to the 'geography of knowledge' is a powerful medium through which to explain and understand the purposes and actions of leadership and management. As Gunter and Ribbins (2002) explain, mapping as an exercise reveals the topography or relief of the conceptual domain; it allows for the charting of knowledge positions in relation to a bedrock of knowledge claims; it offers a political description of the knowledge producer's drawing of boundaries, bases for entry and border skirmishes in the development of theory and explanation; and it is, finally, a tool to be used for the purposes of exploration and charting routes, erecting signposts and direction finding in the pursuit of knowledge creation. In this world of knowledge, paradigm and perspective, the map is a very useful tool for planning a way forward.

Table 3.1 Leadership knowledge domains in education

Conceptual Knowledge	• Focuses on issues of ontology, epistemology and conceptual clarification in leadership.
Descriptive Knowledge	• Focuses upon factual reporting of one or more aspects of leadership.
	• Identifies patterns of features or characteristics in leaders, leading and the led.
Humanistic Knowledge	• Focuses upon perceptions, experiences and understandings of those involved in leadership and the led;·
	• Reveals how role incumbents in leadership experience or facilitate leadership.
Critical Knowledge	• Focuses upon revealing and emancipating practitioners within the power structures of organization or society.
	• Identifies patterns of power and distribution of leadership or work amongst leaders and the led.
Evaluative Knowledge	• Focuses upon effectiveness and efficiency of performance and outcome.
	• Identifies patterns of success or quality assurance.
Instrumental Knowledge	• Focuses upon method and approach in goal-directed leadership and management.
	• Identifies tactics or strategies for leaders and leadership.

A management framework, however, is not only a theoretical tool but is also pragmatic. As Fidler (1996) describes it, mapping is part of an application of models, concepts and frameworks that involves the creation and adaptation of concepts and ideas for particular purposes in management. It is an invaluable practical tool for use in strategic leadership, direction-finding and the planning of organizational development. A framework contains this process of mapping, as does generating and sharing cognitive schema, thereby providing opportunity to frame and portray theory, actions and practice. It can include a statement describing the arrangements for managing the school and gives an opportunity to clarify relationships and responsibilities, as well as helping to sequence and prioritize activity. In point of fact, co-producing scripts and maps or frameworks of management represents active cognitive schema and quite frequently, a useful form of 'semantic mapping', which contributes to a 'working policy document'. In many respects, this represents the metaphorical 'hymn-sheet' so often referred to in team meetings.

An example of this tool being used in a theoretical context is work completed by Ribbins and Gunter (2002) and Gunter and Ribbins (2002), mapping the field of educational leadership. Several types of knowledge production are identified and these are summarized in Table 3.1. The purpose, value and utility of this kind of summary, charting types of professional knowledge, are to inform greater awareness, use and generation of knowledge and professional learning in the leader's practice. Leadership per se is an exercise in developing practice and the linkage of theory (knowledge) with provision (practice), producing pragmatic theory (*praxis*). (This knowledge and the relationship between theory, values and professional practice are further explored in the next chapter.) Generally, however, professional knowledge that can be either pragmatic or theoretical or a mix of the both is presented here as an important ingredient in any 'transformative or empowering function' in an educational setting.

Knowledge and knowing – leading managing

Mapping is a very a useful exercise in the work of management. It enables the possibility of charting and co-ordinating multiple sources and types of professional knowledge. A practitioner using such knowledge can engage with a task and think through the exercise of management. Sallis and Jones (2002) provide another example of this tactic in a useful introduction to the recently developed field of *knowledge management*. Globalization, macro-economics, and capital in the form of 'an asset' are core ideas in the field of knowledge management. There are several forms of formal and informal knowledge identified in this theory, all relevant to the task of managing change and development in the school setting. For example, several types of working knowledge, such as knowledge that is critical, embedded, creative, explicit or tacit, are relevant to the learning organization. Tacit knowledge, in particular, is informal knowledge that is often referred to as *know-how* and regarded as a hidden but vital knowledge indispensable to an organization.

The importance of knowledge might appear at first glance self-evident for the world of education. However, it might seem as apparent on a second glance that educational organizations are not very good at knowledge management. As Daniels and Garner (2000: xvi) comment:

> Schools encounter great difficulties when they attempt to become learning organisations. From the point of view of those concerned with schools as organisations there is a need to shift schools from positions of passive compliance and/or resistance to change and ask how best they might be transformed.

This concept of transformation, however, needs careful explanation. It is perhaps more helpful to think of this idea as a transformative and 'bottom up' growth rather than a 'top-down', imposed alchemy or instant transformation. The importance of evidence-based research and constructed knowledge to help practitioners better understand and contribute to strategic leadership and SEN policy is really self-evident. The theory of the learning organization, organizational learning and reflective practice describes complementary ideas in a knowledge-based approach to management. A learning organization, according to Senge (1993), will adopt the following actions in their management:

- introduce systems-thinking aimed to integrate disciplines into a coherent body of theory and practice;

- encourage workforce members to strive for personal (professional) mastery;

- identify existing mental models and subject these to scrutiny or challenge;

- build a shared vision;

- structure team work throughout the organization.

The concept of 'life-long learning' and a belief in continuing workforce development are central to the idea of the learning organization. Many of the issues related to this knowledge-orientated approach in educational management can be seen to resonate with those surrounding the development of inclusive education.

Daniels and Garner (2000) return to the question of knowledge-production and schooling to point to socio-economic trends and a developing knowledge society affecting the policy of inclusive education in the global context. They refer to a need for re-orientating education so that it accepts and exploits three key premises required for a knowledge-building organization – namely, that:

- Learning occurs through engaged participation in the activities of knowledge communities.

- Teaching involves informed interpretations of and responses to students' orientations to knowledge.

- Schools, as sites of teachers' knowledge application and production, need to understand the range of orientations to knowledge held within them and how these originated.

Such a treatment of knowledge as forms of distinctive systems, furthermore, leads to adopting a generalized and collaborative knowledge-building approach to learning in the classroom. Daniels and Garner (2000: xviii) argue such an approach represents an 'inclusive-sensitive re-orientation to knowledge, cognition and pedagogy', pointing to a widening recognition that schools today are changing in the wake of an expanding knowledge-based society. Containment of knowledge, however, as well as its delivery in forms of transmission that entail flexing and transfer across traditional social and physical boundaries should be carefully managed. The conversion of knowledge into economic or social capital and as packaged byte-sized assets conforms to a contemporary trend in defining learning and curricula as a transmission delivery. While transmission is one element in the learning process, it is only one of several kinds of communication necessary for deep learning or sustainability in organizations. It is important that new technology is not used to create a misleading metaphor for describing post-modern definitions of learning or to justify developing a commercialized pedagogy available only, to those who can plug into it.

Making sense: a working model for educational leadership

In making this argument for valuing professional knowledge, teacher leadership and learning, I want to re-emphasize the notion of the 'thinking practitioner' and the value of the independent learner. I suggest that this represents a continuing development of the original idea of a 'reflective practitioner' (Schon, 1983) and organizational learning (Schein, 1985). In a direct reference to leadership and management, it reflects an emphasis upon how sense making and making sense are essential thinking for modern school leadership.

In a critical analysis of contemporary educational leadership, Simkins (2005) explains how suggesting leadership is based upon identifying 'what works' so that it may be prescribed and replicated can often be inappropriate and unhelpful. In the leadership world 'making sense of things' is at least as important as 'seeking what works'. The contemporary policy environment in education places expectations on those charged with leadership that can seem almost intolerable, given its range and complexity and the internal tensions and even contradictions within it. An easy example is educational inclusion. The leader practitioner is faced with the challenge of making sense of a highly contested political arena as it is experienced in a particular context. There is therefore a making-sense agenda for educational leadership comprising the following tasks for understanding and knowledge building:

- establishing ways in which leadership itself is conceived;

- marking the role and purposes of the organization within a dynamic and conflictual policy environment;

- identifying ways in which leadership roles are changing and should change;

- agreeing ways in which power and authority are and should be constituted and distributed in educational organizations;

- making sense of 'other worlds' across inter-professional and organizational boundaries;

- using leadership development to understand sense making itself.

This agenda serves equally well as a blueprint for proposing the development of organizational effectiveness and inclusive provision. Inherent in both is a continuing and fundamental tension between concern for individual needs and social responsibility. More and more, an inclusive form of leadership is required to assist the integrative management of increasingly fluid, dynamic and interactive learning contexts. In a very immediate sense, traditional workforce boundaries are evaporating with the impact of new forces of change, such as the increasing levels of mobility and diversity in a global society.

MANAGING INCLUSION AND SPECIAL EDUCATION: THE MISE MODEL

This final section presents a conceptual framework for explaining and framing the action of effectively managing inclusion and special education. It takes the form of a schematic model made up of five levels that is intended to work as a rational representation of fundamental structures, principles and agency at play in the process and practice of the management task (see Figure 3.1). As a framework, it is intended as both a prompt and a template for framing an integrative approach to managing special and inclusive education. The MISE model formed the rationale and structure for a CPD course managed in partnership with a West Midlands LEA for five years (see Whittaker, 2004) and I have also used the MISE framework to structure this book. I hope to demonstrate a relevance and utility in this model for guiding the practitioner in thinking about managing diversity and differences in the educational setting. This forms part of a continuing process of learning, making sense and knowledge production.

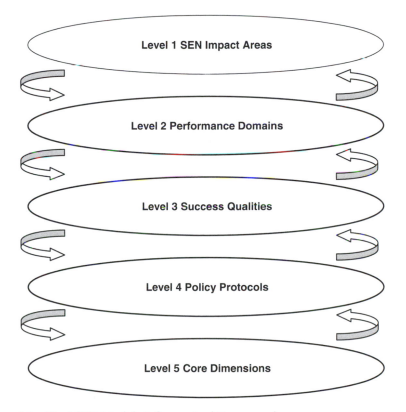

Figure 3.1   The MISE Model: A Conceptual Framework

It is in following and revisiting this model at the various levels of activity that issues surrounding process and organization can be identified, integrated and managed. Each level in the model is two-sided, and the task of managing SEN provision is much like working with a series of spinning 'conceptual coins' as the currency of an integrative management. For example, at Level 5 (See Figure 3.6) in the model, while strategy might be the prime focus at a particular point in the work of a team, it should not be separated from issues of provision or operation. In the same way, it is nonsense to suggest that in the educational context, leadership should be separated from management. It just does not work this way and if such an artificial separation is pursued as a working model, it will invariably lead to poor practice.

The MISE model is made up of five vertical but inter-relating and interactive levels of managing inclusion and special education. It offers a 'jo-hari type window' at each level along intersecting axes that create four quadrants of space within which two dimensions of management are set to interact (see Luft, 1970). The model describes a conceptualization of intention (horizontal axis) and task (vertical axis). Blending these produces both a functional process and integrative management.

The binary representation of an inter-play between structure and agency is repeated as the practitioner tracks up or down each level of the model. I imagine it working much as a series of 'spinning plates', reminding me of this same simile being so often used to describe the teacher effectively managing the various aspects of the working classroom. It is possible, at this and every level in turn, to locate specific tasks that form part of the managing process in each quadrant. In a manner reminiscent of the jo-hari window, different stages of a management activity can reflect different levels of an activity portrayed in the MISE model and reflected in the context of a particular project or task.

For example, at Level 5 (see Figure 3.6), work located in the left-high quadrant (involving deliberate questioning and a challenge of a problem-posing kind, as well as decision-making in its earliest stage of group-storming and creative conflict) is likely to occur at the start of a project or programme. With a relocation of task and actions in the lower left quadrant (involving deliberate resolution, compromise and problem solving that lead to closure and decision taking), work shifts towards completion of a particular stage in a project. If there is over-commitment to an activity located in one quadrant, for example, reflecting a preoccupation with problem posing, this will inhibit problem solving, knowledge production and/or decision taking. Conversely, too great an emphasis upon strategic management will result in excessive 'blue sky thinking' or 'out of the box' creativity and an operational tragedy.

While this level (5) describes a broad basis for defining management in a fundamental and functional way, it also represents core action and key processes that will occur and recur at every level of the management task. The MISE model operates at each level in an independent but complementary way. It offers a conceptual framework made up of the following five levels of managing the task of inclusion and special education.

Level 1 – Impact areas of inclusion and SEN

This is the uppermost level of functioning and is located in the surface aspects of an inclusive and special educational provision. It is this face of

SEN provision which is most easily and readily experienced as real-life work. It is the part of management that is context-dependent and sensitive to changing priorities. The impact areas will change in definition over time, but those identified here are set to dominate in the next decade of modernizing development. This is already evident and gathering pace in the remodelling agenda of the school workforce, the emerging pressure for the extended school, in descriptions of the statutory framework for ECM and the new arrangements for school self-evaluation (see Cheminais, 2006).

Level 1 is made up of two dimensions: the first is the organizing structure of collaborative or inter-agency working provision. It includes work linked to partnership and service compacts at one end of a continuum, and at the other in work associated with networking organizational learning designed to offer support for learners, teachers, and learning leadership. The second dimension describes qualities associated with the process of reflecting the values and principles necessary to engender an inclusive culture in the educational community. At one end of a continuum is a concern for (and an enabling of) participation in learning opportunities and a parity of esteem irrespective of individual or social difference for all members of the school community. This position should arguably be clearly maintained as an explicit value-set in the school culture. At the other end is work focused upon understanding and providing for diversity in the community. This invokes a continuing concern and construction of method for reducing barriers to learning and ensuring access to the curriculum.

Realizing this organizational culture and the nurture of an appropriate climate implies a particular ethos for an organization and points to the crucial role of pastoral care and the vital work associated with a pastoral curriculum. Working successfully within what is often a hidden and neglected part of the curriculum has in point of fact a maximum impact upon inclusion and the learning experience of pupils with SEN (particularly EBSD – see Chapter 7). Most of this work will reflect a pervasive requirement for parity of esteem, and enabling levels of participation which in turn will lead to initiatives that will see community practices enabling or creating new points of access to the formal or academic curriculum. This process reflects on-going provision for diversity and will thus raise issues surrounding the development of personalized education and a bespoke pedagogy. The dimension as represented is a mirror image of the whole school curriculum (pastoral + academic).

It is also a missing consideration in the apparent rationale for teaching and professionality underpinning the UK government's remodelling of the school workforce. Logic infers that freeing teachers to teach means no involvement in pastoral care, that teachers should not be concerned with the personal, social and emotional development of learners. It certainly infers that none of these form part of the learning process! The modernizing policy agenda focuses more or less exclusively on a traditional model of knowledge transmission, learning and academic performance. It is then given further

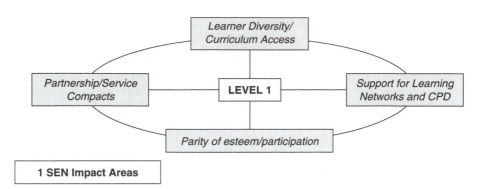

Figure 3.2   The MISE Model: Level 1

reinforcement in a technical and managerialist paradigm associated with a producer and consumer-driven notion of public service (see Chapter 10).

The evaluative and instrumental knowledge required for this level of managing policy and developing provision includes an up-to-date use of information technology, advancing support for learning networks that are both interactive and trans-disciplinary (see Chapter 6). Perhaps somewhat ironically, the ECM agenda encourages the notion of child development as an holistic concept. What is at odds with this, however, is a compartmentalization and commodification of the many aspects/services that support this learning which are packaged as a form of delivery to users. Networking and establishing working compacts will rely upon servicing interactive relationships that ensure secure and trustworthy communication, quick transmission of information and an exchange of knowledge with perspective-sharing between specialists utilizing different sets of expertise and skills.

An interesting example illustrating the context for this level of the MISE model also captures the origin of 'parity of esteem' as an idea. A cluster of secondary schools in Northern Ireland collaborated in a project aimed at nurturing inclusive education with a particular bias. The pressure point for segregation experienced in this area was social and religious rather than disability or 'race'. Parity of esteem emerged as a key concept that could be used as a distributive standard for developing integration of school admissions and school programmes, irrespective of background.

A second example is provided by a special school in an English Midlands LEA winning a bid for money to develop networking. The example is from a student assignment submitted as part fulfilment of the Birmingham University MISE programme. An ICT support manager was appointed on a cost-centred basis to develop and facilitate networking, using information technology to support curriculum and pedagogic knowledge transfer to mainstream schools.

A third and final case example is reported, describing new provision at Port Phillip Specialist School in Melbourne, Australia (Burnett, 2003: 14). The project, involving the 'fully serviced school' concept, includes a head of integrated services, a professor with expertise in all aspects of paramedical service delivery, and workforce members with extensive experience in the use of ICT to optimize outcomes for pupils with special needs.

Level 2 – Performance domains of inclusion and SEN

This level of MISE is located just beneath the surface of provision and represents the intersection of key aspects of performance in educational enterprise. The horizontal axis describes a continuum of function ranging from stated policy such as aims, declared standards and levels of measured achievement to organizational structures of systemic organization, procedure, protocols and discipline. The vertical axis represents the cultural and ethical arrangements triggered in the management of change, as well as an affirmation of professional identity, role definition and empowerment linked to strategic options and decision making reflected in organizational planning. As Fullan (1991; 1993) explains, sustainable change in the educational setting is very much a moral and values-driven process – something frequently forgotten in a managerialist paradigm dominated by a technical, target-driven mind set framed in the transformational leadership model.

Interestingly, even this model strains to integrate with a functional schema as targets require a wider performance management framework in which to work. The schema, however, as is powerfully explained by Tallis (2006) in a critical review of the UK's National Health Service, is clearly not fit-for-purpose in sustaining effective public service. For change leadership to be successful, both dimensions of this level need to be integrated in a way that is increasingly characterized by an exploitation of new forms of distributed leadership (see Gronn, 2002; Rayner and Gunter, 2005a).

It is also necessary for change to link directly with strategic and operational thinking identified in the deeper levels of the MISE model. Evaluative and instrumental knowledge is still required for this level of managing policy and provision but this is both informed and reinforced by critical and humanistic knowledge. The latter is evidenced in both formal and informal or tacit forms of knowledge, involving work aimed at enabling and exploiting the experience, expertise and skills of the workforce. Management activity at this level is often largely perceived as 'leadership'. Such an organizational dynamic, as I have previously explained, is what Ainscow et al. (1995) called the 'moving school'. It subsequently shaped several developmental projects associated with the Improving Quality of Education for All (IQEA) research based at the Institute of Education at the University of Cambridge (Hopkins, 2001).

A case example describing the work of one special school in the UK (the Transforming School Workforce (TSW) project) shows how this level of activity can produce both short- and longer-term restructuring (see Rayner et al., 2005). These changes included the appointment of a full-time Bursar,

Figure 3.3   The MISE Model: Level 2

changes to the teachers' workload balance and teaching time and most interestingly, pressures beyond the immediate project pressing the school management to continue to redistribute leadership through an established
change management team. In curricular areas, as well as in planning and
management, wider and deeper involvement of the para-professional members of the school workforce was substantially extended. Overall, concerns
for sustainability were evidenced in a persistent effort to integrate strategic
and operational factors, such as finance, staffing, purposes and benefit
analysis related to the TSW project.

   While the project had a specific focus on workforce remodelling, it quickly
became apparent that it was in fact about whole school development. The
need to conceptualize a functional management with integrative leadership
surfaced time and again throughout the life-span of the project. Where the
project failed, conspicuously, was in ensuring a close linkage with the core
purpose of teaching and learning, and an inclusion policy. This was in large
part attributable to the technical emphasis of a transformational model of
change management found in the project, led by the Learning Leadership
Centre (see Collarbone, 2005; Gunter and Rayner, 2006).

Level 3 – Success qualities in inclusion and SEN

The mid-level of the MISE model describes a fulcrum point at which inter-
sects qualities and values integral to success and the assurance of quality.
The first dimension is made up of work related to assuring good quality and
enabling the institution's or individual practitioner's function, namely realizing efficacy and efficiency. Both concepts are measures of performance and
represent a set of factors necessary in any work and the continuing evaluation of success or worth. Efficacy has to do with how well an organization is
realizing its purpose and function, efficiency with it offering value for
money and the best use of resources.

To realize each of these 'quality marks', however, the managing of inclusive policy and provision must also include qualities associated with ethical considerations of equity and empathy. This dimension refers to all of those ideas and values identified by a number of educationists as essential tell-tale indicators of an inclusive community. The need for equity, evidenced in access, participation, and support for learning, is balanced by a complementary need for empathy evidenced in an unconditional regard for the worth of the individual, an appreciation of multiple antecedents for difficulty and a parity of esteem for social and learning differences reflected in diversity.

As the dimension is located mid-point in the MISE model, it is a significant source of multiple effects and will affect any of the other levels of managing policy and provision. In this respect, it also describes activity that represents a confluence of types of knowledge identified by Ribbins and Gunter (2002).

A previous case example, from the Birmingham MISE course, of this level working in a West Midlands pimary school involved its school workforce participating in a project with a recently appointed school improvement partner to establish a new relationship between the cycles of school improvement and self-evaluation (see DfES/Ofsted, 2004; 2005). A particular focus for the project was the management of specific, practice-based data to inform levels of access and participation of disadvantaged groups within the school community (SEN, English as a Second Language (ESL), Ethnic Minority). This was part of an holistic renewal of the school profile aimed at establishing a foundation for working towards better provision, as well as the communication of options to access this provision as provided for the wider community. Emerging from this work was a strategic decision to move towards strengthening targeted aspects of provision that would form part of the profile of an extended school (see DfES, 2005b). This included a review of the network for collaborative partnerships with other agencies and schools in the district. The indicators of performance employed in the final part of the project included efficacy statements, VfM counts, as well as evidence of equity and empathy in terms of stakeholder views and levels of satisfaction (NB: including the perspectives of children, parents and external agency workers).

Level 4 – Policy protocols for inclusion and SEN

This level of activity is more closely focused upon the relationship between resource management and policy. It requires generating and acquiring types of knowledge that are conceptual, descriptive, fiscal and critical. It is essentially about bringing and sharing meaning to the work of managing social justice and equity in education. Critical knowledge, and in a wider perspective the paradigm of critical theory, are particularly important in enabling evaluative research to inform inclusive and special education in the 'transformative mode' as described by Mertens and McLaughlin (2004). In the operational dimension, funding structures, wherewithal and resources that are both human and non-human are factors flowing up from previous levels

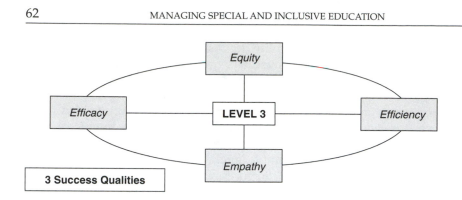

Figure 3.4   The MISE Model: Level 3

to represent a finite constraint on what it is that can be achieved. Interestingly, teachers have a firm tradition of enabling policy that to all intents and purposes is resource-neutral. However, when applied consistently, resource and funding should re-feature at each level of the MISE model as a planning question and an operational issue in the decision making and operation of policy and provision.

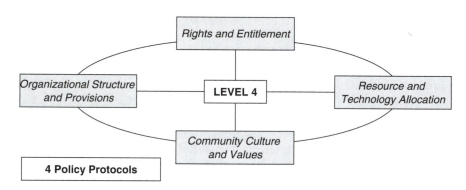

Figure 3.5   The MISE Model: Level 4

At this level (4), the horizontal axis supports a dimension that refers to the arrangements and practices making up the various aspects of provision in an organization. Professional codes of practice and conduct are an example of this formal structuring of the managed context, and in the case of SEN provision, might for example include formal use of the SEN Code of Practice to secure specialized technology.

At the far end of this same axis sits work involving the structuring of resource, albeit financial (as in the case of budgets) as well as material such as information technology infrastructure, human resources and the built environment.

In an English school, and the SEN context, this is the 'department' or 'management zone' of the SENCo or the 'Inclusion Leader'. Yet, interestingly, the influence of the SENCo generally in matters financial and resource management is often severely constrained (Cole, 2005).

The vertical axis of this level represents a dimension containing less easily measured (but for inclusive leadership essential) phenomena in an educational context. In terms of an inclusive policy protocol, it marks referential aspects of an educational organization. These include the nature of an organizational culture that exists in the institutional setting, captured in the feel of a place, its organizational climate, ethos and the basic values shared by the community. Policy protocols generated by work in this dimension include articulating individual and community rights, responsibilities and entitlement. These are especially important for the pastoral curriculum and most particularly impact upon students experiencing EBSD. Again, such work engages with types of knowledge that are conceptual, descriptive and critical, but also can greatly benefit from humanistic theory. Counselling and human relations represents one specific discipline that is relevant in this area.

Several case examples of schools applying the more recent version of the 'Inclusion Index' (Booth and Ainscow, 2002) provide an opportunity to see leading work focusing on re-shaping culture, reflecting this level of the managing task. A medium-sized primary school in a West Midlands new town used the MISE Leadership Course with Birmingham University to redevelop a parent partnership (example from a student assignment submitted as part fulfilment of the Birmingham University MISE Programme). The aim was to include a number of ethnic minority groups who had previously been marginalized in spite of a considerable effort to include them in the school community. A drop-in café organized twice a week on mornings in the autumn term was so successful it was extended into the school year and expanded to include parent volunteers running a cost-centred enterprise.

Level 5 – Core dimensions of the managing task

At the foundation Level 5, the key axes represent the intersection of a strategic-operational structure with a cyclical process of problem posing, decision making, knowledge acquisition moving towards, problem solving, decision taking, and the application of knowledge. Work located in the left-low quadrant at Level 1 (involving deliberate questioning and challenge of a problem-posing kind, leading to exercises in problem solving in its earliest form of storming creative conflict) is likely to occur at the start of a project or programme. With a relocation of activity to task moving in the higher left quadrant (involving deliberate resolution, compromise and problem solving) there is also engagement in a process of decision making. Finally, activity is further progressed with a movement in the cycle toward operational management of the decision-taking kind and the eventual completion of task, beyond which review and problem posing re-trigger the cycle of management. Knowledge types most relevant at this deepest level of the core dimensions of MISE are conceptual and humanistic.

Figure 3.6   The MISE Model: Level 5

An example offering context for this level at work is provided by the headteacher of a rural primary school in the MISE Leadership Course with Birmingham University (example from a student assignment in the Birmingham University MISE Programme). A practitioner enquiry project was launched setting up an inclusion and SEN project to review whole school approaches to a fit-for-purpose curriculum. Combining materials from the course and the Inclusion Index provided a framework that interestingly led to early questioning about how to best facilitate management of change. The work involved in this activity would pre-empt tactics later associated with the remodelling school workforce initiative, and strategies identified as good practice.

A small working group met to explore a number of developmental activities aimed at reflexive thinking about how leadership and management in the school were deployed. Techniques including SWOT (a management audit exercise involving an analysis of strengths, weaknesses, opportunities and threats associated with any specified aspect of provision), as well as the five Whys and brown paper process mapping, tactics later recommended by the TDA (2005), were used to encourage the whole school staff to contribute to this work. The school subsequently created a new change management team tasked with redefining roles and responsibilities for member groups of the school community (including pupils and parents as well as the professional and para-professional members of the school workforce).

The MISE model: a Gestalt in flow?

Finally, returning to the MISE model, it is evident that moving upwards from Level 5–1 mirrors a traditional development of project management. The model also works by moving downwards from Level 1–5, and in fact might conceivably be triggered by focusing in upon any level of the managing process as represented in the MISE structure. This can be achieved by selecting an 'inclusion touchstone theme' and using it to fasten a sharp focus on how inclusion or SEN policy travels through the school community. Such themes might include a number of different topics, all of which are identified by reviewing the MISE policy context (see Chapters 1 and 2), as well as responding to local issues.

The following represent touchstone themes that have worked successfully in this way as part of Birmingham University's MISE Course:

- Exclusion.

- Disability and Social Justice.

- Identification and Assessment of At Risk Learners.

- Young Carers in the Community.

- Bullying and Alienation.

- Truancy.

- Change Management and Distributed Leadership.

- Inter-agency Interaction.

- Personalized Education.

- Pastoral Care and Curriculum.

The tactic works by creating a focal point for a leadership group or groups (for example, Change Managememt Team (CMT), Senior Management Team (SMT), or Pastoral Team) to explore the theme, by referring to the MISE model over time and linking specific actions at one level with other levels of activity. New knowledge is identified, acquired and generated by revisiting and unpacking the linkage between levels of the MISE model as a set of steps in project management. The model, like the Gestalt model, is in constant flow in which the constituent parts do not in summing up explain the final operation. This final figure of integrative management is created by the conceptual field of a situated context. An inclusive form of leadership is also required to drive and steer this use of what is understood to be a functional and integrative model of management for inclusion and special education.

Part II

Inclusive Leadership, Managing Change and Networking?

The second part of this book is about managing inclusive education and SEN provision in educational organizations and the wider setting of the local community. The way in which change is perceived and strategic decision-making is carried out is crucial to shaping and reshaping the nature of a school community. A predominant value at the heart of an inclusive leadership ethic is a belief in an expansive process of learning, tied to the idea of leadership occurring in distributed forms of professional activity. It also rests on an understanding of learning that sees change as mutability, an eco-systemic process in which seeking sustainability and security as well as adaptivity and continuity is paramount. In this way there is a recognition of learning as growth, that is in part developmental, in part systemic, and in its totality is always social but ultimately individual.

I am reminded of a previous analogy of horticulture and gardening to describe the job of education and teaching. In the following three chapters, the focus is on how this garden should be tended during the work of reform, and it is tied to a notion of change characterized in the rhythmic flow of mutability represented in the seasons of the year. The management task is one that involves cultivating a rich diversity in flora and fauna (personal and social differences), bound by a cyclic change of growth, but combined with new opportunities to design a landscape for the learning community in the twenty-first century.

Chapter 4 introduces the idea of inclusive leadership as a distinctive form of professional activity in the educational setting. It is defined as a form of dis-tributed leadership that is also by definition a form of professional learning necessary at every level of provision in a learning organization and learning community. Central to this definition is the action of sense making and knowl-edge acquisition. It is linked to a number of key issues in an explanation of how leadership operates as a key dimension in educational management. It is also defined in particular as contributing to integrative management, pre-sented in Part I as the most appropriate approach to developing and main-taining SEN policy and provision. Implicit in the learning of inclusive leadership is the growth of personal and collective *praxis* and the professional ethic grounded in a notion of the professional learning community.

Chapter 5 is about change management and its role in education reform, school improvement, workforce remodelling and new forms of policy and provision for managing diversity and difference in the school population. An emphasis upon the importance of change in the work-place and society is linked to the nature of knowledge and its accessibility, and is seen to be impacting upon the basic function and purposes of schooling, and the reconstruction of the school setting. A second set of implications in a post-modern setting reflects a demand for utility in education, with increasing emphasis on accountability and school improvement. Implicit in this latter movement is a concern to ensure that the set of success qualities identified in Level 3 of the MISE model is being evidenced. The question of how best to manage change as both a part of strategic leadership and a response to changing policy contexts is also considered. The definition of a desirable change process is linked to the notion of growing the learning community.

Chapter 6 introduces the concept of networking to support learning and knowledge management. Multi-agency issues relevant to developing special and inclusive education are considered in this chapter. The policy backcloth is the continuing drive in an initiative aimed at 'excellence for all' and 'every child matters', both centered in a standards policy agenda aimed at modernizing the education workforce and extending the school system. A recurring theme running through this chapter and the book is a focus on learning in which members of the school workforce openly work together to support each other, establish shared norms and values and continually improve their practice in professional learning. All three chapters reflect the importance of sense-making in leadership and the developing work associated with production of *praxis* as a particular form of practitioner-based knowledge.

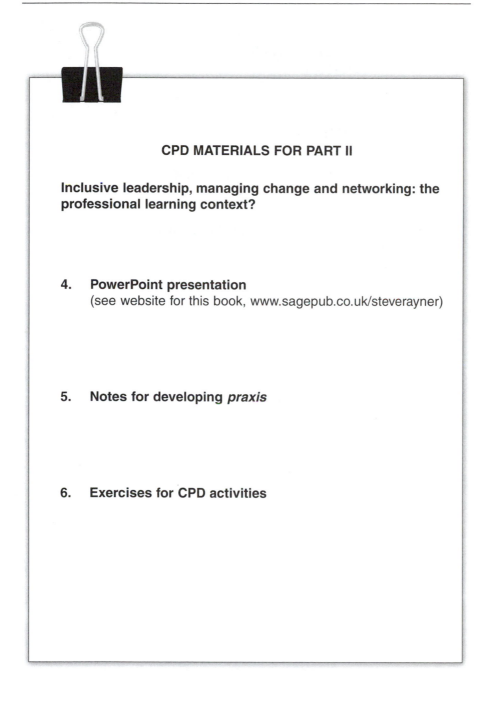

CPD MATERIALS FOR PART II

Inclusive leadership, managing change and networking: the professional learning context?

4.   **PowerPoint presentation**
     (see website for this book, www.sagepub.co.uk/steverayner)

5.   **Notes for developing *praxis***

6.   **Exercises for CPD activities**

5. NOTES FOR DEVELOPING *PRAXIS* [1]

KEY ISSUES/QUESTIONS

1. Discuss the following issues as a workforce or small group exercise – aim to relate each to your work-place and your own role in the workforce:

   - global learning and the knowledge society;
   - reform and modernizing education;
   - transactional leadership;
   - transformational leadership;
   - leadership forces and inclusive leadership.

2. Try and answer the following questions:

   - SEN provision – are you assessing for needs, difficulties or differences?
   - Inclusive education for all needs inclusive leadership in all?
   - Learning leadership – what is knowledge management?
   - Ensuring success qualities – equity and empathy (rights, responsibilities and roles). Can we do it better?
   - Sustaining the learning community – developing *praxis* for inclusive leadership – how can I do this and share it in a learning group?

5. NOTES FOR DEVELOPING *PRAXIS* [2]

CORE CONCEPTS

Explore how the following concepts actually work in your own practice.

1. PROFESSIONAL *PRAXIS*

Three types of core knowledge exist in the pursuit of an educated and good society:

- *Theoria* – the pursuit of theory and truth.
- *Poiese* – the production of a craft or object.
- *Praxis* – the basis of proper action for social well-being and freedom.

Three forms of process occur in thought and action:

- *Eidos* – a guiding idea or intention.
- *Techne* – a practitioner disposition or technique/procedure.
- *Phronesis* – a practical action informed by a moral *eidos* and experience.

Two forms of outcome are created:

- *Object* – a product, artefact or construction.
- *Telos* – practical wisdom located in the social context (leadership).

2. INCLUSIVE LEADERSHIP

Inclusive leadership comprises the following three action principles:

- **Integrative** – as a strategic process which is problem-posing and knowledge-based.
- **Relational** – as activity focused upon ways and means and always situated in contexts defined by purpose, people and evolving *praxis*.
- **Functional** – as reflective enquiry and a research-led applied discipline used to understand, facilitate and evaluate structures, agency and outcome.

5. NOTES FOR DEVELOPING
PRAXIS [3]

KNOWLEDGE SOURCES – KEY READING

Anning, A., Cottrell, D., Frost, N., Green, J. and Robinson, M. (2006) *Developing Multiprofessional Teamwork for Integrated Children's Services*. Maidenhead: OUP, McGraw-Hill Education.

Atkinson, M., Wilkin, A., Stott, A., Doherty, P. and Kinder, K. (2002) *Multi-agency working: A Detailed Study*. LGA Research Report 26. Slough: NFER.

Bennett, N., Crawford, M. and Cartwright, M. (2003) *Effective Educational Leadership*. London: Paul Chapman.

DfES (2004) *The Management of SEN Expenditure* (LEA/0149/2004). London: DfES.

Fullan, M. (2003) *The Moral Imperative of School of Leadership*. London: Paul Chapman.

Hartle, F. (2005) *Shaping Up to the Future: A Guide to Roles, Structures and Career Development in Secondary Schools*. Nottingham: National College for School Leadership.

House of Commons (2006) *The SEN Select Committee Report, HC478–1. Special Educational Needs, Third Report of Session 2005-06, Volume I*. London: The Stationery Office.

Sallis, E. and Jones, G. (2002) *Knowledge Management in Education*. London: Kogan Page.

Stoll, L., Fink, D. and Earl, L. (2003) *It's About Learning (And It's About Time). What's In It For Schools?* London: Routledge-Falmer.

PricewaterhouseCoopers (2007) *Independent Study into School Leadership: The Main Report*. Nottingham: DfES.

Websites at: www.michaelfullan@ca
www.ofsted.gov.uk
www.ace-centre.org.uk

5. NOTES FOR DEVELOPING PRAXIS [4]

ACTION PROMPTS

1. Focus upon developing self and working with others as a theme for a learning group/INSET activity linked to inclusive leadership (from the middle up and down, in and out and back again) and explore how to:

   - Manage your own workload and time effectively to allow for an appropriate work/life balance.
   - Give and receive effective feedback and act to improve personal performance.
   - Support staff in developing constructive working relationships with SEN pupils and their parents/carers.
   - Develop and maintain a culture of high expectations for self and others working in the SEN team, and take appropriate action when performance is unsatisfactory.
   - Collaborate and network with other SENCos and SEN professionals within and beyond the school.

2. Develop an INSET day programme to use the inclusive leadership wheel as a tool for problem posing and exchanging perceptions on how an aspect of the school community is being managed (for example [A] School-Parent Relations or [B] School Experiences of Immigrant Children).

3. Set up a learning group to draft out a plan for networking and evolving an extended school service involving new intervention frameworks to support at-risk children (evidence-based rather than entitlement-based service provision).

6. ASSURING QUALITY AND ACCOUNTABILITY IN SEN PROVISION

1. Organize a group to conduct a benefit analysis/quality assurance check in one or more areas of the school community, for example:

   - arrangements for change management and strategic review;
   - work/life balance for individual groups of the workforce;
   - role responsibilities in the self-evaluation/school inspection process;
   - CPD deployment and the fit with strategic development in the organization.

2. Target the 'removing barriers to access' and/or 'every child matters' agenda and create a practitioner-enquiry group to conduct an action-leadership project to involve some or all of the following:

   - review the cultural climate and ethos of the community as fit for function and purpose;
   - collect and analyse relevant practice-based data as an audit of existing provision for diversity and difference in the community;
   - appraise stakeholder views and contributions (existing and potential);
   - consider the school profile and 'position' in the local community;
   - Identify change management recommendations for the organizational community.

6. REMODELLING THE SCHOOL WORKFORCE AND MODERNIZING REFORM

Workforce remodelling and SEN provision – what do you know?

1. Get up-to-date knowledge of the following policies in the government's statutory framework:

   - Disability Discrimination Act 1995 and 2005
   - SEN and Disability Act (SENDA) 2001
   - SEN Code of Practice 2001
   - Government Strategy for SEN, RBA four key areas
   - *Every Child Matters* five outcomes for children
   - Ofsted integrated inspection framework for Children's Services
   - National Service Framework for Children, Young People and Maternity Services.

2. An up-to-date knowledge and reference to the following (QA) Quality Assurance frameworks:

   - Standards White Paper (2005)
   - National Service Framework Standards
   - (SENSS) Special Educational Needs Support Service Quality Standards
   - (HLTA) Higher Level Teaching Assistant Professional Standards
   - CPD Professional Standards.

Map out the implications and possible options for school development in this new policy arena – how does this fit into the wider school community/local community?

6. SCHOOL IMPROVEMENT AND SELF-EVALUATION: LEARNING AND CHANGE

Complete these tasks as part of a CPD team or working group. How do any of these suggestions link to the work of specific groups in the school community (parents/governors/pupils and so on)?

Assuring Quality Checks

- agreeing standards criteria for assuring quality in provision;
- agreeing effectiveness indicators for the inclusive school;
- managing and motivating performance and accountability in SEN provision;
- defining quality or success frameworks (benchmarking growth);
- understanding the new school inspection relationship and self-evaluation.

Managing Change and Improvement Priorities

- reaffirming an inclusive culture, values and attitudes in the community;
- sustaining stakeholder participation, enablement and voice;
- transforming leadership for re-modelling the school workforce;
- establishing and maintaining an inclusive leadership ethic;
- modelling professional values for leadership and change;
- developing professional identity and trust.

Developing a Professional Knowledge/Learning Network

To develop SfL (Support for Learning) networking and partnership in the learning community:

1. Acquire an understanding and organizational approach to the key aspects in knowledge management.
2. Explore the idea of an extended school structure in relation to your own institution (school/service/college).
3. Create an inter-professional support for a learning team/ network in the school setting (develop role remit in liaison with a change management team/stakeholder groups in the school community).
4. Create an inter-professional CPD group to consider ways of developing new knowledge associated with multi agency working, supporting approaches to removing barriers to achievement in the school setting.
5. Explore potential for knowledge and support for learning networking with other schools in the local community (co-configuration with primary/secondary/special pyramid or cluster). Explore the potential for extending this to the wider LA school community.
6. Strategic leadership – identify building blocks/change agents/growth points.
7. Establish continuity in professional learning and CPD for producing *praxis*.
8. Re-assert the need for a 'moving culture' and adaptivity in the organization.
9. Establish organizational structures for learning (teams/ projects/tasks).
10. Develop cultural artefacts and tools for supporting and managing diversity.
11. Link distributing leadership and integrating management in strategic and operational actions/projects in the school community.

4

Inclusive Leadership

This chapter considers the inter-relationship between two key terms used throughout this book. The first is inclusive leadership; the second integrative management.

Inclusive leadership is a professional form of learning necessary at every level of provision in a learning organization and school community. It is a form of leadership that is concerned with educational theory, professional knowledge and the growth of *praxis*. It is, equally, leadership that is concerned with people, systems and context. It is, however, ultimately a mode of action that enables access to learning at every level of provision and deals in diversity and difference.

Integrative management requires inclusive leadership. It is functional management tied to a school's most challenging task – reaching the hard to teach and teaching the hard to reach. The difficulty encountered in this task is in part a product of persona and social diversity in cognitive style, intellectual capability, social identity and individual difference. It is also in part a product of social diversity, human rights, equity and entitlement.

The career journey for the learning professional is described in terms of a 'relational practice' and the production of a 'professional *praxis*'. The key to this approach to learning leadership is the concept of a professional ethic grounded in a notion of the professional learning community.

A NEW WORLD: CHANGING CONTEXTS FOR SCHOOL MANAGEMENT

The work of managing education is at present dominated by a policy context associated with an expanding knowledge society and structured by a market-led ideology. This approach is continually represented in the field of educational policy as modernizing reform. It is an emphasis which has led to a global domination of transformational leadership in educational management. Murphy and Hallinger (1992: 86) attribute the popular adoption of transformational leadership to '. . . changes in the policy context of schools' but argue, like Draper (2005: 81), that this is a normative change in which school leaders are being asked to '... undergo a metamorphosis, to change from transactional to transformational leaders'. Any meaningful approach to developing an inclusive leadership in SEN provision must ideally take account of these recent trends in leadership and related developments in what is now often called the knowledge society.

An awareness of social and economic trends in this way mirrors a similar sense of the social impact upon schools of demographic change and mass migration across the globe. Grossman (2004: xxi) argues that this reality is fast becoming the most striking feature in the classroom today:

> People in the developing world are emigrating to industrialised countries to better their economic prospects. Persecution and war refugees who leave their homelands are seeking safety and freedom in new countries. Immigrant and refugee children have very different ways of functioning in a school, as well as many problems that require special handling by school systems and teachers ... A one-method-fits-all-students approach is unacceptable in today's world.

Istance (2002) reinforces this sense of a wider implication of social trends across the western world for the core function of schooling and education. He identifies firstly a growth of 'individualism' in which activity is increasingly solitary rather than communal, further reinforced by an erosion of traditional values associated with the family. A second trend is the hardening of social exclusion and widening gaps between the affluent and those in poverty. Again Istance draws upon his work with the OECD (Organization for Economic Co-operation and Development) to spell out an immediate implication for education. He suggests that:

> At the very least, schooling should not be a mechanism for exacerbating these divides, including those arising from residence and the exercise of choice. Much better that it should be a force for inclusion in society. (Istance, 2002: 3)

As Istance argues, educational systems and communities should not be merely reactive to external pressures and changes as strategic leadership seeks to inform an understanding and decision regarding future policy developments in schooling. Gronn's re-definition of leadership involving a phenomenon identified as a distributed property is presented as an emerging and evolving requirement in post-modern management practice (Gronn, 2000; 2002). It is, however, apparent that continuing pressure for a proscribed policy and managerialist control of performance accountability in workforce remodelling, as pursued by national governments across the globe, is at present replicating a notion of distribution in yet another form of delegated managerialism tightly coupled with a global model of transformational leadership (Gunter, 2005; Gunter and Rayner, 2006; Harris, 2005).

The underlying momentum of inclusive leadership is mostly located in a process of mediation exercised by the practitioner and utilizing different ways of knowing and the application of both experience and knowledge to

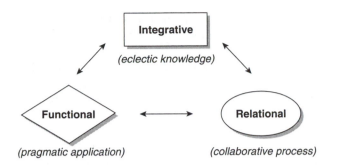

Figure 4.1 An Inclusive Leadership Style: Action Principles

a situated context. It might well include a new emphasis upon individual difference and personal psychology that is distinctively sensitive to distrusted notions of cognition and leadership rather than the individualized ideal of a transformational leader. In a way alluded to by Daniels and Garner (2000), it is particularly germane to explanations of managing change and promoting SEN policy as part of an approach advocating education for all (EFA).

To this end, it is useful to think of inclusive leadership as a key aspect of integrative management and structured around three core principles as described in Figure 4.1. These are:

- **Integrative** – as a strategic process tied to managing actions and practice which is problem posing, knowledge-based, aimed at synthesis and always learning centred.

- **Relational** – as an activity focused upon ways and means and always situated in contexts defined by purpose, people and evolving *praxis*.

- **Functional** – as reflective enquiry and a research-led applied discipline used as a tool to understand, facilitate and evaluate structures, agency, and outcome.

Professionality in education is reflected in this concept of inclusive leadership. It produces opportunity for personal development that does not infer that leaders are born, nor that leadership is the preserve of an elite caste. It is in essence leadership in all and concomitant to the aspiration of education for all. It is also presented here as the basis for an examination of leadership in this chapter, reflecting an attempt to further develop key themes revealed in the MISE model – particularly at levels 5, 4 and 3 – focusing upon the drive for change and efficacy in special inclusive provision.

DEVELOPING LEADERSHIP: USING
KNOWLEDGE AND MEANING

An understanding of leadership is in many respects a pursuit of knowledge as defined by Simkins (2005). He identifies three key examples of this particular form of knowledge as they are found within the arena of professional development:

- *Knowledge for practice* – technical, associated with a formal kind of procedural knowledge and linked to evidence-based research.

- *Knowledge in practice* – tacit, associated with professionality and professionalism, experience and wisdom.

- *Knowledge of practice* – critical, associated with enquiry, purpose and nature of leadership.

Simkins offers a useful example of how leadership preparation might be understood in relation to this knowledge. He suggests that leadership coaching might be conceived as:

- Instilling knowledge about 'good practice' (knowledge-for-practice).

- Encouraging reflection on a leader's own practice, perhaps through discussions with an 'effective' leader (knowledge-in-practice).

- Challenging the underlying basis on which practice is founded, in relation, for example, to the assumptions about power and influence on which it is based (knowledge-of-practice).

Following Simkins, I argue that my own definition of inclusive leadership does not take on one perspective but some parts of several explanations for how a successful leadership does work. However, for a synthesis to occur that is meaningful and practical, the assumptions underpinning these types of knowledge must be more carefully articulated. The mix involved in such a synthesis is not simply 'spontaneous' or 'transformative'. Nonetheless, as stated by Simkins, 'each of the three relationships between knowledge and practice may contribute to the development of leadership' (p. 21) In a review of the field, Simkins (2005: 12) identifies a traditional and an emergent definition of educational leadership. These are described in terms of key features in Table 4.1.

A traditional definition of leadership reflecting a hierarchy and a powerful redistribution of role responsibility is usefully described in a history of the English school headmaster (Grace, 1995). As previously explained, this tradition is a powerful legacy creating a stubborn residue in thinking around an understanding of leadership and subordinate agency. It is a 'traditional' conception of leadership, described by Gronn (1999) as grounded in 'naive

Table 4.1 Explanations of educational leadership

The Traditional View	The Emerging View
Leadership resides in individual systems	Leadership is a social property
Leadership is hierarchically based and linked to office	Leadership can occur anywhere
Leadership occurs when leaders do things to followers	Leadership is a complex mutual process of influence
Leadership is different from and more important than management	The leadership/ management distinction is unhelpful
Leaders are different	Anyone can be a leader
Leaders make a crucial difference to organizational performance	Leadership is one of many factors that influence organizational performance The context of
Effective leadership is generalizable	leadership is crucial

realism' and Ogawa and Bossert (1995) as a 'technical-rational' perspective on leadership. This is in contrast to an emergent view reflecting Gronn's account of the structural evolution of leadership. Gronn (2002) argues leadership as a unit of analysis should be more usefully construed as a distributed and common phenomenon rather than an individualistic phenomenon. The perspective presented here is one of an integrative synthesis and a need to utilize both of these traditions in restructuring our idea of leadership so that it will work in the context of managing inclusion and special education. To this end, many of the issues and ideas involved in forging a leadership approach involve deliberate problem-posing and decision-making processes associated with strategic leadership. These are immediately relevant in balancing a similar set of questions necessary for understanding a construction and implementation of SEN policy, for working with an inclusion imperative and most certainly securing the place of the special school in future provision.

Understanding educational leadership – models and meaning

There are three distinctive models of leadership influential in developing an applied model for managing education. These are:

1. Transactional Leadership – a leadership method aimed at ensuring performance by achieving motivation with stability.

2. Participative Leadership – decision-making processes are foregrounded in this model and collegiality is one example of an applied version of this approach in which formal leaders espouse consultation and collective decision-making.

3. Transformational Leadership – the leader's agency is emphasized as a means of enabling vision, values, beliefs, behaviour and attitudes in the organization.

These may be seen as contributing to a fourth kind of leadership presented in this book:

4. Inclusive Leadership – reflecting contextual, functional, and distributed aspects of educational leadership and tied to developing professional *praxis* specifically linked to a model of integrative management (MISE).

The following section presents a summary description of each of these forms of leadership and describes a progression toward a particular approach to leadership fit for purpose in managing inclusive and special education.

1. Transactional leadership: Is a broadly defined approach in which relationships with teachers are based on an exchange for valued resource. Sergiovanni (1991) says that leaders and followers in this approach exchange labour and commitment on a mutual basis of meeting needs and providing services, in order to accomplish an *independent* objective and mutual pay-off. Leadership is construed as managerial, hierarchical, powerful, and political. Followers or subordinates strike a working compact based upon self-interest. Contractual deals reflect this 'reality' of a leader-subordinate relationship, with reinforcement or reward given for good work and merit pay for increased performance. Action-centred leadership is a particular and useful version of the transactional form of leading that has its origin in the military context and reflects a practical concern for resource and operational issues surrounding flexibility, efficiency and efficacy. It adopts a pragmatic and situational emphasis but critics have observed that in extreme examples, this can lead to parochialism, technical obsession, military discipline and isolation (Law and Glover, 2000).

Adair argued that in order to be effective leaders must consider *group* and *individual* need, and should harmonize these in the service of the common *task* (see Figure 4.2). The role and work of a leader in this approach to transaction are to facilitate and steer the common task by working as a team, while respecting and developing individual members.

Adair's model works by focusing upon and maintaining three contingent factors in leadership – trait, situation and group – perceived as complementary and interactive. This approach is useful in helping to frame leading within a functional context as part of a wider application of an inclusive leadership and integrative management. (The theme of action and impact is further developed in Chapter 5 and more especially Chapter 7 in relation to the role of a SENCo.)

Adair's three-circles model

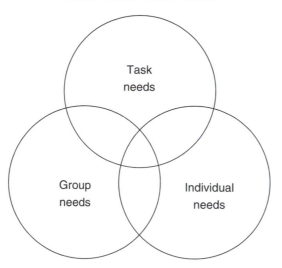

Figure 4.2   Action-Centred Leadership

2. Participative leadership: While this form of leading reflects a 'democratic' and 'shared' progression of transactional leadership, it is, as such, a version more commonly associated with a professional and thereby an educational institution. It assumes that collective decision-making processes are a central focus of the group. Collegiality, frequently espoused in higher education, is one example of an applied version of this approach in which formal leaders espouse consultation and collective decision making. Managing this approach embraces a view that issues may arise from different authoritative or expert parts of the organization and be resolved in a complex interactive process. Alternatively, it is couched as a democratic methodology appropriate for a modern society. Extreme examples of this approach reveal conflict and contested decision making that result in a damaging and destructive inertia.

Developing this approach can sensibly evolve ideas of leadership as 'distributed leadership' (Neuman and Simmons, 2000: 10), reflecting a shift in power away from the 'single person' to 'collaborative' decision taking. Distributed leadership calls on everyone associated with the particular community or school to take responsibility for student achievement and to assume leadership roles in areas in which they are competent and skilled. This expectation points to an inclusive approach. It does not mean, however, the abandonment of formal leadership roles exercized by individuals in an organizational structure and context. It does mean that these may be more flexibly arranged and limited to specific tasks or a time-limited responsibility.

3. Transformational leadership: Is the most recent and comprehensive approach to school leadership. It deals with a technical concern for change processes and a discourse by which leaders seek to influence school outcomes rather than any focus upon the nature or basis of direction. Caldwell (2004: 82) offers the following explanation:

> Transformation means change that is significant, systematic and sustained. Transformation means that the school of the future will look quite unlike the school of the present. The transformation of schools means the transformation of work for those engaged in the core business of learning and teaching. Expressed simply, the transformation of schools means the transformation of the teaching profession. If the profession is transformed then the role of those who exercise leadership will be transformed.

Leithwood (1994) explains that transformational leadership in education is associated with a concern for the following key orientations, which in themselves reveal adaptation of a business model when reapplied to an educative process:

- building a school vision;

- establishing school goals;

- providing intellectual stimulation;

- offering individualized support;

- modelling best practices and important organizational values;

- demonstrating high performance expectations;

- creating a productive school culture;

- developing structures to foster participation in school decisions.

Transformational leadership as applied to educational contexts is surprisingly 'familiar' and 'normal' in English schools, as Bush and Glover (2003) correctly observed. It has become a way of being and of work. The model is often characterized by a concern for pay-off and impact, in language associated with business, commerce, marketing or accountancy; examples include terms such as audit, delivery, product, impact, and these are reinforced by a curious mix of quasi-religious terms such as *transformation* (instant change), *mission, vision* and *charism(a)*.

    Transformational leadership, therefore, describes a particular type of leader-centric process focused on increasing the commitment of followers to organizational goals. Leaders seek to engage the support of teachers and galvanize their acceptance of a vision for the school so as to enhance capacities for goal achievement (Gunter and Rayner, 2006). It is hard to argue against this approach when to do so will appear to fly in the face of a positive and optimistic attitude, a visionary thrust of synergy and modernizing improvement. In fact, 'not signing on' is easily branded as bad 'team play' lacking in a necessary competitive spirit and a winning mentality.

To sum up: change is an essential part of managing educational policy and provision, in 'learning' and the so-called 'business' of education. It is, however, distinctive in its form. It is a *transformative* change that is associated with learning, innovation, empowerment, adaptation, and growth and not easily imposed as a political exercise in policy prescription. For this reason, it is not the same definition of change that is so central to a managerialist-orientated model of transformational leadership existing in many educational contexts. The latter sits square as the basis for 'transforming education' in the UK government's modernizing policy (DfEE, 1998a; 1998b; DfES, 2001a; 2005a). Transformative change is an educative process, and crucial as part of an educational system. This process, when well managed, produces growth in professional knowledge and shapes a learning organization; it facilitates personal growth, independent thinking and learning, critical respect for individual differences, celebrates achievement and is securely set against the backdrop of life-long learning.

INCLUSIVE LEADERSHIP AND MISE: THEORY, *PRAXIS* AND PRACTICE

The idea of inclusive leadership presented here is based on the notion of activating a functional and relational structure described in the MISE model. The press of purpose, role and people creates an early motivation for activity that is invariably a trigger for some form of leadership. This is further reinforced by a constant pressure for accountability leading to a recurring concern for the success qualities identified at Level 3 of the MISE model. According to Cheng (2002) there are a number of forces which exist in the educational setting that shape this action of leadership. These include:

- Human Forces – social and person-centred, motivational, involving work satisfaction, integrity.

- Structural Forces – policy development, technical support and accountability.

- Cultural Forces – ethics, ethos, values and codes of practice (professionalism).

- Political Forces – partnership, collaboration, participation, conflict-resolution.

- Educational Forces – expertise and direction in learning and teaching.

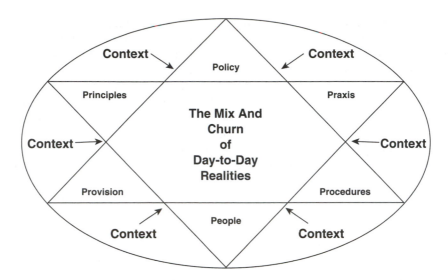

Figure 4.3   Inclusive Leadership and Integrative Management

Cheng's description of these forces and the distinctive action of leadership is traditional insofar as it presumes a leader and subordinate followers seeking purpose and realizing success. A leader is engaged in directing an orchestration of resource and talent in a way that defines this act in terms of influencing people and securing goal development. It is in this sense strategic management in play. Cheng's work is useful insofar as it offers a consideration of the necessary interface between a focus on learning as leadership and a demand of some measure of quality as an outcome in leadership. This involves turning to the way in which a multiple range of approaches form a broad ranging description of leadership:

> Based on different perspectives, different approaches may be developed to lead, to manage, to influence and even to control people and their activities in the educational institution … how to set goals, create meanings, direct actions, eliminate uncertainty or ambiguity and achieve goals is also a core part of leadership activities in education. (Cheng, 2002: 51)

Cheng explains how a series of leadership roles is required for developing an organizational system capable of 'multiple models of educational quality' (2002: 60–6). What is immediately relevant here is a consideration of how to exploit these leadership forces as a potential synergy for activation in the educational setting. Figure 4.3 charts these leadership forces identified by Cheng, locating each in an interactive relationship with others but demonstrating how all are simultaneously bound by the constant effect of a particular context. Leadership of this kind does not separate from a managing perspective and the issues related to operation. An example of this kind of process would be a continuing concern for resilience and sustainability. At the centre of this framework is the mix of immediacy and action – the churn of what many would generally call the real world – and always a constant challenge for the practitioner.

The inclusive leadership process is a continuing interaction of all these forces acting on protagonists and groups playing out the role and actions of leading. It is also the actuality that leaders need to reflect upon as well as think their way through as they make choices about priority, direction and task.

For example, in Figure 4.3, one aspect of leadership activity involving institutional systems and operational method stretches across the three cornerpieces of a triangular zone that deals with structural and educational forces closely linked with resources and the organizational context. These include *policy, provision* and *procedures*. In a second section depicting human relations and the social fabric of a community, *people, principles* and *praxis* are the three cornerpieces to a triangular zone of leadership that deals principally with human, cultural and political forces at play in the organizational setting. A very useful exercise in learning leadership CPD is to interrogate and unpack each of these two inter-related aspects of leadership as an 'holistic interaction' as portrayed in Figure 4.3. For example, how is the first zone of operational leadership currently working in an organization espousing the idea of a learning community (school, college, university)? An interesting start might be to use this approach with the governing body in a school. This kind of 'review' lends itself to action research or more specifically focused forms of practitioner-enquiry/learning group. It is also a useful tactic as a nurturing activity intended to support or benefit from a genuine process of organizational learning (learning groups and/or communities of practice – see Bennet and Tomblin, 2006; Sytsma, 2006; Wenger, 1998).

All members of the school community are both subject to, and in turn contribute to, creating Cheng's range of leadership forces in the educational setting. Leadership involves dealing with different aspects of this 'revolving chart', depicted in Figure 4.3, at various points during the school term. Organizational culture, role definition, position and task will determine how a person taking up a leading role is enacted. The SENCo, for example, represents a role traditionally labelled as middle management (comparable to a subject department leader or a Head of Year in a secondary school in England). The role embraces a need to engage with the entire set of aspects identified in this leadership wheel. It is not possible to successfully fulfil this role and avoid engaging with these aspects of leadership.

A consideration of the wheel and its movement when applied to a particular task is a useful CPD activity. For example, focusing upon identification and assessment of EBSD in the school population, as a learning activity for the workforce, might firstly look at individual practice. This could target what personal theory (ideas, values, explanations) underpins a practitioner's idea of the relevant principles and people necessarily involved in this task. Put simply, as an example should EBSD be regarded as a medical or moral difficulty? Secondly, a focus upon institutional practice, for example, might review practitioner awareness of what procedures are in situ for dealing with violent episodes of pupil behaviour. How in turn does this relate to stated policy and ethos? Is it linked to separate aspects of provision? How does it finally and actually carry through to the centre of the wheel – affecting the mix and churn of day-to-day realities and practice?

A deciding factor in determining the nature of leadership and management is not vision, as is so often suggested, but context. The notion of a leader's vision is important – but only when it is applied to the mix of cultural and social contexts comprising the structure and ethos of an organization or community. Leadership 'forces' and 'vision' interact with this context. The context can range across a continuum of site-based provision, intersecting with social and political activities in policy management. In England, a mainstream school, special school, pupil referral unit, support for learning service, LA children's service, are just some examples of where this SEN context is located. Within this physical provision, the practitioner working with SEN is facing a challenge associated with a moral and professional context that is interactive and simultaneously about the personal and the social. It is immediately holistic requiring a perspective that is whole school, yet individual; it is community-focused but tied to the individual, minority needs and social justice. It is inseparable from a concern for learning as process, intervention and an equality of opportunity. Community and culture therefore become additional concerns as the impact of leadership on a mind set reflecting beliefs, attitudes, and behaviour grows increasingly evident in any educational setting.

Inclusive leadership, professional knowledge and *praxis*

The core principle emerging from a consideration of SEN policy in the first part of this book is equity in education. For the individual practitioner, this means exploring diversity and integration in relation to the meaning of leadership as part of a personal and professional learning exercise. Acquisition of professional knowledge is in large part also about knowledge creation in work usually associated with CPD. An important foundation for this learning is practitioner enquiry and education research (Bennet and Tomblin, 2006; Sytsma, 2006). This does not simply mean applying an approach associated with evidence-based practice and performance management, but is more genuinely grounded in the need for the creation of a community of practice (Wenger, 1998). It also incorporates the renewal of professionalism and curriculum development as originally described by Stenhouse (1975) and re-presented by Elliot (2004). For the SEN context, it importantly extends the previously explained notion of the 'transformative principle' explained by Mertens and McLaughlin (2004).

Recent developments in CPD and research in the UK, however, resist this kind of educative process or an integration of theory and practice that can be tied to knowledge management. The approach, instead, leans too heavily on the political aims associated with enactment of national policy. This, in turn, is shaped by the combining of demand for accountability, transformational leadership and performance management. The use of evidence-based practice, for example, represents in some extreme examples of research a scientific veneer for extending this very same approach to accountability and school improvement (particularly evident in the wake of the *No Child Left Behind* statutory framework in the USA).

It is useful at this point to refer to the early work of Usher and Bryant (1989: 6) and their consideration of a utility of research, theory and practice in further and adult education. The approach described by these educationists emphasized the idea of critical reflective practice and how '... to encourage a 'coming together' of practitioner and researcher, and of research and practice'. A triangular structure depicting the relationship between theory, research and practice is offered as a basis for explaining a complex interaction between each and the existence of different forms of knowledge. Of particular relevance here is the suggestion that practical knowledge is distinctive but closely related to other forms of theoretical knowledge. The nature of this relationship, if too great an emphasis is laid upon one particular form of knowledge (say abstract principles of a knowledge discipline), is a failure in adult education to interlink its study with its practice. Usher and Bryant argue that the field:

> By vainly seeking for knowledge in disciplines it has failed to see that there is knowledge in its practice, and that generating its own theory must start from that knowledge. Adult education as a field of study must therefore be located in the 'practical'. (Usher and Bryant, 1989: 179)

What is applicable here for adult education is equally applicable to SEN provision and managing leadership. What the practitioner knows is used as a basis for learning more about leading and renewal of both policy and provision. In this respect, the core process at work in all of this is a development of an individual's *praxis* in leading and leadership. It is transformative as a learning experience, not transformational as a management tool, and when part of an integrative action it has the capacity to be both transformative and transforming. To achieve the latter requires an educative process, an emphasis upon organizational learning involving knowledge creation, and a dynamic engagement in leading learning and learning leading. This in turn creates the need for ensuring a distributed opportunity for leadership in the work setting. The opportunity for leadership is a potential (or fuel or resource) for managing any kind of educational system, but especially an holistic provision such as cross-phase inclusion and special education. An interesting and pertinent challenge is to consider how we can involve different member groups of the educational community including children in this learning and knowledge production.

Working with theory, *praxis* and practice: learning leadership

Educators are always involved in developing and using their own *praxis*: this pragmatic knowledge is defined as practical action based upon critical thought which shapes and changes the world. Managing inclusion and special education is quite literally intervention intended as a transformative process producing learning and change (Bayliss, 1997; Mertens and McLaughlin, 2004). Yet few educators speak of *praxis*. Those that do tend to link it to the work of Freire and a concern for the 'education for the socially dispossessed' (Freire, 1972).

While *praxis* may not form part of many practitioners' overt vocabulary, it is most certainly a useful concept, in large part defining as 'practical wisdom' a knowledge combination of theory with practice and the desirable outcome for CPD in education. Importantly, it is as a term and a concept comprising much more than only technical knowledge. It is also much more than practical knowledge.

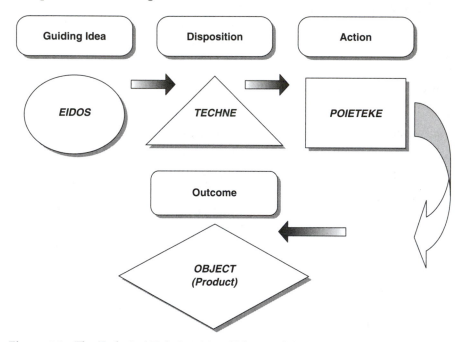

Figure 4.4   The Technical Relationship of Ideas and Action

The origin of *praxis* as an idea and theory lies in Aristotelian ethics/philosophy. Aristotle proposed that there were three basic activities of man: *theoria*, *poiese* and *praxis*. He identified three types of knowledge in correspondence with this activity: theoretical, to which the end goal was truth; poietical, to which the end goal was production; and practical, to which the end goal was action. This was to suggest that practical activity involved an application of ethics to inform 'correct and useful action' and this was seen in turn to form the basis of citizenship. Educators are by definition and function involved in each of these basic activites in their work.

The main focus in ITE (Initial Teacher Education) and CPD is generally on the second form of activity, in which *poiese* strives to achieve production. This involves an individual in creating and making a product. It is an exercise in construction, drawing upon technical skills and expertise. Pedagogy forms the product or object in this context – the combination of *techne* and the exercise of skill with *eidos*. This includes not only the original guiding idea or purpose, but the wider backcloth of knowledge – paradigm or classification – in which the idea is embedded (a bridge, for example, must serve the function of traversing a barrier or gulf between two sides in a line of progression, as well as reflect particular applications of physics, the aesthetic and the utilitarian).

The progressive structure of this process is described in Figure 4.4, and is adapted from Grundy (1987: 24). While *techne* is identified as the main form of knowledge underpinning pedagogic endeavour, learning and teaching is construed as pedagogy plus theory (*eidos*) and moral/ethical informed knowledge (*phronesis*). Being an educationist, however, becomes more than an exercise of these constituent parts when it is applied as provision or practical action (*praxis*). This entails the transformative essence or change found in learning and teaching as a process and in *praxis* itself as a particular form of educational knowledge. In many respects, this reflects a shift of perspective usually associated with the theory-practice relationship found in traditional approaches to understanding practitioner expertise and professional development. It reflects a move away from believing that theory simply drives practice towards an idea of the practitioner using technical knowledge, but also combining this to produce practical wisdom and in this way to generate new forms of applied theory. *Praxis* is therefore always linked to the social context and is crucially shaped by a consideration of ethics or social well-being.

This is *praxis* not as it has been more generally defined in neo-Marxist critical theory as political empowerment and economic or social process. It is rather, as Grundy (1987: 65) argues, *praxis* understood in a way that is closer to the original meaning of the practitioner's work as civic responsibility. It is illustrated in Figure 4.5. To seek social justice, empowerment and equity as structural features in the process of education and as an outcome of a transformative effect of learning is exactly this same process. In Aristotelian terms, the knowledge required and acquired in this process is *phronesis*.

It is this knowledge that forms the basis of the practical action of the professional and the leader. It requires a trust and an autonomy in the practitioner that allow for deliberation, choice and decision as part of a moral act seeking what is right in a particular situation. It also infers that the practitioner will by learning and leading facilitate further improvement or enable empowerment in a 'curriculum subject or situation'.

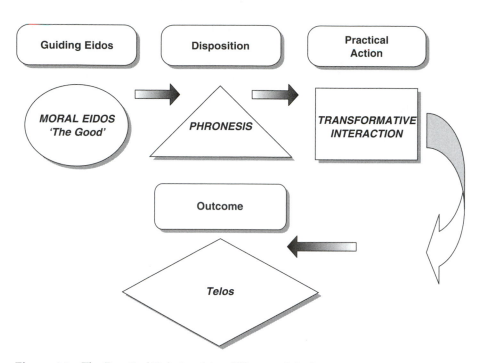

Figure 4.5   The Practical Relationship of Ideas and Action

The outcome achieved is called *telos* and represents a kind of 'practical wisdom'. As Grundy comments, the need for practical action or *phronesis* in teaching and developing the curriculum is why the professional practitioner should be encouraged in work that requires a particular form of leadership and development. Grundy (1987: 65) explains that:

> ... a practical interest initiates the sort of action which is taken as a consequence of deliberation and a striving to understand or make meaning of the situation on the part of the practitioner rather than action taken as a consequence of a directive or in keeping with some pre-specified objective.

The implications for learning leadership rest in how this explanation of the theory–practice relationship forms part of a definition of learning and education. It is this transformative aspect of learning that is so relevant to a belief in inclusive education, or the desire to manage diversity more meaningfully in the learning context and most importantly remove barriers to learning experienced by the disabled or disadvantaged. In this respect, it can actually offer opportunity for facilitating 'emancipatory *praxis*'.

Inclusive leadership is in this way reliant upon a developing professional *praxis*. It is no coincidence that Freire's work is so frequently cited by writers addressing issues related to *praxis*. In *Pedagogy of the Oppressed*, Freire explored the idea of pedagogy and learning. Schooling is identified as serving the interests of privilege in society, played out in an established professionality and pedagogy reflecting the work of oppressors controlling the oppressed. Learning, in contrast, is presented as a world-mediated mutual process and a response to an impulse to become more fully human. *Praxis* is identified as a particular and more authentic method of teaching, involving the use of 'dialogics'. It is described as the essence of education when it is adopted in working toward empowering practice or independence for the learner.

Inclusive leadership is action that presumes an existing set of functional limitations for those experiencing learning difficulties in the school context. In its most advanced or effective form, an inclusive leader aims to achieve a transforming and transformative effect in the work of making provision for the most vulnerable in the learning community. This is also, however, the work of any teacher. It is described by Grundy (1987: 191) as a combination of professional knowledge, action and reflection:

> This is a reflexive process rather than a linear process, with the transformation displaying itself in increasing moments of emancipatory *praxis* rather than developmentally improved practice. The process of professionalisation is a pedagogical process, not a developmental one.

Inclusive leadership is therefore in essence a professional form of learning that is necessary at every level of provision in a learning organization. It is leadership that is concerned with educational theory, professional knowledge and a growth of *praxis*. It is, equally, leadership that is concerned with people, systems and context. It is, however, ultimately a mode of action that enables access to learning at every level of provision and deals in diversity and difference.

5

Growing the Learning Community

Managing change is a lead task in the present day work-place. This is as true for school settings as it is for other sectors in the public services, business or industry. In many respects it is a necessity for professional and organizational survival or at least in retaining institutional relevance in a fast changing world.

At a macro level, the emergence of digital media and the globalization of a knowledge society have contributed to a rapid expansion of access to information. For educationists, this social shift has had several implications, some reflecting the nature of knowledge and its accessibility, some reflecting the function and purposes of schooling, and some affecting innovation and the reconstruction of the school setting.

A second set of implications in a post-modern setting reflects a demand for utility in education, with increasing emphasis on accountability and school improvement. Implicit in this latter movement is a concern to ensure that the set of success qualities identified in Level 3 of the MISE model (equity, empathy, efficacy and efficiency) is being evidenced.

The question of how best to manage change both as a part of strategic leadership and as a response to changing policy contexts is considered in this chapter. The definition of a desirable change process is linked to the notion of growing the learning community.

MAKING CHANGES IN THE WORK-PLACE

There is in the contemporary work-place an orthodoxy that seems to demand all change is good, and necessary, while any resistance to change is bad. Such a presumption is reinforced by a preoccupation with efficacy in the change process as a design issue and a technical operation. In terms of *praxis* this focus represents a limiting concern for *techne* rather than *phronesis*. Preoccupation with operational efficiency or efficacy can impede original purpose or value and worth and can create a perverse outcome. This attitude to change and effectiveness is perhaps a *zeitgeist* in need of careful assay. Constant change is debilitating and invariably inhibits learning and performance. Reorganization of services or structure and busy activity can also mask indecision when dealing with failure. Managing change, nonetheless, is a necessity for professional and organizational survival or at least for retaining relevance in a fast changing world. This *zeitgeist* is forcibly presented in the introduction of a recent key study of school leadership in which it is stated that:

> ... the social and policy landscape has changed completely, so that what school leaders are expected to do now and in the future is significantly different from what it was even a few years ago. (PricewaterhouseCoopers, 2007: v)

Change as a process is most certainly crucial too in any learning or development in the human world. It is nonsense to argue that education is not 'in the job of managing change'. The dynamics of growth, development, schooling, training and teaching all involve an intention and presumption for realizing change and innovation. Yet, at the same time, for both personal and organizational learning to occur, there is a need for regulation, routine and a form of stability that enable capability, engagement and sustainability in performance. Dismissing the need in a learning community for a carefully managed mix of structural stability and flexibility, coherence and continuity, as well as control with autonomy of practice, is to incur change leading to dissipation, failure and organizational breakdown. Managing change is not simply about coercion or persuasion and motivation but crucially is also about moral purpose, pragmatic leadership, organizational function and professional learning.

Growing an inclusive learning community

The first important step in managing change is purpose and strategic direction. The national and international policy arena described in Chapters 1 and 2 forms the 'topographical landscape of SEN policy and provision' in which navigating a 'professional journey' is the process of managing change. This is an important point and I will return to it later in this chapter. In terms of a process, emphasizing the ideas of inclusive leadership, as explained in Chapter 4 and located in the MISE model described in Chapter 3, provides a tool with which to prioritize aspects of change management. In particular, this involves a focus on the educative endeavour being best served in an approach involving the nurturing of personal and professional growth in a learning community. To facilitate this kind of growth necessarily entails working with diversity and difference.

The task of managing this approach is perhaps helpfully summed up as 'growing the learning community'. Moving between policy, provision and practice entails managing change that is quite literally 'learning' and an 'acquisition of knowledge' as well as 'sense-making reflection', and 'action or doing' is what in turn produces both an individual and collective form of

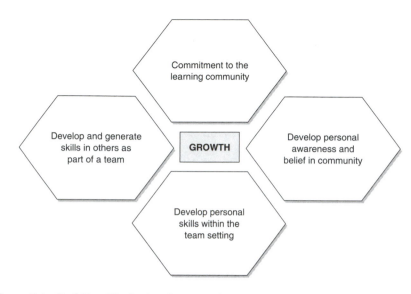

Figure 5.1 Building Blocks for Growing the Learning Community (Adapted From Kenning, 2002)

reflexive *praxis*. The concept of a learning organization is helpful here too if it is taken literally to mean a deepening notion of community activity enabling individual contribution to an organization. The aim is education as learning: the objective, to encourage adaptation, responsiveness, creativity and growth in the community. Opportunities to contribute to this process should stretch across the organization and reflect individual engagement with both leading and managing appropriate roles, functions and other aspects of provision.

This kind of 'growth' as applied to leadership is identified by Kenning (2002) as a firm basis for modelling individual contribution to a school community (see Figure 5.1). Kenning's research, sponsored by the NCSL, is concerned with understanding what leaders do when they lead in a learning community.

The construction of team-work and the collaborative process are identified as the building blocks of organizational growth. A knowledge of group dynamics is obviously helpful in this process, but so too is a recognition that team-work should not be simply regarded as a form of delegated instruction or dedicated task. (The process is reminiscent of Adair's model of action-centred leadership.) Leadership is part of a repertoire of activity that expects individual contribution in role or function as part of a developing notion of the team, group or community. For Kenning, the process ensures a positive attitude to potential and encouraging individuals to see value both in their own and community development.

Participation and engagement in change

As an action, managing change is interwoven with strategic work. Dimmock and Walker (2004) explain this emphasis upon learning centredness – which also reflects moving up or down the levels of managing described in the MISE model. It means that:

> ... strategic intent and leadership for school improvement is thus value driven, learning focused and culturally contextual, and one that essentially provides a long-term trajectory, while offering resilience, flexibility and considered responsiveness to engage the vagaries of government policies and short-term fluctuations of student success. In these ways, we argue that strategic leadership is most likely to contribute to school improvement, ensuring that schools achieve their goals while truly reflecting the cultural diversity of their communities. (Dimmock and Walker, 2004: 54)

Gunter (2003) argues that inclusivity or equity in an educational community requires an understanding of leadership as being educational rather than simply organizational or institutional. She suggests that social justice should strongly feature as a motivation for change, and as part of a focus that steers 'work for those who are currently othered' (p. 125) in terms of their social identities and so disenfranchized from engagement with school. I suggest that by default this actually forms a large part of the strategic agenda in the change process for education and necessarily involves issues of critical theory and concern for diversity. The emphasis here, however, is in integrating this social concern within a functional and personal perspective to ensure inclusive leadership and an integrated management of individual differences in the educational setting.

MANAGING DIVERSITY, EDUCATION REFORM AND CHANGE

Managing diversity is often identified as a major goal in education reform and a key plank in school improvement. This is somewhat ironic, given a widely held opinion amongst practitioners that school improvement sits in damaging contradiction to an SEN and inclusion agenda. Nevertheless, educationists repeatedly point to the need for change in order to better manage diversity in the school population. Leithwood et al. (1999) tell us that continuing diversity will require schools being able to thrive on uncertainty, having a greater capacity for collective problem solving, and being able to respond to a wider range of students. A standards-driven inclusivity is actually identified by Caldwell (2004) as the key driver behind a political impetus, international in scope and pressing for educational reform. He points to the 'reality' of economic, social and technological change as an inescapable pressure impacting upon education as a service sector.

Caldwell calls this approach a new 'globalization, localization, individualization' :(p. 83) paradigm and explains how it is linked to remodelling and a new professionalism.

A new approach: leadership distributed and distributing

An alternative form of shared leadership grounded in the idea that a fast changing world is a reality and requires a new form of educational leadership is described by Hartle (2005: 18):

> It is evident that the function and form of secondary schools is changing and that school leadership pathways will become more complex as a result of a more diverse work environment. Internally, there is a drive towards shared leadership, which in theory will create more opportunities for leadership development.

This kind of leadership is anticipated as necessary in the post-modern workplace. A current example of this approach is a desire for workforce flexibility and work aimed at systemic 'co-configuration' occurring in public service reorganization. This changing face of work-place leadership is usefully critiqued by Gronn (2002: 428), who argues that leadership should be construed as a unit of analysis and the property of distribution created by the 'fast capitalism of late modernity'. Gronn extends an early explanation for this notion of leadership as a common property situated in the labour force. There are, however, several working definitions of the term in contemporary literature that describe distributed leadership as a form of delegation or dispersal spread along a spectrum, forming at one end a tightly coupled direction of staff in the work-place (Hargreaves and Fink, 2006; Harris, 2005), and at the other social and workplace practices linked to the process of professional learning and knowledge development in a learning community (Rayner and Gunter, 2005a).

    The most influential early research into distributed learning as it features in managing change in the school setting is reported by Spillane et al. (2001). These researchers theorize how situated cognition in an organization is an interactive 'web of actors, artefacts, and the situation is the appropriate unit of analysis for studying practice': (p. 23). Spillane et al. argue that such a construction of leadership phenomenon is best understood in the action contexts of the work-place. Cognitive activity is conceived as 'stretched over' the artefacts and actors that make up an organization.

    In terms of reform, the implications of acknowledging and exploiting distributed leadership as a model of 'reforming leadership' are evident in the conclusions of the PricewaterhouseCoopers (2007) Study of School Leadership. Distributed leadership is presented in this study as diversifying leadership and a key device in the necessary dispersion of leadership and management in extended and increasingly more complex school organizations, encompassing new roles, tasks and networks for knowledge production and delivery. Leadership is offered as a method of delegated responsibility and devolved resources for schools to enforce an implicit policy aimed at de-professionalizing the school workforce.

Educational leadership draws upon researching and theorizing in education, is practised within education and is intrinsically educational. The Pricewaterhouse Coopers' brand of school leadership appears to contradict this view. It is not surprising to see the same study recommend a marked increase in the 'outsourcing of educational work' and the import of business practices and business leaders into the developing education service. Following Gronn (2000), in contrast, distributed leadership is presented here as a relational interaction, and reflective of an inclusive leadership that is only realized in a complex inter-action of structure and agency, thereby contributing to an integrative manage-ment of learning and education. In this way, perhaps, it is more closely positioned to the original concept presented by Spillane et al. (2001).

Managing change – leading learning in the vortex

The exercise of inclusive leadership is inescapably about managing change and sustaining a culture described as the moving school (Rosenholtz, 1989). There is, however, the force of gathering consensus that post-modern society demands an organizational structure and systems capable of total flexibility and constant but smart change management in the educational setting. There is in the transformational leadership perspective an argument that effective change management requires full-on abandonment of the status quo and the quick fix turn-over. There is no sense of learning a lesson here or the engagement of individuals as learners in a process – simply design, execution and impact and a building vortex of change. (I have heard it described as 'fire, aim and change'.) Navigating change in contexts that are increasingly characterized by turbulence and uncertainty requires much more careful balance and control and is captured in Glatter and Kydd's analysis of Fullan's model of a culture of change:

> Like a great deal of other contemporary research and writing in the field it diverges sharply from some current official positions, for example, with regard to the assumed potency of the transformational model of leadership … Arguably it expounds a well-founded view of good leadership practice, espe-cially as it offers a holistic approach to understanding and managing complex-ity, avoiding the reductionism which through simplification and fragmentation cannot meet the challenge. (Glatter and Kydd, 2003: 234)

In Fullan's view, to manage change successfully requires a fuller apprecia-tion and use of this change knowledge. He stresses a deep concern for the ethical aspects of leadership, identified as a first base in any programme of school improvement and reform (Fullan, 2003). The broader and inclusive aspects of this description of educational reform are firmly connected with moral purpose. This is very close to Aristotelian notions of *phronesis, telos* and *praxis*. Fullan et al. (2005: 54) insist that:

> The first overriding principle is knowledge about the why of change, namely moral purpose. Moral purpose in educational change is about improving society through improving educational systems and thus the learning of all citizens.

Professionalism and professionality are important ideas in this argument, but rarely receive direct consideration. Professionalism – reflecting a set of beliefs, attitudes and values about learning, teaching, pedagogy and the curriculum – is plausibly being stripped out of the new versions of education presented in the literature describing education reform.

Remodelling the school workforce and managing diversity

The form of leadership being presented within the national reform agenda and remodelling agreement in England (DfES, 2002b) is largely about organizational efficiency and effectiveness rather than about learners and learning or what might be defined as educational leadership (Gunter, 2005). The Transforming School Workforce Pilot Project in England typified this approach with its emphasis upon policy prescription, managerial control and directed change in targeted activity. Collarbone (2005) explains the win-win, five-step change formula given to school leaders to follow in the project. It comprised the following actions:

1. Mobilize – recognize the need for change, a school change team and opportunities for delivery of change.

2. Discover – focus on workload, assess the change readiness and build staff commitment.

3. Deepen – develop the scale and scope of the change and confirm a change initiative plan.

4. Develop – develop a vision and strategy for change and potential solutions, combined with a delivery plan.

5. Deliver – implement the change initiative plan and monitor effectiveness.

School leaders were trained in the operation of this change management scheme at global training events in the project. Collarbone makes several claims about this transformational approach. Firstly, it is self-directing as it places the school in control of planned change and through the devices of a 'change management team' and the writing of a 'change plan' also involves the whole school community. Secondly, the scheme is tried and tested, both in the commercial sector and in education. Finally, the process exploits consultancy – a strategy repeated in the recently proposed new relationship with schools evaluation framework (DfES/Ofsted, 2004; 2005) and in the work of the National Remodelling Team, established in England to oversee the 'roll-out' of workforce remodelling (DfES, 2005a).

Developing this idea of making change work in relation to managing education should hopefully turn the debate towards purpose and professionality and issues of inclusion, diversity and difference. As Evans and Lunt (2002: 12) argue, the standards driven agenda for managing change neglects educational functions linked to reducing barriers to access for many young people in the curriculum. An analysis of the state of the art in respect to teacher leadership shows over time how designated teacher leadership roles have become heavily dominated by prescriptive policy implementation beyond the control of reluctantly compliant teachers (Little, 2003). In an even more damning article, Ball (2003) describes how a continued remodelling drive towards a resource-focused operational excellence and a target-saturated culture of performativity is threatening the soul of the teaching profession.

Managing with an inclusive leadership ethic

Managing change is only successfully taken forward when it not only embraces the need to 'win hearts and minds' as part of a change process and conversation but is also concerned to reaffirm culture in a community (values, attitudes and beliefs shared as a social compact). The collaborative nature of culture in the successful inclusive school has clear implications for the nature of leadership and decision making in the management of diversity and difference (Kugelmass, 2003). The importance of collaborative processes points in turn to the relevance of distributed leadership and participative decision making described in Level 1 of the MISE model.

The 'inclusive' leaders described by Kugelmass in an account of case studies collected in three different countries (see Chapter 2) were consistently observed to be supporters and enablers of staff as they engaged in a collaborative process of school development. They would not, however, as Kugelmass stresses, hesitate to be autocratic when faced with decisions impacting on the foundation of their schools' inclusive cultures. The questions left hanging here are about ownership and power and more particularly about establishing just whose values and beliefs represent the policy and purpose of a community. Fullan's rejoinder to this question and the task of managing change is to suggest that school leadership is moral work entailing the following key aims (Fullan, 2002):

1. Making a difference in the lives of students.

2. Committing to reducing the gap between high and low performers within your school or district.

3. Contributing to reducing the gap in the larger environment.

4. Transforming the working (or learning conditions) of others so that growth, commitment, engagement, and a constant spawning of leadership in others are being fostered.

Table 5.1   Values in Educational Leadership

Transformational Values (direct action and impact)	Transformative Values (interactive empowerment)
West-Burnham (1997: 95) Leaders should develop 'moral confidence', the capacity to demonstrate causal consistency between principle and practice and create shared understanding and a common vocabulary.	Foster (1989: 49) Leadership, then, is not a function of position but rather represents a conjunction of ideas where leadership is transferred between leaders and followers, each only a temporary designation ... Leaders and followers become interchangeable.
Hopkins (2001: 2) It has always been the prime duty of schools to educate young people to cope with the future. This is a demanding task at a time of constant, unpredictable and accelerating change .... But nothing will ever change the fact that at the heart of every good school is a human being with a passion to transform children's lives.	Fullan (2002: 3b) You cannot accomplish the previous three levels of leadership without the trans-formative powers of creating growth oriented learning conditions of others in the organization.
Fullan (2002: 3b) We are now working with the British to determine what policies would transform the working conditions of teachers. Such trans-formation requires passion, commitment, and sustained energy. In short, you need many leaders working with moral/spiritual force.	Lambert (2003: 425) (1) Leadership may be understood as recipro-cal, purposeful learning in community. (2) Everyone has the right, responsibility and capability to be a leader. (3) How we define leadership frames how people will participate.
Caldwell (2004: 87) The successful transformation of schools calls for a 'new professionalism' in which teachers' work is increasingly research based, outcomes oriented, data driven, and team focused at the same time as it is globalized, localized and indi-vidualized, with lifelong professional learning the norm for the specialist in school education as it is for the specialist in medicine.	Dimmock and Walker (2004: 39) Leaders formulate their holistic school designs and exercise strategic leadership around a coherent set of values and the fol-lowing key features: learning for all as the centrepiece of the design; connectivity and consistency between the elements of the school in order to achieve synergy ... and the reflection of, and responsiveness to, social–cultural context, increasingly important in contemporary multiethnic communities.

Learning sits at the heart of this process as it is described, inferring creativity, contribution and adaptation both in the individual as well as organizational growth. The notion of transformation recurs in this approach and it is useful to re-check what it is we actually mean by the idea or the process. In Table 5.1, a comparison is presented in an attempt to distinguish the values underpinning two approaches to managing change and educational leadership. On the one hand is an approach that is prescriptive and a top-down directed transformation as change impact; on the other hand is the idea of a polysemic, transformative process dealing in participation, involvement and empowerment and focused upon learning as a change outcome.

Implicit in much of this discourse regarding forms of leadership and change is a desire to foster an inclusive ethic, professionality and leadership based upon trust. The cornerstone in such an approach is integrity. The need for integrity features in human relations and in the structural coherence of systems and practice. I have always been struck by the way in which the first and last cause for dissent or discord, in groups of children who are only just learning to socialize or young people who are at work or play, is the notion of fairness. The cry – 'it ain't fair' – is so often the individual's explanation for problematic or inappropriate behaviour.

The same need for social justice has in my experience always been key to dealing with issues surrounding the management of personnel. Morale, commitment, well-being, sustainability, understanding, communication, and performance across the workforce are key factors as well as indicators of success in the management of change and institutional improvement. All of these rest on establishing moral purpose, trust and preserving integrity. An inclusive ethic is in large part about fair play as it features in professionality and an educational purpose and attitude reflecting a set of agreed values. It is therefore about integrating and working and re-working the qualities of this ethic into the fabric of the culture of an organization. To do this well means incorporating the success qualities identified at Level 3 in the MISE model and applying these to every aspect of work in an organization. Each of these aspects or qualities when unpacked as an exercise can in turn form a useful 'litmus test' for any particular development of policy, provision or practice. Finally, to achieve any of this work at any level of professionality is also most emphatically about establishing and managing trust in people and in the system.

Bottery (2003) offers a useful analysis of trust in the management of education. In an elaboration of different kinds of trust he reaches the conclusion that in the educational setting it is necessary and inevitable. This inevitability is linked to the realization that less certain, more flexible working contexts demand greater levels of trust in the workforce. The establishing and deepening of trust, however, will reflect attitudes and values inherent in policy assumptions about learning and teaching. It will also heavily influence morale. While Bottery makes a strong case for reclaiming a place for trust in educational management, this is confounded by an establishment policy agenda dominated by excessive emphasis upon audit and accountability. In terms of the relationship between trust, leadership and professionality, Bottery and Wright (2000) argue that a:

> ... combination of directive government policy and acquiescent professional culture generates a monolithic approach to education, silences alternative voices and contributes to a form of corporatism in which genuine democracy is radically reduced. Basic changes are therefore needed in professional orientation, in particular a much more 'ecological' approach to professional work and identity.

A second illustration of this interaction between integrity and success qualities forming an inclusive ethic for leadership and management is found in the research reported by MacBeath (2005), looking at contemporary examples of early forms of 'distributed leadership' in schools. MacBeath concludes that 'distributing leadership' is premised on trust but this in itself presents a dilemma. Without mutual trust, relationships and respect are compromised and mistrust exerts a corrosive influence on every aspect of working life in a school setting. Headteachers in this study repeatedly reported a belief in the importance of trust but felt constrained by the pressure of accountability from external sources, so that trusting others to deliver was a calculated but necessary gamble but one which they felt they had to take in order to sustain professionality and learning. Distributed leadership, however, is no guarantee of quality. It can it is argued, compound the dilemma of trust or mistrust and in fact reinforce or spread bad practice via the process of distribution, that is, dissemination and dispersal (Timperley, 2005). It is nonetheless a necessary aspect to developing an inclusive ethic and an integrative style of management.

QUALITY ASSURANCE: STANDARDS AND SELF-EVALUATION

An implication of my argument here is that an 'inclusive school' is actually grounded in an ideal of education reform, change and school improvement (just not always the version promoted by the government in England). The importance of this idea is that a desire to raise or sustain standards and ensure flexible adaptivity as an organization is very much a part of the process of building inclusive practice. Ofsted (2000: 4), reinforced this point in a framework document for school inspection:

> An educationally inclusive school is one in which the teaching and learning, achievements, attitudes and well-being of every young person matter. *Effective schools are educationally inclusive schools.* This shows, not only in their performance, but also in their ethos and their willingness to offer new opportunities to pupils who may have experienced previous difficulties. (Emphasis author's own.)

A working agenda for school development (improvement) is now a statutory requirement in England and Wales. However, to what extent and how does this activity currently incorporate principles of equity and educational inclusion? A mainstream or special school should equally consider this question and ask how the school community manages diversity and difference. The tell-tale features of an effective school bear an uncanny resemblance to those used to describe the inclusive school (see Table 5.2). The tensions so frequently cited by teachers when justifying a need for exclusion or selectivity to ensure academic standards perhaps do not actually apply, or more likely reflect difficulties and tensions per se that are more closely linked to a quasi market-place ideology rather than a pressure for educational effectiveness and/or school improvement.

Table 5.2 School effectiveness indicators

The Effective School	The Inclusive School
• Professional leadership that is purposeful and participative	• Choice for students
• Shared vision and goals reflecting unity of purpose and collaborative practices	• Co-operative and collaborative activity amongst learners
• A learning environment reflecting an emphasis upon teaching and learning	• In-class support arrangements for teachers and pupils
• Purposeful teaching reflecting efficient and effective organization	• Experimental, inductive, hands-on learning
• High expectations and positive reinforcement in response to success and failure	• Independent learning emphasizing learner responsibility
• Monitoring, evaluation and practice-based data management	• Active learning with pupils engaged in doing, talking and collaborative learning
• Emphasis on pupil rights and responsibilities	• On-going concern for the processes of learning
• Working home-school partnership as a key aspect of the learning community	• Concern for formative and authentic assessment rather than standardized
	• Stakeholder engagement and participation

Policy and provision that are working to sustain an inclusive identity are clearly values-driven, and resonate with ideas surrounding equity and empathy for individual difference. There are distinct differences in underpinning values on the one hand, in leadership that is transformational and managerialist, and on the other hand, in the transformative, integrative and functional (see Table 5.1). This concern to 'transform' in 'learning' is arguably an essential ingredient in successful educational leadership. It is, however, much wider than only a transformational directive aimed at winning hearts and minds as part of a declared mission statement.

Assuring quality, managing performance and accountability

It often seems that a need to demonstrate accountability and assure quality in all aspects of provision – both in education and other public services – has created a managerialist bureaucracy and an industry in its own right. While debate might focus upon the size, scope and exercise of such activity, there can be no issue with a need to ensure standards in provision and realize good practice. As to the volume of paperwork, energy expended in generating and recording practice-based data and then an ultimate exercise in target-setting and performance management, none of this is a bad thing but all of it can create self-inflicted harm in both the individual (stress-related burnout) and the organization (toxic distrust embedded in a corrosive audit culture). It is useful when navigating a way through this landscape of inspection, standards, accountability, review, quality kite marks and evaluation to seek perspective and locate such work in the arena of assessment, learning and growth. The final caveat should always arguably be to test proposed actions and method in any form of QA for fitness of purpose.

Table 5.3 An SEN policy framework – Standards and Evaluation

Educational Standards	Self-Evaluation
Standards White Paper (2005)	**The New Relationship with Schools**
• Personalized education – no failure • Parent power as consumer and client • Stakeholder engagement • Local community empowerment • Schools evolve into multi-service providers	• Shorter school inspection (two days) • School inspection partner (SIP) • The SIP 'Single Conversation' • Increased use of practice-based data analysis • Self-evaluation cycle/School evaluation forms (SEF)
National Service Framework Standards	**Key Issues for Managing Diversity (Ofsted)**
• Early intervention to promote health and well-being of the child • Support for parenting • Family and child wraparound services • Cradle to adulthood support service • Promoting personal welfare	• Zero intolerance for pupils experiencing SEBD • Reduced rates of exclusion of SEN pupils • Improved rates of attendance for SEN pupils • Improved SEN data management linked to school development plan
SENSS Quality Standards Evidence of:	**School Self-Evaluation (SSE)**
• Interpersonal and collaborative working skills • Assessment and progress monitoring • Parent partnership skills • Contribution to the networked learning community	• Pupil Achievement Tracker (PAT) • SE-cycle (should be tied to school development cycle) • SEF – (Ofsted) • Survey participant voices (e.g. students/parents)
CPD Professional Standards	**Practice-based Data Management**
• Qualified teacher status • Performance Threshold • Excellent Teacher Status	• Pupil achievement and attainment data (over time/progress and added value) • Personal development in pupils (social emotional and behavioural) • ECM outcomes monitoring • Organizational data/finance data
HLTA Professional Standards	**Annual School Profile**
• Professional values and practice • Professional knowledge and understanding • Partnership working	• School's service statement (aims etc.) • Organizational data/Comparative review of SE data/Pupil attainment data • Curriculum provision statement • Community function statement • Improvement plan summary

For example, the theories of quality associated with developing the strategically focused school (Davies, 2004) or in terms of managing quality – Total Quality Management (TQM) (Deming, 1986; West-Burnham, 1997) – provide a clearly established basis for acknowledging the place of assessment in assuring quality. This shows itself in the workforce learning as a task is completed. While the over-arching definition of quality in TQM theory is perhaps problematic – given its ephemeral nature and notwith-standing a near total emphasis upon process that is attractive but limiting – measuring success using benchmark indicators combined with some of these principles in a more general approach to assuring quality can be useful and effective in a school setting or learning community. Similarly, generating, collecting and analysing practice-based evidence can be time-consuming but extremely useful if tied to strategic processes located at Level 5 and moving through to Levels 4 and 3 in the MISE model. Conversely, reducing QA process to so-called SMART targets (see for example, Gibson and Blandford, 2005) in a target-saturated environment (see Tallis, 2006) or to sets and series of criterion-referenced bulleted lists (see Gunter, 1997) can simply stifle good or mask bad practice. Calibration of purpose and design in the QA process is crucial in advancing strategic and operational dimen-sions of change management and success in the performance domain.

Again, when following the MISE model, developing an inclusive ethic links Levels 3 and 4 in work progressively focusing upon assuring quality and projects aimed at enhancing both dimensions of the performance domain. This includes working directly with both the internal shape of QA (role responsibility, procedures and the change process) and the external face of accountability in the form of evidence and reportage (aims, standards and outcomes). A running thread connecting all levels of the MISE model and linking interaction between managing change and organizational growth is actually work with the implementation of government policy. In terms of inclusive leadership and managing diversity this includes taking decisions about how to interpret and implement some fundamental issues in a fast changing educational system. A summary of this changing policy infra-structure is shown in Table 5.3. Self-evaluation and assessment are an integral part of educational leadership, just as it is a part of the process of learning. Quality assurance and standards of performance as evidenced in monitoring, review and evaluation inspection are features of an audit culture underpinning government policy and the expectations of educa-tional management. The infrastructure is in part outlined in Table 5.3 and will ideally feature in any approach to accountability and organizational development attempted in the school or service setting. It is a clearly stated policy context for schools in England.

Further, a careful deliberation in strategic terms is required for managers responsible for SEN provision when planning school development. Key issues in this strategic scoping are part of the change management process. For example, can the governing body of a special school ignore the looming re-categorization of SEN and the apparent demise of the current identification and assessment of SEN apparatus in local authority structures involving the SEN statement and placement? Secondly, can a special school or for that matter a mainstream school afford to ignore the implications of a policy-provision convergence in the Every Child Matters policy agenda with the standards agenda involving personalized education and extended schools legislation? Thirdly, the remodelling exercise for all schools is described by the DfES (2004b; 2005,) as a self-directed approach based upon the idea that a one-size to fit all policy will not work. It is based upon a 'tried and tested way of managing change in schools' that also relies upon recognizing that change management lies at the heart of the school remodelling process. The rollout of the reform is supported by the National Remodelling Team.

Remodelling reform is the vehicle for driving change in the educational system in England. Change and adaptivity are clearly important organizational features in a post-modern society. Certainly, the post-modern shifts in knowledge construction and social structures characterized by ambiguity and fluidity impacting upon education leadership are making it necessary to develop more flexible and distributed kinds of practice. It is probable that growing a remodelling leadership might usefully develop a role function and new leadership ethic not dissimilar to a leadership model in Native American tribes reported by Bryant et al. (2003). What is essential, however, in the growing of such distributed practice is a consistent and coherent set of values that in the Native American example of a non-hierarchical and function-related system of leadership was provided by tribal culture and religious belief. In our own context, this set of values should ideally reflect an inclusive ideal and an educational professionalism and professionality.

6

Networking Support
for Learning

A key concept and structural device in the management of new knowledge identified in this chapter is the network. Van Loon (2006: 307) explains that:

> A network is a device for organizing and conceptualizing non-linear complexity ... Networks problematize boundaries and centrality but intensify our ability to think in terms of flows and simultaneity. As a concept, a network has been highly conducive to theorizing phenomena and processes such as globalization, digital media (Internet), speed, symbiosis and complexity. This in turn enables us to rethink what constitutes the foundations of intelligence, knowledge and even life itself.

Multi-agency issues relevant to developing special and inclusive education are considered in this chapter. The policy backcloth is the continuing drive in an initiative aimed at Excellence For All and Every Child Matters, both centered in a standards policy agenda aimed at modernizing the education workforce and extending the school system. I follow the logic of developing leadership *praxis*, described in Chapter 3, and look at how knowledge management is linked to professional learning in an integrative management of inter-agency working.

STRUCTURE, AGENCY AND NETWORKS

Engaging with both Levels 5 and 4 of the MISE model necessitates thinking through the organization and deployment of resource and knowledge in the community. The overall purpose for this work is educational intervention to enable learning. The content in a network for this context includes processes and procedures that will provide *support for learning*, enabling access to the curriculum for the learner irrespective of individual or social difference. A range of theories associated with distributed cognition and socio-cultural theory, encompassing organizational learning and inclusive leadership (see Chapters 4 and 5), helps to explain how this kind of networking can be managed. In this chapter, a brief consideration of knowledge and learning networks is examined, followed by a consideration of recent research targeting professional learning utilizing socio-cultural activity theory (Engestrom and Middleton, 1996; Warmington et al., 2004). This also includes a consideration of how knowledge networking affects an organizational structure and can structure managing inclusive and special education.

The need to develop, sustain and maintain working structures within an organization is self-evident and yet more crucial in periods of accelerating change and uncertainty. In a learning organization, the primary focus in developing infrastructure by definition should remain one that fastens on the task of knowledge creation and management. The principal form of structure constructed and adopted for this task in the recent past is the network. This is a concept originating in commerce as a structural system for streamlining trade, supply and delivery. In organizational theory and management, it is a term associated with how the flow of communication has operated in the work-place and society. A network is a system made up of a series of nodes connecting and interconnecting in a grid, mesh or matrix across place, space and time. Centralizing networks usually emphasize a hub or centre responsible for a linear flow and control of the system. Decentralizing networks emphasize a greater fluidity, adaptivity and inter-connectivity that often work without a controlling hub (nodes exist as a loosely coupled array rather than a sequence of satellites). More recently, the digital net has become an international network and global pipeline, hugely increasing the scope and speed and volume with which storage and communication of information occurs in the work-place (witness the email mountain replacing the memo pile).

The communication network as a structural device has traditionally been used to reorganize organizational infrastructure in the work-place. Examples of communication infrastructure and related organizational cultures are shown in Table 6.1. All of these structures are a rational and/or linear construction designed for transmission and delivery. The shape of the network is geared to achieving a strong and unbroken flow of content, ideally securing flexibility, adaptability and continuity in communication. This shapes infrastructure in an organization and is in turn often shaped by ideas of authority, power and control, determining the culture of an organization. A widely observed description of culture as either 'open-door' or 'closed-door' epitomizes this shaping effect of structure upon culture. Communication flow, traditionally, is a basic requirement in the establishment of line management and so tied to the managerial exercise of authority, direction, instruction and administration. Information and knowledge flow have always been part of this arrangement, reflecting systems, protocols and procedures forming the administration of work in an organization.

Table 6.1 Examples of networking infrastructure (see Law and Glover, 2000)

Communication Network Linkage	Structure	Organizational Culture	Structure
Star (Centralizing)		Web	
Chain (Centralizing)		Heirarchy	
Circle (Decentralizing)		Cluster	
Star/Circle (Decentralizing)		Net	

The relevance and utility of the network as a structure in education are reflected in the take-up of networking as a tool in the education reform movement across the globe. In England, this is exemplified in the policy landscape of SEN provision and inclusion frame-working. One recent example is the drive to create an integrated children's service. Networking in SEN provision, however, is not a new idea. It has been most evident in the UK as a form of multi-disciplinary agency located in Early Years provision (0–7 years of age). This has involved a range of statutory and voluntary sector organizations in a number of collaborative ventures developing a more unified service provision (for example, Portage, SureStart, NSPCC, Children's Trust). The SENCo in a mainstream school setting has also been traditionally encouraged to develop a networked whole school approach to SEN provision. In the typical LEA in England, support services of various kinds have existed since the 1981 Education Act, and more recently most have operated as a cost-centred consultancy network, working with individual schools as clients and contracting work on the basis of service-level agreements in the quasi market-place of a local educational community. More latterly, these services are being subsumed by (or in some cases running in parallel with) the emerging integrated children's service.

As with special schools, the future for this kind of support provision rests largely on the reconstruction and definition of the local school community, and the decisions reached about how to best manage learning differences and diversity in this same community. For example, in a positive review of

Behaviour and Education Support Teams by the DfES (Halsey et al., 2005), it was found that the question of funding continues to leave such services vulnerable to the decision making of individual schools rather than at the level of a local authority. Generally, the distribution of funding to support policy decision making is vital to any continued support service provision. In England, the implementation of this policy is currently being managed by the LA and members of the elected County Council. For a SENSS or indeed a special school, the future must involve an increasing awareness of how the knowledge and expertise it possesses can be extended or presented as a contribution to maintaining a community-based SfL network.

A second example of a learning network is the trend towards setting up new forms of Lifelong Learning Networks, for example, the Carmarthenshire Lifelong Learning Network in Wales. This is a services structure being pioneered and enabling a range of education and training providers to work with community-based bodies, including the voluntary sector, to develop provision in communities aimed at reaching and engaging with people who have not recently taken part in any formal learning. Managing effective networking is now part of a policy rhetoric often presumed to be a best way forward, however, creating and sustaining organizational networks that actually work is perhaps not an easy matter. It requires new partnerships in agency and continuing professional learning (CPD). In the same way, mainstream schools will need to follow a similar kind of growth, albeit more distinctively focused upon the learning community within its own organizational framework. Those boundaries, nonetheless, are likely to be increasingly 'flexed' in the face of pressure for the 'extended school'.

This policy directive in England (see DfES, 2005c) is similar to the 'full service community school' provision already established in the USA (see Gallagher, 2006) and Australia (Burnett, 2003). The ECM initiative creates the concept of full service or extended schools in which the school is the hub of all children's services. Hartle (2005) predicts that this will mean:

- Teachers in more regular contact with other professionals and new ways of working.

- School staff taking up consultant placements and professional secondment.

- Staff 'cross-over' between several career pathways inside and outside the school sector.

- School leaders having new opportunities to exercise leadership of other agencies.

- Children's services staff (social care/health professionals) having the chance to work in extended secondary schools.

Interestingly, all of these predicted changes have been common practice in effective special schools for more than two decades. Partnership, collaborative practices and inter-agency working all fall into a networking pattern of communication and organizational structure. The network is fast emerging as both an indispensable tool and an integral structure in managing knowledge and diversity in the learning organization within an expanding and changing schools' community.

Networking organizational learning in an inclusive learning community

The development of community-based networking is applicable at many different levels of provision existing in a local authority or school district. It can involve a series of interconnecting matrices combining to create a loosely linking super-structure. It might in turn therefore include a number of different complementary and interactive networks such as those summarized in Table 6.2.

SfL networks are essentially local to the schools community and exploit a linkage to any or all of the types of network described in Table 6.2, in a wider super-structure. An easy example would be the ICT infrastructure or learning grid set up in an individual school. SfL networks are distinguished by an explicit aim of intervention to support learning and ensure access routes into formal education. In fact, the examples in Table 6.2 are only an illustration of some of the multiple sets of networks that exist and continue to spring up from week to week. While these are, in general, knowledge networks that support learning, it is when knowledge flow from the wider series of networks triggers more specific local networks informing individual interventions that an SfL network is established. These include examples of both networking that is a top-down or centralizing control of information and operation, as well as examples reflecting a less formal operation involving exchange of implicit knowledge. The latter are usually self-regulating and independent forms of networking that frequently characterize the way in which tacit knowledge is shared and transferred from place to place.

These exchanges have been greatly accelerated by the advances associated with ICT and the so-called digital revolution. ICT and the underlying structures of communication can be seen to shape and re-shape organizational learning, knowledge creation and professional learning. Types of networks are increasingly important in how and what is exchanged as a form of knowledge. The purpose and intended outcome in such work are pivotal to good integrative management. I suggest that in an inclusive setting and when managing diversity it should always be about developing both an individual and collective *praxis*. This blending of theoretical and practical knowledge is an essential ingredient in any transformative learning that is by definition the 'stuff' of interventions aimed at support for learning.

Table 6.2   Forms of Network in the Learning Community

Network Type	Description and Examples of Network
Knowledge/ Organizational Networks	These are formal network structures usually built upon digital technology platforms, reinforcing a managed organization of knowledge flow and working practices. • DfES TeacherNet in England (see www.teachernet.gov.uk) • Networked Learning Communities initiative pioneered by the NCSL (130 networks linking 1300 primary school leaders (see www.networkedlearning.ncsl.org.uk) • There are several regional partnership in England, for example, The West Midlands SEN Regional Partnership (see www.westcmidlands.org.uk) • Durham Schools ICT Portal (see www.durhamlea.org.uk) • Diversity in Education (see www.multiverse.ac.uk)
Learning/Community of Practice Networks	These networks are associated with both tacit and explicit knowledge as it exists in social agency. Such groups include, for example, informal to formal opportunities to learn in the work-place setting. Examples include: • SENCo Forum in England – an informal professional learning mail-base (see lists.becta.org.uk/mailman/listinfo/senco-forum) • Principal Professional Learning Community (PPLC) in New Zealand – reported by the Ministry of Education as a highly valued and supportive programme (see Piggot-Irvine, 2006) • The Carmarthenshire Learning Network (www.clnweb. org.uk) • Educational partnership across national boundaries (www.globalgateway.org)
Social/Peer-related Networks	These formal and informal action groups for practitioner/ stakeholders include affiliation to friendship groups, leisure activity groups, support groups and interest groups. Examples given here are more formal as they extend beyond the school setting and include: • Teacher Support Teams (see Daniels et al., 2000) • Charitable bodies, for example the British Epilepsy Association, Dyslexia, and MENCAP (see respectively www.epilepsy.org.uk, www.bdadyslexia.org.uk, and www.mencap.org.uk) • The Foundation Stage Forum – an online community for those involved in the education and care of children up to the age of five (the Foundation Stage) at www.foundation-stage.info/index.php • Young Minds Info Centre – contains detailed information organized by topics relevant to children's mental health (see www.youngminds.org.uk/infocentre/)

Table 6.2 (Continued)

Network Type	Description and Examples of Network
Agency Networks	These are networks set to advance the organization of inter-agency and inter-professional work in a unified approach to educational and childcare provision. Examples here are national in scope, some aimed at professionals, others at parents and allied stakeholder groups, but there are many local networks forming as part of the ECM initiative: • SureStart – UK government programme working for improving outcomes for children, parents and communities (see www.surestart.gov.uk) • BILD – a membership community and partnership network with a desire to improve the lifestyles of people with learning disabilities (see www.bild.org.uk) • Working Together With Parents Network at the Norah Fry Research Centre at Bristol University (www.bristol. ac.uk/norahfry/right-support/membership.html) • National CAMHS Support Service (www.camhs.org.uk)

Managing the knowledge flow in an inclusive community

Part of the challenge presented by networking is the issue of quality control. All information is not by definition useful or sound. Nor is the over-whelming flow of information afforded by digital technology always helpful. Intensification of work created by ICT systems always seems an ironic if not perverse outcome in the face of expected benefits and the dazzle of new time-saving technology. Critical in managing knowledge flow, however, is the exercise of purpose and operation as it is shared across the community. For the inclusive setting, leadership that is distributed but purposeful is a necessary part of this networking management. It is also useful to have a sense of the kinds of information and knowledge that are fit for purpose in the exercise of inclusive leadership.

The 'content' of such a network repository for the inclusive school combines 'specialist knowledge' with generic 'operational knowledge'. This 'gateway' and/or 'gateway keeper' should also ideally include signposting sources and switching the direction and acquisition of the knowledge flow for the community. This is a leadership role that combines facilitating knowledge flow with strategic and operational knowledge management for an organization.

Examples of some of the SEN content for this knowledge network are summarized in Table 6.3, based upon traditional SEN categories as a starting point. This approach might then form an exercise in CPD, combining professional learning and organizational knowledge creation. It could usefully extend the knowledge network to include additional categories of learning differences and difficulties associated with widening participation and equity (for example, gender, personal capability, ethnicity). Alternatively some of the inclusion touchstone themes identified in Chapter 3 might also be usefully added to this knowledge pool.

A second knowledge content stream relevant for networks in the school community as a whole, and particularly for managing personal differences and diversity, is resource management and budgetary finance. The exercise of financial management is lowly rated by school leaders in an appraisal of their role (PricewaterhouseCoopers, 2007). There is a need at this point to emphasize that finance data management should ideally be the responsibility of a bursar or administrator. The action of combining strategic and operational management is a trigger to refer to finance and utilize resource data which need to be networked in such a way that they can be accessed and used at differing levels of the organization and educational system. It is impossible to work toward VfM or added value if this referral option is not open and transparent to leadership at every level of an organization.

Managing resource information and the network

The history of SEN policy and provision since the Warnock Report in England is one of an expensive financing of special school provision and to a lesser extent the SEN assessment and identification administration, but this is in stark contrast to a tendency for establishing resource neutral policy initiatives aimed at SEN provision within a mainstream setting. Overall, recent spending patterns reported to the SEN Parliamentary Committee (HOC, 2006) noted spending predictions of £4.1 billion for 2005–06 in contrast to £3.8 billion in 2004–05. The breakdown provided for the £4.1 billion was:

- Special education (£1.4 billion).

- Mainstream education (£2.0 billion).

- Independent/non-maintained schools (£481 million).

- LA duties (£264 million).

The issue of finance and resource allocation to support inclusive education is a difficult conundrum. Increasingly, finance is subsumed in the general schools' budget, and statutory legislation, inspection and audit are used to ensure that schools and LA organizations fulfil obligations to properly fund SEN provision. This has obvious dangers for ensuring continuity and regulation in the management of SEN provision.

However, more recently the government has ring-fenced funding to support the ECM policy initiative. The government in England, for example,

Table 6.3 Knowledge Sources for Learning Differences

Learning Difficulties/ Differences	Knowledge Sources
Autistic Spectrum Disorder	Autism Independent UK: www.autismuk.com Autism Connect: www.autismconnect.org The National Autistic Society: www.nas.org.uk Asperger's syndrome: www.practicalparent.org.uk
Cystic Fibrosis Cerebral Palsy	Cystic Fibrosis: www.goodgulf.com Cystic Fibrosis: www.cysticfibrosis.com Cerebral Palsy: www.cerebralpalsyfacts.com Cerebral Palsy: www.scope.org.uk
Down syndrome	Down syndrome: www.downs-syndrome.org.uk Down syndrome: www.43green.freeserve.co.uk Down syndrome: www.ndsccenter.org
Dyslexia Dyspraxia	Dyslexia: www.bda-dyslexia.org.uk Dyslexia: www.dyslexia-teacher.com Dyslexia: www.dyslexia-inst.org.uk Dyspraxia: www.dyspraxiafoundation.org.uk
Emotional, Social and Behavioural Difficulties Eating Disorders	AWCEBD: www.awcebd.co.uk DfES: www.dfes.gov.uk/sen ADHD: www.addis.co.uk Tourette's syndrome: www.tsa.org.uk Anorexia Nervosa: www.anorexia.com Bulimia: www.nhsdirect.nhs.uk
English as a Second Language	Asylum Seeker Children: www.ofsted.gov.uk Asylum Seeker Children: www.Dfes.gov.uk National Association for Language Development: www.naldic.org.uk
Epilepsy	Epilepsy Association: www.epilepsy.org.uk National Society for Epilepsy: www.erg.ion.ucl.ac.uk Epilepsy Association for Scotland: www.epilepsyscot-land.org.uk
Multiple Sclerosis	MS Overview: www.spotlighthealth.com MS Society: www.mssociety.org.uk
Profound, Multiple and Severe Learning Difficulties	Teaching Children with PMSLD: www.equals.co.uk British Institute of Learning Disabilities: www.bild.org.uk MENCAP: www.mencap.org.uk Disability World: www.disabilityworld.com
Sensory Impairment	Hearing/Visual Impairment: www.ability.org.uk Hearing Impairment: www.careline.org.uk Visual Impairment: www.rnib.org.uk
Speech, Language and Communication Difficulties	ACE Advisory Centre Trust: www.ace-centre.org.uk TeacherNet: www.teachernet.gov.uk Helping Children to Communicate: www.ican.org.uk

has committed £680 million between 2006 and 2008 to directly support the setting up and embedding of extended services – at least £250 million of which is to go directly to schools. This is being made available through local authorities, who will be developing, in consultation with schools and other partners, a strategy for how funding will be allocated (HOC, 2006). There is a clearly stated expectation, however, that schools should 'charge' parents for many of the new services that will be offered as schools are extended into 'full service schools'. There are three levels of finance knowledge management crucial to achieving successful integrative management. These are:

1. *The Institutional Level* – That is, within the community or organization that will be administered by the governing body. A useful ICT system that helps administer and support this knowledge management is SIMS but there are other platforms for accounting school budgets. It is important too that the administrative structure in the school setting can provide information and advice and support strategic and operational decision making. Bursarial provision identified in the transforming school workforce pilot project (Thomas et al., 2004) and the evaluation of the roll-out of the workforce remodelling agreement (DfES, 2004c), are absolute necessities if financial information is to be effectively networked to support a pattern of distributed and inclusive leadership. The bursarial role should also interface with the role of managing the administrative office in the school setting, further reinforcing the systems in place for administering allocation and deployment of non-human resources throughout the school organization.

2. *Local Authority Level* – Arrangements for the distribution of resources at the level of the LA are complex and vary widely throughout the country. However, LEAs are required under Section 52 of the Schools Standards and Framework Act 1998 to prepare a budget statement before the beginning of each financial year. An account of the main sources of funding available to support the schools' budget will typically include LEA level information, a list of schools' budget shares, the calculation of each school's budget share and the LEA's allocation formula. In general, schools are in a bidding situation to compete for any additional funds for SEN provision (MacBeath et al., 2006). Much of the current funding is distributed according to the formal identification and assessment of SEN, creating perverse incentives that prevent schools 'moving' children up the SEN scale as described by the SEN Code of Practice, by working to resolve learning difficulties or reduce 'barriers to achievement'. To do so would mean losing the resource attached to the child. Networking within the schools' community is clearly a crucial part of navigating the funding arrangements in the LA which is going to be even more important in the near future. Such knowledge will increase in complexity and importance as unitary children's services are progressively developed across the country over the next two to three years.

3. *National Level* – Incentives for schools to implement particular policies rolled out by the government form an important need-to-know content for school leaders and governing bodies. One recent example is the specialist school scheme in which schools bid for the status and if successful receive additional funding to support nominated, specific, school-based improvement or developments. For special schools, the designations for which they can bid are the SEN Categories listed in the SEN Code of Practice (cognition and learning needs; behavioural emotional and social development needs; communication and interaction needs; sensory and/or physical needs). In 2005, the government announced new school funding arrangements to be introduced from April 2006. It is important that a bursar or equivalent keeps a tracking brief on how these arrangements will be managed by LAs as they are phased in across the country. Crucially, a particular note should be kept on planning for SEN expenditure and how any new initiatives aimed at improving the management of diversity and difference in the schools' community are to be resourced.

REMODELLING REFORM AND INTER-AGENCY PARTNERSHIP

There is compelling evidence that the landscape of the schools system in England is undergoing massive shifts in terms of its expected structure, identity, function and practice. The inter-disciplinary working practices familiar to special school staff for two to three decades are set to sweep over mainstream education. The press for 'joined-up provision' is reflected in the ECM agenda and a policy rhetoric that demands inter-professional working practice 'wrapped around the child'. Lacey (2001: 135), prefacing much that was later to appear in the ECM initiative, argued passionately for the enhancement of support partnerships between families and professionals, focusing upon the qualities and strategies necessary for genuine collaboration between partners to successfully support the vulnerable child's learning. Such vulnerability includes all children at risk of failing to achieve their potential because of social and learning differences or disability. The wide range of professional partners who can be involved in this work is summarized in Table 6.4.

The preferred relationship of special and mainstream education, as well as different agencies resembling two sides of the same coin, captures the distinctive and symbiotic structure of an integrated schools community. (This notion reflects an alternative to the either/or discourse summarized in Chapter 2.) Personal difference is accepted; it is accommodated and valued as distinctive but perceived as a potential rather than a deficit or liability.

Importantly, this integrative valuing must pervade the leadership ethic or *phronesis* being produced in a multi-agency working context. It is captured in the principles described in Level 3 of the MISE model, but particularly

Table 6.4   Multi-Agency Partners

EDUCATION

Local school	Special school	Local FE college
ICT specialists	Mobility instruction	Educational psychology
Portage	Home visiting service	Hospital school
Services for sensory impairment	Specialist FE College	Learning or behaviour support service (SENSS or BEST)

HEALTH

Nursing	Physiotherapy	Speech therapy
Medicine	Psychology	Psychiatry
Audiology	Orthoses	Orthoptics
Dietics	Dentistry	Occupational therapy
Health visiting	Complementary therapies	

LEGAL SERVICES

Education Welfare Office	Police	Guardian Ad Litem
LEA/LA Solicitor	Probation	Supervision

SOCIAL WELFARE

Family social work	Residential social work	Local fostering team
Respite care	Support workshop	Job coaching
Day care centre	Benefits	Home help
Housing		

VOLUNTARY SECTOR

Independent schools	Charities	Private homes
Arts therapies	Alternative therapies	Private respite care

in the concept of empathy. The counselling notion of unconditional regard for human differences is particularly relevant to this principle being put into practice. It is, however, extremely difficult to operationalize in a typical educational community that is organized on an increasingly selective basis as curriculum specialisms occur, and academic judgements of worth are made contributing to exclusionary and discriminatory practices in grouping children or young people in the community. A second and equally difficult aspect to this same issue is around the social and cultural differences related to race, ethnicity and religion. Again, the concept of empathy becomes a central value in the inclusive leadership ethic that must be nurtured throughout the school community.

REMODELLING THE FULL SERVICE
EDUCATIONAL COMMUNITY

Using the network as a structure and managing information flow in a way previously considered, the following three examples offer an idea of how the new multi-agency infrastructure in a modernized educational community might look (comprising the reformed special school, mainstream school, and LA service provision).

Example 1: the modernized special school

The reformed special school is expected to be a centre of excellence offering expertise and knowledge in educational provision for managing learning differences in the school community. This idea of the modern special school will sensibly involve integrating existing special school and SENSS functions specializing in the same area of SEN provision. This model might include, but does not presuppose, site-based co-location as it is being applied at present in a great deal of modernizing reform (see for example, The Darlington Village described in PricewaterhouseCoopers, 2007: 76–7). The structure of the modernizing special school might therefore include re-establishing itself as a multi-purpose provision that includes some of the following:

- **Specialist Special School** with an admissions policy offering fixed-term renewable placements for children with specific and extreme learning differences.

- **Schools Community Support Service Base** offering delivery of centre to peripheral support for learning in the form of flexible and dual placements for individual children in the school community experiencing extreme learning difficulty.

- **Specialist Professional Learning Centre** inter-professional accredited training and consultancy service to other teams/services in the educational community.

- **Specialist Community Advisory Centre** providing complementary knowledge, expertise and support for managing personalized educational systems/differential pedagogy.

- **Specialist Advocacy Centre** enabling access, voice and participation in support and advice on SEN/inclusion matters to stakeholder groups/individuals in the school community.

This change strategy would require expansion and an extension of the role of the special school. It would require careful consideration of remodelling training needs of the special school workforce. A second crucial consideration would involve strategic decision making in relation to the structure of funding in the LA. Finally, it would reposition the special school at the heart of the schools' community and the LA children's workforce network.

Example 2: the extended mainstream school

The full service school concept is usually understood as a co-ordinated and integrated educational experience provided for the 'client', that is, the pupil and their parents. A working model for this kind of school in England is the SureStart Children's Centre, catering for the Early Years pre-school population, typically open from 8.00 a.m. through to 6.00 p.m. all year round, and offering a range of health, social and educational services. The concept of an extended school provides an opportunity for school leaders to develop multi-agency collaboration, promote an extending notion of inclusive leadership and operate as agents of social change and community renewal. This will entail, however, new ways of working and a shift in style from school to community-based education. The networking structure outlined in Figure 6.1 on page 125 offers a structural template for the modern mainstream school. It assumes the creation of a dedicated team that Cheminais (2006) describes as wrap-about provision operating around the child. One of the key functions of this team would be key work. This extends a traditional, named key-worker structure and offers an invaluable tool for ensuring continuity in approach across and through any trans-disciplinary and inter-agency provision.

A second core function for the team is networking with external agencies, co-ordinating two further functions: one, a deepening level of provision for individual children on a case by case basis; the other, a knowledge management function enabling good levels of data transmission and communication throughout the LA service community. Implicit in this notion is the careful maintenance of a shared common framework for an identification, assessment and intervention protocol for vulnerable children. A considerable amount of continuing effort on the part of the government is currently being spent in developing a common assessment policy framework for the children's workforce initiative that will afford further resources for networking knowledge and information across agencies involved with the development and education of children. Finally, it has been stated that the government intention is that by 2008 most schools in England will be extended schools (DfES, 2003d).

Example 3: the integrated LA services community

Every local authority in England has now appointed an extended schools remodelling adviser (ESRA) to lead the development of extended schools using a developing range of government validated remodelling tools and processes

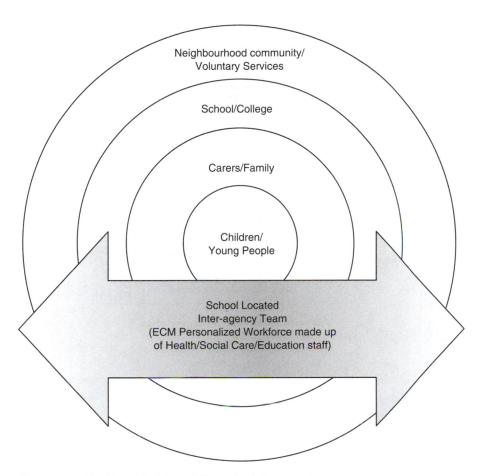

Figure 6.1 The Extended School (Learning) Community

across the local authority (NGA, 2006). The role of the LA in the extended schools reform programme is pivotal. Two current issues will need urgent clarification in the immediate future if the full service concept is to be taken forward. The first issue is to do with the particular structure constructed for the reorganization of the LA children's service community (see Figure 6.2 for an example of an intervention-led structuring of service provision). The second will be the funding formulae designed to resource this community. Some difficulties will inevitably occur in jigsawing funding and organizational structures between the different funding arrangements for health and LA.

This will be further complicated by free market principles that continue to dominate government thinking in terms of public sector financing and organization. One implication of this is the increasing tendency to recommend service charging, which is likely to be taken up in the modernized school setting.

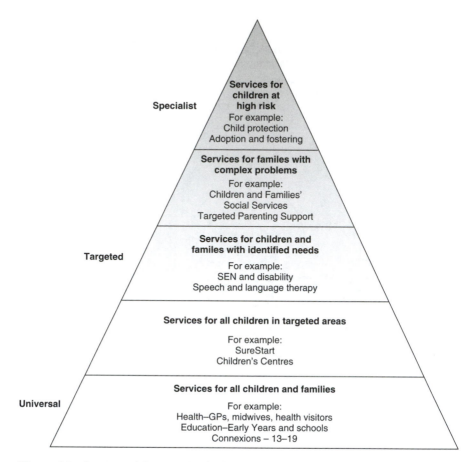

Figure 6.2   Integrated Services in the LA (Source: DfES, 2003d: 21)

Inter-agency working – partnerships and boundaries and learning

One theme running through this book is the central place of *praxis* and pro-fessional or transformative learning in the leadership and management of special and inclusive education. At no point is this theme more self-evident than in a consideration of inter-agency partnerships, inter-professional working practices and related professional learning. The drive toward part-nership teams is described by Burnett (2003) as a key feature in inclusion-led reform because it:

- offers support and diversity in meeting the needs of all pupils;

- attracts more opportunities to access a wider range of additional funding;

- improves service delivery;

- increases productivity potential;

- encourages creativity, and interdependency, as shared goals become established.

The idea of public service joint working is neither new nor necessarily regarded as a positive success. Lacey (2001) provides a useful explanation of the rationale behind services working together, as well as some of the established benefits for working in a collaborative 'support partnership' with their client base. Intervention and community-based support typically involve one or more of the following kinds of collaborative agency:

- networks;

- clusters;

- federation;

- consortium;

- support partnership;

- teams (multi-disciplinary);

- teams (inter-disciplinary);

- teams (trans-disciplinary).

Lacey explains how a process continuum flowing from an open and loosely coupled system (liaison) through levels of increasing specification (co-ordination and co-operation) to a tightly coupled system (collaboration) characterizes the partnership concept in an inter-agency context. The shift from 'multi- to trans-disciplinary' team working reflects a similar continuum, involving increasing levels of professional identity shift, boundary crossing and a re-blending mix of professional knowledge/practice in the specific context (team function). The trans-disciplinary setting perhaps represents the greatest likelihood of achieving joined-up, seamless, front-line delivery of a wrap-around service provision.

In developing effective multi-agency work, a clarification of the following key issues recurs in studies evaluating service provision (Anning et al., 2006; Atkinson et al., 2002; Lacey, 2001):

1. **Structural**: fiscal and non-fiscal resources; role definition; organizational remit; operational prioritization; communication systems; confidentiality/ informational sharing protocol.

2. **Process**: understanding remit responsibilities; professional identity; professional agency cultures; leadership commitment; key personnel involvement; mutual resource sharing.

The development of new ways of working generates a need to refocus on how this can be best achieved. Multi-agency working has revealed the need for an understanding of forms of knowledge distributed across traditional boundaries and groups of people in multiple settings. A new form of distributed knowledge is identified by Puonti (2004: 44) as challenging the conventional assumptions of individualized learning at the heart of developmental psychology. Further distinctions are made between a formal, codified knowledge associated with professional discipline and an informal personal and experiential knowledge. The application of this knowledge in the work-place reflects a *praxis* that is the product of a cycle of theory–practice process running through a career-long accumulation of learning.

In recent research examining how inter-agency teams can improve and develop their working practice, theories of distributed cognition have been employed in two cutting-edge forms of participatory research. Groups of participants from a range of agency settings have been engaged in each project: the first involved professional learning intervention groups (Warmington et al., 2004); the second, selected inter-professional teams in focus groups who were presented with critical incident scenarios used to produce practice-based data (Anning et al., 2006). Key concepts emerging from this work, in large part informed by socio-cultural activity theory, include:

- *Boundary crossing* – a means of challenging existing professional identities and reconceptualizing the ways in which collaboration between workers from different professional backgrounds might generate new professional practices.

- *Conflict as a catalyst for learning* – socio-cultural theory is adopted to reveal the surfacing of contradictions, tensions and dilemmas that occur in inter-professional teams with a view to generating new understandings and inter-professional knowledge.

- *Knot-working* – an intensely collaborative activity that relies upon constantly changing combinations of people grouping together for a fixed period of time.

A new approach to professional development is emerging from this research that indicates the need to think in terms of producing a collective *praxis* and utilizing the new concept of *expansive learning*. This kind of learning is a collaborative construction of new forms of activity, often initiated by individuals making modest innovations in the course of their work. It is, furthermore, equally important that utilizing an individual's *phronesis* forms a deliberate part in the process of creating *praxis* for the continuing development of inclusive leadership and the exercise of an integrative management. It is clear from reading the literature that there is, on the one hand, a huge gap between policy rhetoric and an over easy reference to the idea of networking and partnership as the way forward in securing joined-up professional practice, and on the other, actually making it work. Partnership is not easy. Lacey (2001: 172) concludes in a manner reminiscent of my own comments on inclusive education that:

> Very few people need to be persuaded of the importance of working together and providing 'joined up services', but what still seems to be missing is the willingness of large organizations like schools, hospitals and service to change. Collaboration cannot be tacked on to traditional ways of working. It demands fundamental change.

Developing both individual and collective *praxis* by combining theory and practice in new forms of professional learning is an important part of developing new forms of inter-agency work in the management of special and inclusive education.

Part III

Inclusive Leadership and Managing Change: Enabling the Learning Professional?

The third part of this book is a discussion of SEN policy and provision in the school context. Its primary focus is on the management of inclusive learning and pedagogy. The focal point for this discussion is professional learning and leadership knowledge applied to the practice of managing educational inclusion. This will include a consideration of learning, teaching, behaviour management, pedagogy and the curriculum. It examines the ideas behind personalized education and the tensions inherent in managing diversity and differences in the school community.

The backcloth to working successfully in this context is the SEN and inclusion policy described in Part I and the professional learning context presented in Part II. Together with Part III, it is hoped that a new context is beginning to emerge, describing an inclusive leadership and an integrative management of SEN provision. In many respects it is perhaps a perspective that opens up the possibility of moving beyond a special needs perspective to one embracing developing concepts of social diversity and personal differences in the learning community. The opportunity to challenge fundamental notions of special education that have existed for several decades involves what Florian (2006) has called 're-imagining special education'.

She suggests that addressing three basic questions might facilitate thinking of this kind. The first is to define special education. The second is to challenge the long-established basis for organizing teaching and learning on ideas of fixed ability or intelligence. The third is to determine exactly what is special about special education. Each of these questions have in one way or another been raised and addressed as part of the developing approach to managing special and inclusive education in this book. The future for SEN policy and provision has been deliberately located in the context of organizational learning and the learning community. Leadership and change are featured as key aspects in driving forward, to secure better access to an education for all that offers effective support for learning, particularly for those who for reasons of difference experience difficulty or alienation.

To succeed with inclusive leadership in the current policy setting of an international educational standards agenda and post-modern remodelling of the school system is a considerable challenge in its own right. Ainscow

(2006) calls for a deeper emphasis upon 'school improvement with attitude' as a way forward, a renewal of inclusion values and intention associated with the original index for inclusion. Leadership is presented as part of a requirement for managing change and the search for key levers in realizing social justice. An emphasis upon communities of practice and networking as one method for implementing such change is in part reflected both in the next four chapters and Part II of this book. Burnett (2003), however, correctly argues that acknowledging diversity should lead to differences being recognized and celebrated.

What is described in the following chapters is an approach to success management and a defining of individual differences rather than special needs, as a deficit-less strategy for organizing learning that works to potential rather than limitation. To do this is not to propose full scale abandonment of practitioners' professional experience or a status quo in terms of policy or knowledge. Neither does it propose rejecting a recent past, but its does look towards a future that is predicated in notions of educative growth rather than instant transformation, or personal fulfillment rather than disposable commodity. In a policy context that intends public service to be driven by the economics of consumption, this is no easy task.

Chapter 7 considers the role of the SENCo in the English school system. The role is examined in the light of new and increasing demands created by modernizing reform. A SENCo's responsibility reflects an ever-widening remit, encompassing diversity and inclusion in the school community. This entails a continuing involvement in strategic and operational issues that are whole-school and reflect the need for an inclusive ethic (success qualities in Level 3 of the MISE model). Together with an emphasis upon success management, the inclusive ethic is presented as a key ingredient in developing the SENCo's role as a knowledge network broker and manager of support partnerships within and, if required, beyond the school community.

Chapter 8 addresses leadership questions related to moving forward on the issues surrounding SEN, inclusion, diversity and difference in the school community. In particular, it focuses upon a paradox of inclusion in the form of the dilemma faced when managing difference and controlling the pressure of a set of exclusion forces prevalent in both the school community and wider society. This means dealing with the management of human behaviour and well-being, both on an individual basis as well as part of a collective phenomenon in the school setting and as part of the wider community. A way forward is proposed comprising a fourth strand or dimension to the special-inclusion debate – offering an alternative paradigm to those previously described. An integrative approach is one that can lead to constructing new post-modern approaches to diversity and difference in the school/learning community.

Chapter 9 is a consideration of how to manage a developing knowledge of learning differences and social diversity. An implication of recent trends in approaches to teaching and learning is that the school workforce, as a learning community of the future, will need to develop a differential pedagogy. Such an approach might well offer a basis for moving beyond ability-based conceptions of education and needs-led, deficit-orientated forms of assessment in SEN provision. A discussion of how this development should entail organizational commitment to professional learning and developing *praxis* to be utilized in distributed leadership across the school community is presented. Central to this approach is the notion of working with rather than denying individual differences in the classroom.

The final chapter begins by examining a vision of education in England by the year 2020 as described in a recent report published by the DfES (2006). Many of the ideas reflect key themes developed throughout this book. In conclusion, a final review is made of the core concepts for developing the management of inclusion and special education as illustrated in the MISE model, as they relate to the emerging policy agenda in England of a personalized education in which every child is meant to matter.

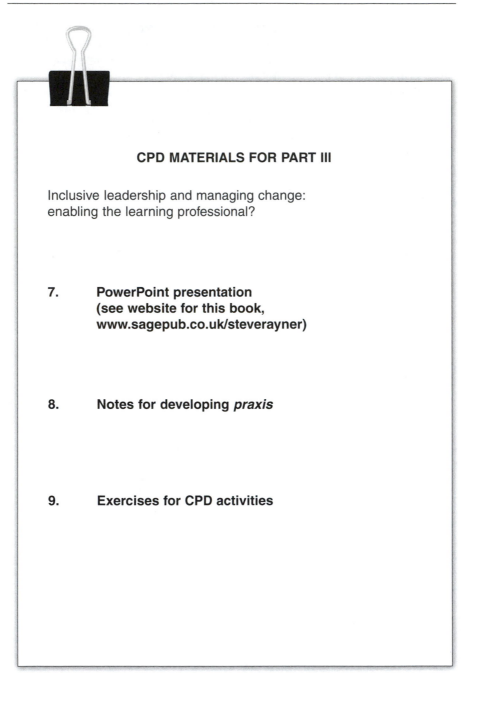

CPD MATERIALS FOR PART III

Inclusive leadership and managing change:
enabling the learning professional?

7.   **PowerPoint presentation
(see website for this book,
www.sagepub.co.uk/steverayner)**

8.   **Notes for developing *praxis***

9.   **Exercises for CPD activities**

8. NOTES FOR DEVELOPING *PRAXIS* [1]

KEY ISSUES/QUESTIONS

Examine the following issues as a workforce or small group exercise:

SEN/INCLUSION TEAM REMODELLING

- Professional learning and developing *praxis* for the TA.
- Strategic leadership in developing participation and partnership in the school community.
- Networking and evolving the extended school service.
- Managing local and national policy priorities.
- Advising and leading on personalized educational and professional learning for diversity and differences in learning and teaching.

TEACHING, DIVERSITY AND DIFFERENCE

- Conceptions of ability and learning capacity/capability.
- Learning how to learn (process and product).
- Multiple functions of assessment in the learning community.
- An SEN specific or differential pedagogy.
- CPD and professional learning in the learning community.
- Connectivity, network and partnership – enabling access and engagement.

MANAGING DIVERSITY AND SCHOOL BEHAVIOUR

- Team-work and partnership in behaviour management ensuring coherent consistency, mutual support and mediation.
- Enabling and using community participation and collaborative activities aimed at supporting inclusive school behaviour, personal well-being and security (pupils, parents, governors, voluntary workers, external agencies).
- Emphasis upon restorative intervention rather than punitive sanction in the implementation of pastoral care before behavioural penalty.

8. NOTES FOR DEVELOPING *PRAXIS* [2]

CORE CONCEPTS

Managing inclusion and special education effectively involves encouraging a discourse in the following concepts. The inclusion touchstone themes listed in Chapter 3 are all relevant to this kind of community-based activity.

SUCCESS MANAGEMENT

- Action-centred leadership for building inclusive leadership groups.
- Action-centred leadership for sustaining task groups/ distributing leadership.
- Success management working with expectations, challenges and achievements in the team/learning group.

MANAGING DIFFERENCES IN LEARNING/TEACHING

- Understanding new aspects of differential psychology (multiple intelligences/learning styles).
- Generating new knowledge and practice-based evidence about differences as they impact upon learning outcomes (attainment/achievement by gender/ethnicity/style).
- Revisiting the uses and abuses of assessment in learning and teaching.
- Ensuring access and participation in the learning community.
- Developing differentiated classroom/differential pedagogy.

MANAGING DIVERSITY AND SCHOOL BEHAVIOUR

- Clearly stated and communicated school discipline/ behaviour management policy and related protocols giving rules, rights, responsibilities for all members of the school community.
- Clear policy statement and supporting protocols describing rewards, penalties and a system of sanctions, consequences and support or intervention in the case of EBSD.

8. NOTES FOR DEVELOPING *PRAXIS* [3]

KNOWLEDGE SOURCES – KEY READING

Best, R., Lang, P., Lodge, C. and Watkins, C. (1995) *Pastoral Care and Personal-Social Education.* London: Cassell.

Black, P. and Wiliam, D. et al. (2002) *Working Inside the Black Box: Assessment for Learning in the Classroom.* King's College London.

Cheminais, R. (2005) *Every Child Matters: A New Role for SENCOs.* London: David Fulton.

Cowne, E. (2003) *Developing Inclusive Practice: The SENCO's Role in Managing Change.* London: David Fulton.

Desforges, C. (2003) *The impact of parental involvement, parental support and family education on pupil achievement and adjustment*, DfES Research Report 433, Nottingham: DfES.

Gibson, S. and Blandford, S. (2005) Managing Special Educational Needs, London: Paul Chapman.

Greenhalgh, P. (1994) Emotional Growth and Learning. London: Routledge.

Hart, S., Dixon, A., Drummond, M.J. and McIntyre, D. (2004) *Learning without Limits.* Maidenhead: Open University Press.

Nind, M., Rix, J., Sheehy, K. and Simmons, K. (eds) (2005) *Curriculum and Pedagogy in Inclusive Education: Values into Practice.* London: RoutledgeFalmer.

Reid, G. (2005) *Learning Styles and Inclusion.* London: PCP.

Riding, R.J. and Rayner S.G. (1998) *Cognitive Styles and Learning Strategies.* London: David Fulton.

web-sites at:

www.multiverse.ac.uk.
www.antiracisttoolkit.org.uk.
www.teachingexpertise.com
www.assessment-reform-group.org.uk
www.parentscentre.gov.uk

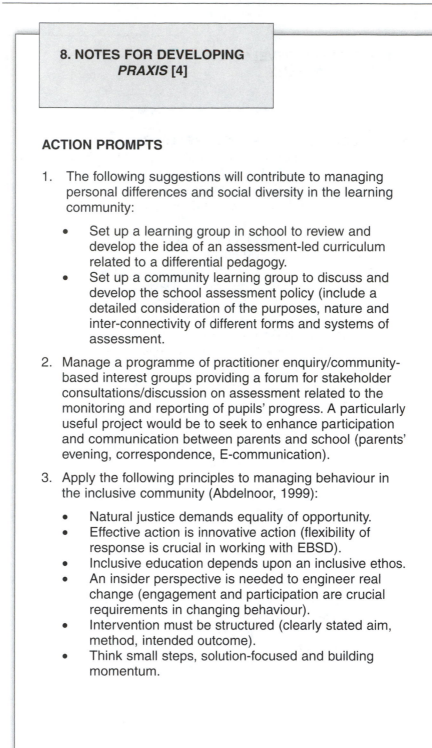

8. NOTES FOR DEVELOPING
***PRAXIS* [4]**

ACTION PROMPTS

1. The following suggestions will contribute to managing personal differences and social diversity in the learning community:

    *   Set up a learning group in school to review and develop the idea of an assessment-led curriculum related to a differential pedagogy.
    *   Set up a community learning group to discuss and develop the school assessment policy (include a detailed consideration of the purposes, nature and inter-connectivity of different forms and systems of assessment.

2. Manage a programme of practitioner enquiry/community-based interest groups providing a forum for stakeholder consultations/discussion on assessment related to the monitoring and reporting of pupils' progress. A particularly useful project would be to seek to enhance participation and communication between parents and school (parents' evening, correspondence, E-communication).

3. Apply the following principles to managing behaviour in the inclusive community (Abdelnoor, 1999):

    *   Natural justice demands equality of opportunity.
    *   Effective action is innovative action (flexibility of response is crucial in working with EBSD).
    *   Inclusive education depends upon an inclusive ethos.
    *   An insider perspective is needed to engineer real change (engagement and participation are crucial requirements in changing behaviour).
    *   Intervention must be structured (clearly stated aim, method, intended outcome).
    *   Think small steps, solution-focused and building momentum.

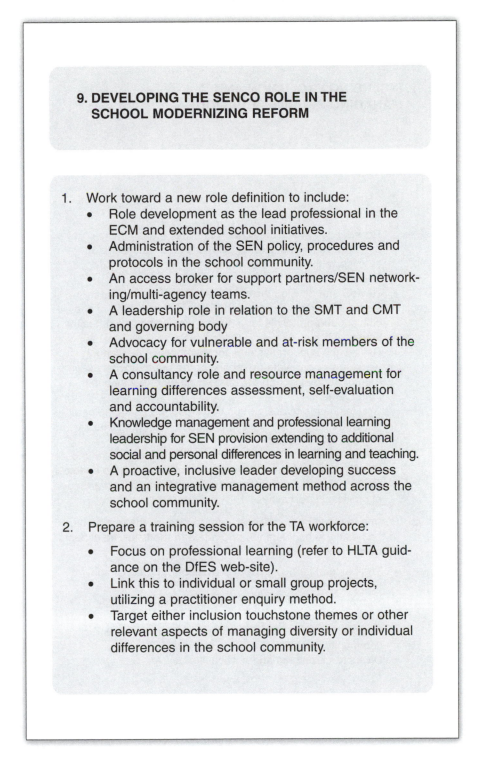

9. DEVELOPING THE SENCO ROLE IN THE SCHOOL MODERNIZING REFORM

1. Work toward a new role definition to include:
    - Role development as the lead professional in the ECM and extended school initiatives.
    - Administration of the SEN policy, procedures and protocols in the school community.
    - An access broker for support partners/SEN networking/multi-agency teams.
    - A leadership role in relation to the SMT and CMT and governing body
    - Advocacy for vulnerable and at-risk members of the school community.
    - A consultancy role and resource management for learning differences assessment, self-evaluation and accountability.
    - Knowledge management and professional learning leadership for SEN provision extending to additional social and personal differences in learning and teaching.
    - A proactive, inclusive leader developing success and an integrative management method across the school community.

2. Prepare a training session for the TA workforce:

    - Focus on professional learning (refer to HLTA guidance on the DfES web-site).
    - Link this to individual or small group projects, utilizing a practitioner enquiry method.
    - Target either inclusion touchstone themes or other relevant aspects of managing diversity or individual differences in the school community.

9. INCLUDING EXCLUSION AND MANAGING SCHOOL BEHAVIOUR

1. The following suggestions form a basis for managing school behaviour in a diverse learning community:

    *   Review and develop the school behaviour management policy and provision, drawing upon ECM outcomes and inclusion touchstone themes to evaluate existing principles, *praxis* and practice.
    *   Review and develop the school systems for attendance, exclusion and child protection (these are examples of specific support protocols for personal well-being and a healthy school).
    *   Review the support systems for members of the school workforce and restate protocols for the peer support roles of mentor and adviser on day-to-day issues of behaviour management.
    *   Create/change teams/groups dedicated to enhancing participation from community stakeholders in managing diversity and school behaviour.
    *   Create a citizenship team to address issues of culture and identity, to establish a Citizenship programme and to enable student engagement through the school council and a range of political opportunities.

2. Form a learning group/change team to discuss matters relating to the healthy school agenda and relate to the following aspects of the learning community:

    *   The pastoral curriculum and provision for personal and social education;
    *   Mental health and well-being in the school community (affective education);
    *   Personal dignity, social respect, friendship and individual/ community identity;
    *   Diversity, citizenship and political literacy.

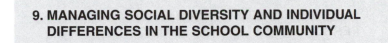

9. MANAGING SOCIAL DIVERSITY AND INDIVIDUAL DIFFERENCES IN THE SCHOOL COMMUNITY

1. Complete these tasks as part of a CPD team or working group.

   - Agree and articulate the place and purpose of special education in an inclusive policy context.
   - Record a shared understanding of the meaning of SEN and inclusion policies and or provision.
   - Formulate a policy for CPD, change management and project leadership in the academic year.
   - Develop the role of the special school or support service for children with SEN.
   - Create a policy for developing data management and evidence-based practice for service improvement.
   - Make a strategic plan for inter-facing with a Common Assessment Framework and building inter-agency action.
   - Clarify the kind of knowledge production or management required for improving SEN expertise and the implications for CPD.

2. Revisit the following questions and discuss how to advance on:

   - Affirming the nature and purposes of assessment in the curriculum?
   - Pupil profiling for learning preferences, strengths and interests?
   - Adaptation in pedagogy and teaching practices?
   - Developing *praxis* linked to teaching, diversity and *praxis*?
   - Joining up parts to make the whole lot work together – integrative management?

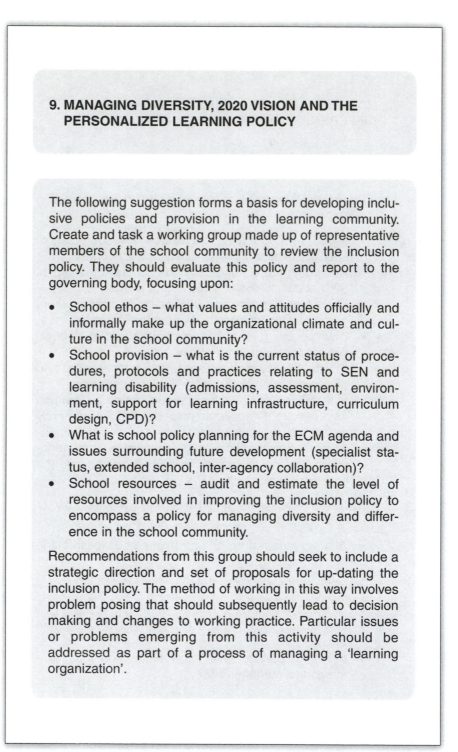

9. MANAGING DIVERSITY, 2020 VISION AND THE PERSONALIZED LEARNING POLICY

The following suggestion forms a basis for developing inclusive policies and provision in the learning community. Create and task a working group made up of representative members of the school community to review the inclusion policy. They should evaluate this policy and report to the governing body, focusing upon:

- School ethos – what values and attitudes officially and informally make up the organizational climate and culture in the school community?
- School provision – what is the current status of procedures, protocols and practices relating to SEN and learning disability (admissions, assessment, environment, support for learning infrastructure, curriculum design, CPD)?
- What is school policy planning for the ECM agenda and issues surrounding future development (specialist status, extended school, inter-agency collaboration)?
- School resources – audit and estimate the level of resources involved in improving the inclusion policy to encompass a policy for managing diversity and difference in the school community.

Recommendations from this group should seek to include a strategic direction and set of proposals for up-dating the inclusion policy. The method of working in this way involves problem posing that should subsequently lead to decision making and changes to working practice. Particular issues or problems emerging from this activity should be addressed as part of a process of managing a 'learning organization'.

7

Managing Support for Learning in the School Community

In this chapter the role of the SENCo in the English school system is examined in the light of new and increasing demands created by modernizing reform. The traditional role of the SENCo, dating back to the mid-1980s, has taken an increasingly formalized position as the lead professional in the day-to-day management of SEN provision in the mainstream school.

The role's responsibility reflects an ever-widening remit encompassing diversity and inclusion in the school community. This entails a continuing involvement in strategic and operational issues that are whole school and reflect an inclusive ethic (success qualities in Level 3 of the MISE model). The SENCo is therefore presented as pivotal to the task of managing learning differences in the school community.

One approach to this task is to adopt the tactic of blending inclusive leadership with an adaptation of action-centred leadership, and to create a highly focused, group-based form of performance management. This particular approach is a contextualized leadership; it gives the SENCo a method for managing and charting success in the shifting landscape of remodelling the school workforce. With an emphasis upon success management, a key ingredient in the new role of the SENCo is identified as knowledge network broker and manager of support partnerships within and, if required, beyond the school community.

INTRODUCTION

'Is it really a good school?' This is probably the most frequently asked question in the world of education. As a pupil, a parent, teacher, headteacher, school governor, school inspector and an academic, I have over the years, time and again, asked and tried to answer this question. There is no doubt that the answer in large measure rests on what it is that people decide makes a good school. How does the school serve the community?

School prospectuses, and more recently web-sites, offer a source of information for those interested in this topic. A recurring theme found in these booklets, and for that matter in any discussion about good schools, is that schools aim to succeed in realizing the full potential of every individual child in a learning community. Such schools aim to achieve what is in fact an inclusive approach, even if they do not recognize it as such, by balancing the needs of one child with those of many children, and through this approach, establish a diverse and effective learning community. The process of building inclusive practice will actually help realize the aim of meeting individual differences described in the typical school prospectus. The inference drawn here then is that a good school is an inclusive school. Zemelman (1998) identified in research in the USA the following tell-tale features of an inclusive school.

- Choice for students.

- Co-operative and collaborative activity amongst learners.

- In-class support arrangements for teachers and pupils.

- Experimental, inductive hands-on learning.

- Independent learning emphasizing learner responsibility.

- Active learning with pupils engaged in doing, talking and collaborative learning.

- On-going concern for the processes of learning.

- Concern for formative and authentic rather than standardized assessment.

Arguably, effective schools are characterized by these same features – all significant aspects in the process of learning and teaching. What teachers actually do when they are teaching will always remain a major part in any success with school improvement or educational inclusion. This same process or journey toward inclusive education is one that describes school improvement, school effectiveness, and a concern for standards in equity, educational achievement and school performance. There is no contradiction.

This is an important point, as it opens up a way forward to developing and strengthening approaches to diversity in a world dominated by performance management and value for money-driven accountability. The latter are often presented as barriers or forces preventing an holistic approach to educational inclusion in the school community. If there is any conflict in the standards agenda and reform for inclusion, however, it lies more closely in a philosophy of ability-led normative judgements required in traditional examination, the almost total emphasis upon a utilitarian purpose of education and the notion that a public service should be self-financing.

The recent government policy of reform in England is aimed at a modernization which Newman (2001) claims is grounded in the idea of life-long learning. This idea is tied to a concept of the citizen as an active, engaged and informed member of a learning community(ies); of work as task-focused and supported through new technologies providing opportunity for the socially excluded; and of multi-agency approaches involving collaboration and co-operation across different parts of the public sector. Remodelling for the school workforce, particularly in light of the ECM agenda, should therefore be positively framed as part of a wider initiative aimed at a better provision for managing social and personal differences in the school community (see Chapter 6). The intention here is to look more closely at the implications of this change. I will examine in particular the leadership role of the SENCo as it is developing in the English school context in the light of national remodelling reform.

All mainstream schools in England are expected to have a designated teacher acting as the SENCo and that they are working with regard to the SEN Code of Practice. A SENCo is required not only to possess advanced teaching skills for working with children who present SEN, but are also expected to manage SEN provision and policy throughout the whole school. The key features in the SENCo remit include a responsibility for:

- day-to-day operation of SEN policy and provision in a school organization;

- strategic development of SEN provision;

- efficient and effective deployment of resources to support SEN provision;

- administration of the SEN Register (required of all schools) and monitoring the progress of all SEN registered pupils;

- managing support for learning procedures, including liaison with the SEN governor, parents and external agencies;

- management of an SEN or inclusion team (when such a team exists);

- development of leadership skills in the key aspects of a SENCo role (teacher competency, professional knowledge of SEN, communication skills, decision-making skills, and self-management).

I therefore want to consider how the SENCo might realize the aim of developing an inclusive leadership and integrative management in the pursuit of success qualities for the school community (MISE model, Level 3).

The SENCo role is a pivotal one in a whole school approach to effectively managing diversity and difference in the school community. In developing new approaches to inclusion and school improvement, it is useful to refer to the following checklist of critical elements in an inclusive school identified by Schafner and Buswell (1996). These elements reflect the success qualities previously described in the MISE model, that is, the four inter-relating qualities of equity, empathy, efficiency and efficacy. They also reflect Zemelman's findings previously described as features of an inclusive/effective school. These critical elements are presented as an action plan and include taking the following steps:

1. Develop a common philosophy and strategic plan for developing educational inclusion.

2. Provide strong leadership.

3. Promote classroom and school-wide cultures that appreciate and accommodate diversity.

4. Develop support networks.

5. Use deliberate processes that are clearly communicated to ensure accountability.

6. Develop organized and on-going technical assistance (resource networking).

7. Maintain flexibility in procedures, protocols and a general or team-based response to problem solving and decision making.

8. Examine and adopt effective teaching approaches.

9. Celebrate successes and learn from challenges.

10. Be knowledgeable about the change process and avoid resistance to growth.

These actions, identified in schools in the USA, afford a useful fabric for a policy framework in the school organization for any international context. This leads in turn in the next section to a consideration of the SEN policy framework in an English school context. The basic requirements of a shifting statutory framework are further examined in the light of ECM legislation and changes to the school inspection regime. It is the responsibility of the SENCo to lead and manage this SEN policy and related provision in the school community.

THE SENCO AS AN INCLUSIVE LEADER

The provision for SEN in the school community involves the whole workforce and other stakeholders in the community. Pupils, parents, teachers, teacher assistants, governors, agency workers and even politicians are all participants in the process of education. The SENCo represents a focal point and a role remit that involve an orchestration of whole school leadership which should arguably draw upon an awareness and integration of roles, responsibilities and self as portrayed in the model of inclusive leadership principles described in Chapter 4 (see Figure 4.1, page 81). In addition, it involves an integrative management of people, resources and learning (Figure 4.3, page 88).

The SENCo remit formally carries with it an expectation of co-ordinating learning and teaching interventions, managing people, and being competent in budgetary control and resource deployment. Beyond this there remains a deeper traditional expectation that the SENCo will be expert in all matters pertaining to SEN and disability, and further that the SENCo will lead in the development of educational inclusion and the management of diversity in the classroom. This brings a widening brief for other personal and social differences in learning (for example, the gifted and talented, pupils with English as a second language, gender differences and equity, behavioural needs and PSLD). It is no surprise that Cole (2005: 287), reporting on a recent survey of SENCo attitudes and workload, concludes that being a SENCo is often a 'mission impossible'. She argues that:

> ... research indicates that despite the revision of the Special Educational Needs Code of Practice in 2001, many SENCOs are still overwhelmed by the operational nature of the role with little support, time or funding to consider more strategic aspects of inclusion and SEN.

One lead aspect of this operational role is to manage accountability and school improvement in the area of SEN provision. This requires developing and asserting a SENCo leadership identity and an SEN/inclusion action plan, involving demarcation of responsibilities and authority. Mapping this role is all important, as the whole school and beyond represents the SENCo's 'department', creating the possibility of limitless boundaries reaching out to all four corners of the local community. One way of imposing some fixed but flexible boundaries for this role is to contextualize the SENCo role and reapply an integrative approach to the managing success and practice-based evidence. This focused form of performance management is increasingly important as the need to directly manage demands of accountability is increased.

Success management: integrating inclusive leadership

The following suggestion of the SENCo adopting the tactic of success management is not an attempt to play down or simplify the complex mix of realities that is school. Nor is it a suggestion that performance management should dominate an inclusive leadership or integrative management of SEN policy and provision. Recognizing the churn of day-to-day working life is central to understanding inclusive and effective leadership (see Figure 4.3, page 88). The enterprise of learning, by its very nature, is about harnessing mutability and growth. It is, furthermore, important to remember that work in school is about dealing with an ever-increasing number of diverse demands for improvement in challenging contexts.

The challenge, nonetheless, is to make manageable the task of achieving success. The first step in building better practice is to establish or re-emphasize within the community the concept of success. Success, in contrast to quality, or standards, or achievement, is more easily and appropriately measured. Benchmarking progress is an exercise that is useful as part of the process in creating a strategic action plan and monitoring attainment. Much of this is now well established in school development planning – the point here is to avoid becoming dominated by performativity or infected by a sterility associated with completing an endless accounting exercise. The debate surrounding the mandatory IEP offers a case in point. For many long-serving SENCos, the bureaucracy linked to IEP writing and administration has been overwhelming.

In a very useful discussion of IEP administration, Cowne (2003) demonstrates how in relation to the SENCo workload, purpose, design and practice must all be considered in a wider pro-active approach to performance management. The take-up of assessment data for the SEN Code of Practice, the annual review, or for school inspection and more latterly self-evaluation, is another aspect of this same process. Practice-based evidence can always be potentially useful, but must not be allowed to paralyze core activity by creating an unmanageable or irrelevant pile of dust-gathering paper (or neglected email attachments in a networked system). The first step in success management is about the action taken to blend strategic and operational issues in problem-posing and decision-making scrutiny of the SENCo remit. Dealing with these core principles of professional learning as leadership (see Figure 4.1, page 81) and action-centred leadership (see Figure 4.2, page 85) in a focused way described in Figure 7.1, page 151 casts the SENCo in the role of change agent located at the heart of an interactive concern for working with expectations, identifying challenges and seeking to facilitate achievement.

The second step is to agree or renew within school a structure or framework for managing success, change and development. This should involve the identification and co-option of key change agents in the school workforce playing the functional role of leadership in the multi-level and interactive contexts of managing change. They might include:

- Class/subject leader
- Parent
- Student
- Learning Mentor
- Teaching Assistant
- Pastoral care leader
- Member of the SMT

- Governor
- SENCo
- Administration staff
- Bursar
- External expert
- Member of the LA
- Site Manager

The list is endless, the potential huge, but the challenge involved in managing expectation and achievement is considerable. The trick is to involve people at a very real level of leading and managing work. Change agents or leaders nonetheless should in turn take up the task of managing specific aspects of school development. This approach anticipates partnership and collaborative networking as requisites for inclusive leadership. It carries with it the benefits of securing rather than losing tacit knowledge transfer associated with communities of practice. It should be established as a template for defining functions and roles that may or may not be long term, but always link to the design and delivery of school policy. This in turn should reflect a community culture associated with the notion of organizational learning.

The SENCo, however, should always remain aware of how learning and teaching are central to this active leadership stretching across the school organization and should ensure that policy development fits into a *joined-up* set of procedural systems and pedagogy. This overview, reflecting the whole school structure for learning and teaching, should be *inclusive*, an integrated structure combining the traditional divisions of pastoral and academic development. Both of these must 'talk to each other' in the formation of culture, systems and structures in the school curriculum and crucially as part of the day-to-day routine of work in school. The role of the SENCo is extensive, is evolving as I write, and certainly merits and needs greater acknowledgement – but is nonetheless still *not* a mission impossible.

School improvement is really about managing success. Defining success is in part a necessary aspect of accounting for and demonstrating improvement, but perhaps more importantly it offers a way of motivating both an individual and the group. Above all, effective education is a team game aimed at including all of its members in a 'win-win' result. This does not mean everyone realizing the same outcome, but it does mean being clear about wanting to secure equity and sharing the same aim to harness the personal potential of the 'learning community'. The adoption of *success management* is begun with the identification and delegation of three key operations for the school community:

1. Strategic leadership.

2. Resource management.

3. Continued organizational learning.

The nature of each of these operations is process-bound and part of a traditional and continuing cycle of planning, action and review. It means not forgetting that operational issues matter and resources are an important consideration in achieving good management. The most important resource in the school setting is human. The SENCo is dealing with the very same issues of school effectiveness and resource management on a whole school basis shared by only one or two other people in the school organization, namely the headteacher, their deputies and the school bursar. The role, however, as previously stated, is not a mission impossible! The task of success management is one that is applicable to every level of the school organization. It must be shared by and in some way involve every professional stakeholder in the educational community. The headteacher and the governing body in turn share the responsibility of producing a description or protocol that makes visible this process as an interactive relationship between decision making, resources, priorities and purpose.

One way of contributing to this is for the SENCo to visualize the school as a unique 'resource bed' as described in Figure 7.1 below. In an adaptation of Adair's action-centred leadership (see Figure 4.2, page 85), the school is seen as a resource-rich environment made up of four dimensions: time and place, non-human resources, human resources and knowledge systems. The SENCo as leader plays the central role of change agent (CA) in shaping and determining SEN policy, provision and practice. This invokes a leadership role that includes actions at each level of the MISE model and most certainly requires membership in the school's SMT. Following the idea of managing success in SEN provision, the SENCo should be aware that individuals and teams or groups play differing roles within this context in the work of learning, teaching and knowledge management. In fulfilling these roles, different individuals will be engaged in the continuing interactive processes of distributed leadership and success management. Resources, finite in form, are construed in part as a school workforce capacity for work, and in part as the capacity for the SENCo's work. The latter, therefore, is individual and in part spent managing the processes of success management.

In adopting this approach, resources are tied to activity generating and acquiring knowledge. Learning is invested in every member of the school community as part of a continuing community-based agenda for meeting sets of challenges, expectations and achievement (success). Each individual in the school community at some point sits at the centre of these overlapping zones of action and is directly involved in the role and work of a change agent. The SENCo in a very real way is sharing the inclusive work of leadership. This work should reflect and also be deliberately linked to the cultural values that form the school community ethic – and presumably – should be emphatically inclusive. There will therefore be an expectation that such a school community will welcome, acknowledge and celebrate diversity and believe that the educational development and well-being of each individual member of the school community are important and worthy of a universal parity of esteem.

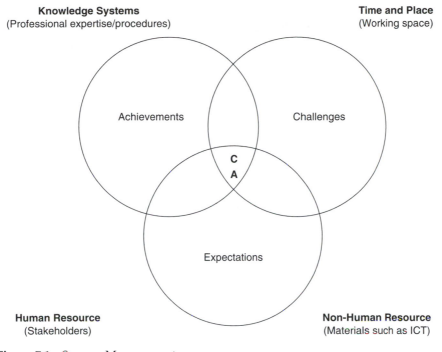

Figure 7.1   Success Management

Remodelling the new SENCo role

Recent government legislation and statutory guidance in the UK carries a considerable set of implications for managing SEN provision and the role of the SENCo in the mainstream school. In many respects, the change reinforces the need for a previously described approach, that of emphasizing inclusive leadership combined with both integrative and success management. The most relevant statutory guidance at the moment is the SEN strategy of *Removing Barriers to Achievement* (DfES, 2004a) and the more recent but closely related *Every Child Matters* policy initiative (DfES, 2003d). This guidance identifies a series of key priorities for action:

- *Early intervention* – taking a lead professional role in multi-agency assessment and intervention (internal and external to the school organization).

- *Removing barriers to learning* – fulfilling the role of access manager and change agent in promoting a support for learning network/professional learning to enable equity and empathy in managing diversity and differences in the school community.

- *Raising expectations and achievements* – providing a consultancy role in advising and leading in the development of organizational learning, an inclusive ethic and the principles of equity, empathy, efficiency and efficacy in the school curriculum.

- *Delivering improvements in partnership* – involving and managing collaborative networking in the creation and exchange of new professional knowledge, distributed leadership opportunities for improving ways of managing diversity and differences in the curriculum and advocacy for the vulnerable or at risk members of the school community.

- *Linking to the National Framework for Children's Services* – developing a brokerage role in linking to and securing a range of support partnerships that reinforce an efficient management of resources to support the inclusion policy in the school community.

- *Managing the ECM Outcomes Framework* – developing and maintaining fit-for-purpose assessment, monitoring and reviewing procedures reflecting both ECM and other educational outcomes (internal and external to the school curriculum involving an holistic assessment of personal, social and intellectual development).

- *Integrated Children's Service* – contributing to a deliberative emphasis away from intervention and toward prevention of at-risk factors in managing diversity and differences in the local community (linked closely to work in ensuring early intervention).

The new role for the SENCo is one that is growing fast and as Cheminais (2005: 2–3) rightly observes, SENCos will:

> … continually find themselves managing across the entire range of personnel in a school, negotiating with and influencing colleagues from the head teacher to the least experienced member of staff. They also liaise regularly with parents, carers and a range of professionals from outside agencies to ensure that children and young people's needs are met, and that the five outcomes of Every Child Matters are achieved. They are also likely to be at the forefront of innovative, inclusive classroom practice in terms of facilitating and enhancing pupils' learning and well-being.

The need to further strengthen leadership and management aspects of the SENCo role has been recently recognized by the DfES who have commissioned the TDA to revise national standards for the SENCo position. Five key tasks have been indicated as a core basis for this framework and include:

- clarification of the meaning of lead responsibility for SEN provision in the school community;

- clarification of the function and key SENCo responsibilities;

- revision of a national standards framework for the SENCo;

- ensuring automatic SENCo membership of the school SMT;

- introduction of a national accredited training pathway for a SENCo mandatory qualification.

Central to developing this new role will be the need to lead people in a number of different learning contexts. Combining this in a pre-emptive adaptation of separate existing standards for the SENCo and for a headteacher in an audit proforma, Cheminais (2005: 38) has produced a daunting and comprehensive description for remodelling the role of the SENCo. This is yet another indication of increasing expectation, challenge and a realization that the SENCo role is fast expanding and becoming yet more pivotal in the integrative management of diversity and learning differences in the school community.

MANAGING SUPPORT PARTNERSHIPS IN A LEARNING COMMUNITY

The SENCo is at present engaged in a series of formal and informal networking in the school community. Increasingly important is working closely with parents and governors as well as other members of the educational community (within and beyond school). This forms an important kind of support partnership in which the SENCo is increasingly taking a lead but always in collaboration with other colleagues across the professional workforce. In the changing world of an integrated children's service and the ECM agenda, this partnership function which pushes beyond traditional boundaries of school and classroom will undoubtedly continue to grow.

The TA Team

Central to this concept of support partnership, the network for SfL and of a related notion of distributed leadership is the role of SEN Teaching Assistants (TAs) or who are in some schools called LSAs (Learning Support Assistants). It is very often the case that the SENCo is the team leader for TAs in the school community. While the role of the TA is moving rapidly away from a traditional idea of highly specific, individualized support for an individual pupil with SEN, contracted for 15 hours or less (the so-called 'Velcro TA' wrapped round the child), towards generic and differentiated support roles covering every aspect of school life, this function demands an inclusive leadership and integrative managing of people. The traditional 'virtual' department of the SENCo has, over the past five to ten years, become a reality, and in secondary settings often involves a large group of staff deployed throughout the whole school. In terms of a traditional approach to support for learning, it might be expected to use the TA and qualified teaching staff to offer the following provision:

- *Pre-lesson preparation* – for example, guidance and collaboration in adaptation or differentiation of materials for use in the classroom.

- *In-class support* – for example, assistance with individual and small group work in the lesson as well as collaboration in designing and maintaining an appropriate learning environment.

- *Withdrawal lessons* – for example, individualized or small group work to complement or extend IEP, skills-based direct instruction or class-based programmes of study.

Further developing this approach takes us back to the idea of success management and Adair's model of action-centred leadership, and the orchestration of distributed leadership. The SENCo is well placed as a 'middle manager' with a 'whole school' remit to organize change agents: nominated people responsible for forming functional teams or local groups designated to develop aspects of school improvement containing reference to educational inclusion. As described in Figure 7.2, a change agent (CA) should be a focal point for shaping up approaches to building such team-work, developing individuals within the team and managing the achievement of agreed tasks (see Adair, 1988). To make this effort worthwhile the CA will need to be concerned about the efficiency, effectiveness and equity of the development led by the team.

Performance will rest on results achieved, in much the same way as a school's performance is ultimately measured in terms of outcome and achievement. To manage success will also involve the CA being concerned to foster team building and role leadership by linking both to a concern for professional learning needs and workload.

The role of leadership both within the team/group and for the SENCo requires bringing together the needs of the group, the individuals within the group and the purpose and function of the group. Adopting this inclusive approach to leadership works to people's strengths and seeks to improve and collectively support aspects of weakness. The requirements of task, group and individuals within the group will actually in part reflect an agenda containing strategic priorities for sustaining change or designated work (see Figure 7.3). Meeting these requirements will regulate how resources are utilized and will include the time and energy expended by the CA.

The final effect of this approach to team management is the continuing learning activity and knowledge creation that characterize a successful

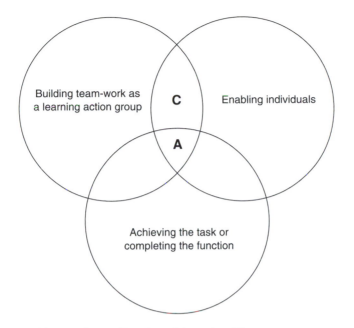

Figure 7.2   Building Inclusive Practice – Managing Change

learning organization and involve a creative synergy that stimulates adaptivity, growth and a dynamic culture. To work in such a team or group setting is a rewarding and at times exhilarating experience. To function well, over time, this partnership demands a growing internal knowledge of group or individual needs as well as external purposes and intentions. To share in this process is to engage in the process of transformative learning – developing *praxis* – generating a leadership dynamic that in turn informs an integrative management of educative endeavour. I am again reminded of the Comenius project in which I participated and was privileged to share just such a process and team/group (Lucietto, 2003).

The SENCo role: reforming extending professional boundaries

A final word should be given to the question of workforce remodelling, professional boundaries and the importance of a secure identity in a trans-professional context. An effective SENCo as acknowledged in the literature (Cheminais, 2005; Cowne, 2003) needs good managerial and interpersonal skills, an ability to understand whole school issues and developments, and the credibility and respect of colleagues in order to take these developments forward. An alternative approach, however, is to consider the development of TAs in undertaking some or many of the bureaucratic tasks of the SENCo

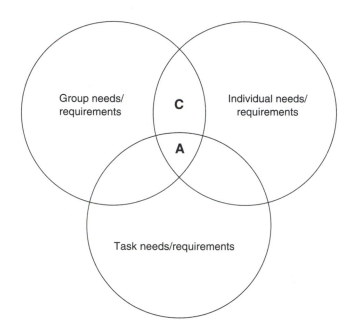

Figure 7.3   Building Inclusive Practice – Sustaining Change

(Cheminais, 2005). This development is clearly in line with the reforming the school workforce proposals (DfES, 2002b), to create new support staff roles at every level in the school, so that teachers can focus on teaching.

What is meant here, however, is clearly open for debate. Such a development could be interpreted as implying that the role of the SENCo no longer needs to be undertaken by a qualified teacher. Indeed Warnock (2005) has argued that the role of the SENCO as teacher is under threat as schools in different parts of the country have begun employing TAs to do the job. She suggests that this casts a dark shadow on the concept of a new professionalism and calls for a reconsideration of the status and training of the SENCo. There is, however, a more positive note within the IRU Report (DfES, 2005c), which recognizes the need to strengthen the role, realizing the benefits of using the SENCo in a strategic role across the school rather than spending time on bureaucracy (see Cheminais, 2005; Gerschel, 2005a). Central here is my continuing concern for enabling a transformative *praxis* in the SENCo role rather than following a conventional transforming leadership model together with the importance of context, that is, a management and leadership role specific to the context of SEN, diversity, learning differences and inclusion. This will involve the SENCo in managing both teaching and non-teaching colleagues and enabling others to work more effectively as managers/members of multidisciplinary teams.

In the final analysis, do we actually need a teacher to fulfil the SENCo role? Or is the more appropriate question to ask if the SENCO role should be completely re-written? What is clearly evident is that dealing with SEN is a challenge for every teacher every day and it is essential that we should not absolve teachers of this responsibility in any way by devolving sole responsibility on one teacher or a TA team. As we have noted, the leadership role of the SENCo is about empowering others in developing innovative practice to further support SEN within their classroom. Gerschel (2005b) reports that TAs expect to be better informed, prepared, trained and supported and have better pay and career prospects. The SENCo leadership role is central in managing this change process, but to be effective must have a strong voice in senior management and be engaged in community-based decision making in order to take a whole school perspective – as this discussion has hopefully demonstrated.

I have argued throughout this chapter that the process of school improvement and educational inclusion is one and the same, and is always a never-ending journey. While there are directions to pursue and priorities to action, the work of enabling educational inclusion is ultimately a continuing cyclical process that mirrors the seasons of growth, and a renewal of the fresh start triggered by the beginning of each new school year. In the next chapter I will consider the most serious threat to inclusion – the question of pupils experiencing EBD – and the dilemma of young people and children presenting self-excluding behaviour, plus the need to counter what can be usefully described as exclusion forces.

8

Including Exclusion, Well-being and Diversity

In this chapter, leadership questions related to moving forward on the issues surrounding SEN, inclusion, diversity and difference in the school community are addressed. An immediate first step is to confront the fundamental problem of exclusion and the challenge of managing behaviour in an inclusive community.

The attempt to 'include exclusion' in this development reveals an ever-deepening paradox at the heart of an inclusion policy in the English school system, revealing a set of contradictions, tensions and dilemmas associated with concepts such as universality and individuality, multi-ethnicity and national identity, assimilation, accommodation and biculturalism.

Including exclusion leads to an unfolding examination of managing policy and provision for personal and social education, pastoral care and the healthy school. A concern for the individual leads in turn to an awareness of personal and social differences, and the need to teach citizenship and nurture tolerance for diverse ethnic and social identities in a changing national context.

A way forward is proposed comprising a fourth strand or dimension to the special-inclusion debate – offering an alternative paradigm to those previously described. An integrative approach to difference and diversity is one that can lead to constructing new post-modern approaches to diversity and difference in the school/learning community.

INCLUDING EXCLUSION: A DEEPENING PARADOX

One of the most difficult decisions I occasionally experienced when working in special education was to accept that an individual child was to be 'excluded'. In what was an 'apparent' contradiction of the core purpose of a special school, euphemisms would be used to explain that the 'placement was inappropriate', 'needs could not be met', or that the individual was 'presenting extreme self-excluding behaviour'. Usually, the problem was that the individual was beyond any control, posing the dilemma of a threat to their own and others' health and safety, and so could not be managed nor any longer tolerated by the institution (community). In the day-to-day language of school, we were not able to help or educate every child all of the time. I recall how colleagues struggled with the feeling that we had failed – that we had literally lost – the child or young person.

Looking back, I can see that the logic of a medical paradigm underpinning special education implied selectivity based on a notion of restorative or palliative intervention and contrastive judgement, thereby determining criteria for admissions and placement-led assessment. Such an approach also provided a recipe for failure. I recall on more than one occasion a visiting (HMI) Her Majesty's Inspector to the special school in which I worked recommending a 'best practice EBSD school', in which it would be subsequently revealed that there was a carefully established selective admissions procedure. In the same way as several psychiatrists and psychotherapists with whom I worked from time to time managed their case-loads, the best practice special school accepted only those pupils they felt they could help. Discrimination formed the basis of what again was perhaps euphemistically called 'assessment' but often seemed to be professional judgements on the 'fit with what we offer' suitability of the 'client' for their school. It occasionally struck me that such practice was simply a selective procedure exercised by the rest of education too, including the best public schools, grammar schools and universities in the country. Special schools, it seemed, when deemed effective and cited as best practice case examples, were no different and not really very special.

In education, as I have previously stated, the irony of such discriminatory practices existing in deeply embedded social and professional cultures, and continually reflected in professional attitudes or educational systems, is profound! The point to all of this, I suggest, is one of a deepening paradox at work in managing inclusive provision that by definition generates a continuing set of dilemmas, contradictions and tension in the school community.

Dyson and Millward (2000) reported on an interesting series of case studies at the end of the last decade in which several English mainstream schools were observed struggling with the inclusion imperative. The research revealed a number of considered compromises in the implementation of inclusion. The researchers concluded that such compromises reflected the irresolvable dilemma of the differences faced in any attempt at constructing school approaches to pupil diversity. In what seems a deeply disappointed voice, the researchers describe a process of unfolding resolutions in managing problems with policy implementation that reflected frustration, failure and compromise. Or, alternatively, as the researchers subsequently claimed, these actions pointed to a continuing process of wrestling with a belief in asserting an excellence for all, in a post-modern context that was expected to shift and change in a constant fashion.

There is no ideal solution in this scenario of the real world, just a best effort in doing the job. There are uneasy echoes, here too, of a similarly reluctant compliance found more recently in teachers' attitudes to implementing reform policy aimed at developing the new professional in a remodelled school workforce, that signal processes much deeper than simply a perverse resistance to change (Rayner and Gunter, 2005b). Firstly, the implications for an inclusion policy seem to be that as an ideal it may well founder upon the need for educationists to discriminate when completing an assessment of pupil worth or quality in work. Secondly, inclusion as a utopian ideal is a romantic rhetoric to which classroom-wise practitioners and school leaders pay lip-service. Thirdly, inclusion will, it might seem, always founder on the issue of behaviour, or more specifically, misbehaviour.

An easy but not the only example of this inherent difficulty is the issue surrounding behaviour and the pressure to exclude from school on the basis of pupil disengagement or disruption. I was surprised some time ago to see a documentary film on British TV featuring one of the schools I visited as an evaluator in the Transforming School Workforce Pilot Project (see Thomas et al., 2004), that preceded the National Remodelling Agreement in England (DfES, 2002b). The film was about recording inclusive education at work. Teachers were video-taped literally spending huge amounts of time continually cajoling and coercing children to stay in school. At the same time, they were busy physically preventing an excluded pupil from entering school. An enduring image from this TV programme is one of senior staff patrolling the school campus, armed with walkie-talkies, shepherding 'self-excluding' pupils back into the classroom.

When parents interviewed in the programme were asked why this breakdown in schooling for their children was occurring, they blamed schools and the loss of 'old-fashioned discipline' for widespread disaffection. Professionals when interviewed blamed 'social instability and low expectation'. The apt title of the programme was 'Classroom Cops'. The ideal of an inclusive learning community seemed to be little more than a vision and pipe dream. Media messages about pupil behaviour may frequently be sensationalized, but they are important. Public understanding and attitudes in the community are reflected in such stories and go on to influence parental perception as well as describe some of the realities of inclusive schooling.

Dilemmas and contradiction are also more widely captured in the recurring story of schools attempting to contain and retain pupils presenting EBSD within the school community. Headteachers are often criticized for a refusal to exclude children. Or conversely, they are singled out for a no-nonsense approach to pupil behaviour and a use of exclusion that maintain the good academic reputation of a school. There is clearly no single approach to the problem of difficult behaviour or the management of educational inclusion. Gaps existing between policies and practice often reflect the same messy mix of contradictions and dilemmas facing staff when dealing with aggression and conflict in the school classroom. There is a sense in which it is not hard to see pupil misbehaviour and EBSD as the 'Achilles heel' of the inclusion ideal. There are those who might even mischievously argue that the implications of EBSD, by their very nature, are 'inclusively exclusive'. Schools facing the threat of out of control, often dangerous, harmful behaviour affecting the safety and well-being of adults, children, person or property, with the resulting disruption or destruction of teaching and learning, will often feel unable to cope, and see only one way out of difficulty – exclusion!

There exists in the present educational system and society at large a combination of structural forces and social attitudes that result in the exclusion of pupils from school. The fictional case study describing the school career and life-story of Billy Bovver, a young person experiencing EBSD and a series of needs-led interventions and placements in the English school system, describes many of these exclusion forces still at work in contemporary society (Rayner, 1999). The strength of these forces appears to have grown rather than diminished during the last twenty or so years, with rates of exclusion rising rapidly in England and Wales during the 1990s (see Table 8.1), then staying comparatively stable at around ten to eleven thousand permanent exclusions per annum over the past five years (2000–2005). These same trends led to the UK Government issuing policy guidance (DfEE, 1997; DfEE, 1998a, 1998b;) and a string of political initiatives subsequently aimed at reducing exclusion and promoting social inclusion.

Table 8.1 Number of pupils permanently excluded 1994/99

Year	Number of permanent exclusions	% Primary pupils	% Secondary pupils	% Special school pupils
1994/95	11084	0.03	0.31	0.53
1995/96	12476	0.04	0.34	0.54
1996/97	12668	0.04	0.34	0.64
1997/98	12300	0.03	0.33	0.58
1998/99	10404	0.03	0.28	0.45

Source: www.dfee.gov.uk *The permanent exclusion rate was derived by dividing the number of permanent exclusions by the number of pupils recorded on the Annual School Census Form 7*

The first set of exclusion forces is associated with explaining the misbehaviour of the individual pupil as a problem caused by 'within person factors'. These may, for example, take the form of psychiatrically diagnosed conditions or medical disorders such as ADHD or ASD. A second set of exclusion forces is associated with social contexts within which the individual is located. Issues that have to do with family, neighbourhood or peer group can dramatically impact upon the behaviour of an individual that leads to the perceived need for exclusion. More often than not, this kind of difficulty is associated with violence and anti-social behaviour. A call by the NAHT (National Association of Headteachers) to have additional powers to exclude parents as well as children illustrates the case in point. A third set of exclusion forces is located in the school system and is closely related to the principles, values and attitudes that form the ethos and organizational culture of a school community. These may be reinforced by school discipline systems and procedures that are often well established and generally unquestioned. These forces can operate to both generate and reinforce the pressure to remove or lose a problem pupil.

MANAGING EXCLUSION FORCES

How can an inclusive school community counter these forces of exclusion? One response is to focus on the following four aspects of behaviour management as part of the aim to establish and sustain an inclusive learning community:

- School behaviour (ethos/climate/culture).

- Professional behaviour (attitudes/values/knowledge).

- Pupil behaviour (attitudes/values/self-perception).

- Pastoral systems (procedures/protocols/practices).

Running through this activity are many of the ideas and principles described by Bill Rogers in a number of publications about behaviour, but generally constructed around the early elaboration of rights, rules and responsibilities in the school context (Rogers, 1990). In adopting this approach, a school staff will directly and positively *include exclusion forces* in its work for school improvement.

Managing school behaviour

Watkins and Wagner (2000) very persuasively describe the benefits of perceiving EBSD through the perspective of 'improving school behaviour'. This perspective, reminiscent of thinking about the corporate intelligences of a school/learning organization (MacGilchrist et al., 1997), rests upon a multimodal structure of behaviour that recognizes EBSD as a product of an interactive eco-system involving three inter-locked contexts – the organizational environment, the classroom and the individual.

Rather than simply seek an explanation for EBSD within the person, Watkins and Wagner argue that we should locate causes in a shifting interaction between all three contexts within school. Part of this corporate deliberation might usefully focus upon the purpose of behaviour assessment, and the way in which the school can know if it is maximizing pupils' progress and achievement. Another part of this reflection is the need to consider various forms of assessment linked to the process of teaching, learning and curriculum development. Definitions of learning informing this activity should seek to link with the ECM outcomes as well as other subject-based, group-based and personal assessment. Developing criteria for assessing emotional and behavioural development rather than EBD, for example, might prove more effective in achieving an inclusive approach to collective behaviour in the school setting. One example of such assessment is the Emotional and Behavioural Development Scale (Grimley et al., 2004; QCA, 2001).

Managing professional behaviour

A second sometimes neglected dimension to behaviour management is the actual approach shared by the adults in a school community (see Daniels et al., 1998). Important professional principles must be established and observed if success in managing pupil behaviour is to be realized. Purpose, consistency, coherence, understanding, reliability, confidence and involvement are all characteristics of effective team-based school discipline and unsurprisingly form key ingredients in the recipe for an effective management of pupil behaviour.

The worse-case scenario is to completely emphasize individual accountability as a mechanism for blame and for the SMT in a school to send out the message that each member of staff is on their own. The senior staff in school should clearly set out the ground rules for a team approach. Support, guidance, tactics, coaching, direction, partnership, as well as individual roles and responsibility are all essential aspects of working this approach (see Abdelnoor, 1999). The place of culture and context is arguably paramount in an effective response to pupils experiencing EBSD. Abdelnoor's ideas of collective responsibility, no blame and fallibility are particularly interesting, emphasizing the relevance of problem-solving approaches to pupils experiencing EBSD. Abdelnoor's step-by-step guide to creating an inclusive culture in school stands side by side with the prevention of exclusion and, arguably, sustaining educational inclusion (see Table 8.2).

Managing pupil behaviour

The day-to-day reality of managing pupil behaviour involves a mix of whole school, team-based approaches and individual intervention. In an 'inclusive' approach to behaviour management a 'catch-all' system, while not being expected to work for every individual, is a vital strategy for ensuring a positive ethos and a proactive prevention of EBSD. Abdelnoor (see Figure 8.1) offers a model describing such an approach in 'preventing exclusions' which is reminiscent of the action-centred leadership structure described in the last chapter as 'success management'. This whole community-based approach should interface with the provision made for pastoral care in the school community. It is the key structural system around which the organizational culture of a school is wrapped and reflects the joined-up thinking behind the ECM initiative.

Table 8.2   Creating an inclusive culture for preventing exclusion
(adapted from Abdelnoor, 1999)

Step 1	Devise a whole-school plan for implementing an inclusive policy for managing pupil behaviour.
Step 2	Ensure staff understanding, involvement and participation in developing an inclusive culture.
Step 3	Consider and agree approaches to change management and the need to work with collective attitudes, values, and belief.
Step 4	Review and develop a code of conduct to be shared by all members of the school community (principles, rights, responsibilities).
Step 5	Review and maintain knowledge networks that support pastoral care, access points to the community and support for learning.
Step 6	Ensure that all members of staff have another member of staff who can actively support and advise them in matters of behaviour management.
Step 7	Review and maintain knowledge networks and professional learning the focus here is behaviour management and pastoral care skills and so on).
Step 8	Target pupil involvement in sustaining good behaviour management (peer support schemes, anti-bullying work, community decision-making groups).
Step 9	Target bullying and reinforce school-based prevention as well as response systems (emphasizing the problem rather than the individual, and collective mediation rather than punishment).
Step 10	Target truancy utilizing DfES initiatives (see www.teachernet.gov.uk/wholeschool/behaviour/truancy/).
Step 11	Review and maintain SEN provision in school as a lead aspect of an inclusive learning community.
Step 12	Enhance the status and extend the operation of the SENCo and SEN networking throughout the school community including liaison between home, community and school (utilizing the extending SENCo brief as a lead professional).
Step 13	Target and co-ordinate an extending programme of community participation events such as support groups, mentoring provision and fund raising (involving parents, voluntary agencies, community groups).
Step 14	Contribute to inter-school partnership and knowledge networking.
Step 15	Develop a protocol for managed transfer of pupils experiencing breakdown of school placement (extending the concept of a learning community).
Step 16	Develop new strategies for opening up and sustaining exchange across the school community and the wider local community in the LA.
Step 17	Reinforce and maintain links with external agencies, voluntary bodies and other community-based groups in the LA (ensure police checks for individuals gaining access to children).
Step 18	Develop opportunities for outreach work and building inter-professional teams to support vulnerable children or young people in the school community.

The pastoral care/curriculum is also a primary source and regulator of school ethos. As long ago as 1989, HMI stated that,

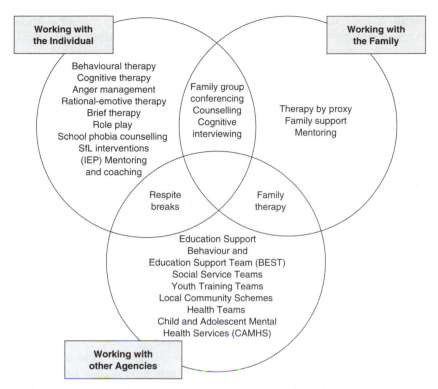

Figure 8.1 Preventing Exclusion and Managing EBSD (adapted from Abdelnoor, 1999: 126)

... the more schools are able to promote pastoral care through the curriculum, the more efficient and effective they are likely to be. Of course, if this is so, there is no place for teachers who claim to be only interested in subjects, not young people, or vice versa. (HMI, 1989: 47)

Whilst these issues become more sharply defined when considering pupils with SEN, and more particularly EBSD, it is also easy to see that pastoral structures, systems and school ethos really do matter in relation to all pupil achievement and school improvement. This, in turn impacts upon teaching and learning. Educational success or failure, pupil involvement or alienation, and school effectiveness or EBD are effects that can be created and shaped by school-based pastoral structures, systems and the school ethos.

Managing pastoral care – systems and curriculum

It is tempting to suggest that an effective education is essentially, completely and simply about human relations. An emphasis upon this aspect of schooling, usually described as welfare or pastoral care, has long been a dominant feature in special education. The pastoral curriculum or personal and social education as it is often referred to in the literature, is understood by Lodge (1995: 26) to be a whole school approach to the management of education and pupil behaviour. It is achieved through processes of co-ordination, good communication, teamwork, clear procedures, integration of approaches and a shared understanding of pastoral goals and how they will be implemented. Following Best et al. (1995: 13), a useful way of conceptualizing the pastoral curriculum is using this equation:

Pastoral Curriculum = Tutor System + Tutor or Key Worker (named professional) + Curriculum Subjects (PSHE/work related education/careers guidance, and so on) + pastoral content/process in other subjects 'across the curriculum'.

There is a basic need, then, for schools and all members of the school workforce to engage with professional learning comprising skills, methods, issues and approaches relevant to personal and social education. Such learning should address the separate areas of social, emotional, behavioural and intellectual development. It is values-laden and careful consideration should be given to the set of collective values formally recognized by the school community as well as the way in which learning based upon these values is constructed. For professional learning to generate *praxis* and contribute to the learning organization, it is important that the moral *eidos* is one that establishes an interaction with the *phronesis* (practical knowledge) developed by the individual practitioner.

Alternatively, the promotion of spiritual, moral, social and cultural aspects of the curriculum may also be used as a conceptual framework for integrating the same elements into processes of teaching and learning. In this sense the curriculum is a process rather than content or product (see Grundy, 1987). An inclusive pastoral curriculum will have a clearly established emphasis upon process. This may mean, in the first instance, teachers surfacing a raised awareness in their teaching of the effects of a school ethos, values clarification, attitude formation, motivation and strategies for managing pupil behaviour. A successful curriculum will be characterized by a regard for the whole pupil, and furthermore, the person as a learner. The notion of emotional growth as a key construct in this theory of learning is a powerful and relevant aspect for such a curriculum (see Greenhalgh, 1994).

Some specific techniques, programmes and examples of intervention relevant to the pastoral curriculum are summarized in Table 8.3.

A human relations approach to the pastoral curriculum emphasizes an affective and social education incorporating a great deal of humanistic psychology and thus encouraging a professional *praxis* associated with counselling and therapeutic intervention (see Decker et al., 1999; King, 1999). The pastoral curriculum should, however, also incorporate target-setting and

Table 8.3 Programmes for the Pastoral Curriculum

Circle Time	A well established technique for group work aimed at relationship building and generating a range of learning processes. The activity seeks to enhance skills in thinking, learning, social behaviour and participation. It is primarily a mechanism for learning how to learn and a preventive approach to EBD, but may also be used as a response or intervention (see Moseley, 1993, and www.teachernet. gov.uk/teachingandlearning/library/circletime/).
Peer Mediation	Involves selected pupils acting as mediators, that is, agents of arbitration with the role of conflict resolution. They engage in resolving disputes amongst their peer group. Pupils acting as mediators are prepared for the role by following a prescriptive mediation-training programme managed by an adult (Stacey, 1996).
Circle of Friends	An intervention used when friendships do not exist or have broken down between a particular pupil and a peer group. A script is provided for the teacher, involving the creation of a socio-metric map of relationships for the peer group (class). The group is then encouraged to think about social responsibility and the teacher forms a smaller support group. The group meets regularly with the isolated pupil during a six-week period to offer help and support friendship making by the pupil (see Turton and Rayner, forthcoming and www.inclusive-solutions. com/circlesoffriends.asp).
Peer Counselling	An approach which adapts theories of counselling to introduce the notion of peers taking up the role of counsellor. Peer counselling comes from previous work carried out in 'befriending programmes' aimed at peers in the role of caring support for peers. These schemes have been found to have a positive influence on the emotional climate of schools and provide a bridge between troubled friends in a peer group and specialized counselling intervention (Cowie and Sharp, 1996; Robson, 1997).
No-Blame Approach to Bullying	A seven-step script for teachers to follow when intervening in a bullying event. The approach is a problem-solving technique aimed at eliciting feelings and concerns for the victim. The aim of the exercise is to facilitate in the group an ownership of responsibility for problem resolution (Maines and Robinson, 1992; Robinson and Maines, 1997).
Self-Esteem Enhancement	Various models of humanistic psychology identify the importance of self-concept and self-esteem in the instinctive attempt to achieve personal potential. Rogers (1983) in particular, links this to learning. Programmes of self-esteem enhancement aim to offer activities designed to build up the self-concept (Bernard, 1997; Fogell and Long, 1997).

(Continued)

Table 8.3   (Continued)

Solution-Focused Intervention	An approach drawn from the work of De Shazer (1988) in solution-focused thinking. It is essentially a problem-solving approach that is deliberately orientated to finding solutions for perceived difficulty (see Metcalfe, 1998). An intervention is characterized by problem free talk, stated goals describing a preferred future, pinpointing exceptions, scaling as a form of self-evaluation and constructive feedback. The approach is practical and user friendly for teachers, insofar as it involves the pupil in planning, and it lends itself to the school context.
Personal and Social Education (PSE) Programmes of Study	Following the re-emphasis upon health education in the form of the Healthy Schools Programme (see www.everychildmatters.gov.uk/health/healthyschools/) PSE elements might include social skills training, anger management, citizenship, health education, and drugs education. (For a particularly useful set of teaching materials on emotional and behavioural development see the SEAL programme (www.teachernet.gov.uk/teachingandlearning/socialandpastoral/sebs1/seal/themes/).
	These represent some of the various initiatives or programmes that might form the content of a pastoral curriculum (see www.nc.uk.net, www.qca.org.uk, www.optimuspub.co.uk and www.wiredforhealth.gov.uk).

bench-marking as aspects of school-based assessment, enabling pupil progress to be monitored in the areas of personal, social, emotional, behavioural and intellectual development (see Atkinson and Hornby, 2002; Grimley et al., 2004; QCA, 2001). Special schools have a long tradition of combining 'care' and 'education' which in examples of best practice reflect an holistic notion of the curriculum that embody principles associated with an inclusive approach to diversity and difference. It is this expertise and knowledge that should be further extended in partnership with the mainstream school community.

INCLUDING DIVERSITY WITH DIFFERENCE: A WIDENING DILEMMA

The challenge of inclusion deepens further in ensuring equity and access to the curriculum for all pupils as practitioners, particularly when we identify additional differences in the school population (such as exceptional abilities, English as a second language) and cultural or social differences (ethnicity, religion, nationalism, social class) to be included in a consideration of managing learning behaviour. There are generally two basic kinds of problem behaviour presented in school: the first are self-defeating or harmful behaviours; the second, behaviours that challenge values or expectation. Grossman (2004) summarizes how managing these behaviours at the classroom level are linked to differing perceptions of behaviour, reflecting values and beliefs associated with a range of individual differences (gender, cultural, moral and personal). In attempting to cater for an increasingly complex mix of social differences in the school population, there is a need to avoid culturally inappropriate educational approaches and the triggering of problem behaviour that is the result of personal misperception or cultural misunderstanding. Central to successfully widening participation is the development of behaviour management that avoids stereotyping and offers a gender positive and culturally compatible approach to relationships, expectations and conduct. This is not an easy task. A summary of some types of behaviour related to social and cultural differences is listed in Table 8.4.

Table 8.4   Ethnic and social diversity: types of behaviour (Grossman, 2004)

Professional skills: avoiding culturally inappropriate educational approaches	1. Misperceptions – non-existent problems (perceptions of assertive behaviour as hostile or aggressive). 2. Misperceptions – unnoticed problems (related to differing attitudes to asking for the teacher's support). 3. Incorrect causes (socio-cultural stresses related to trauma, transition and adaptation to a new milieu interpreted in class and school as non-compliance or disaffection). 4. Incompatible behavioural techniques (clash caused by differing values reflected in social conduct/styles of interaction).
Professional knowledge: understanding diverse student responses to the school community	1. Motivational setting (barriers to success created by ability streaming and labelling for grouping learners together). 2. School success (reflecting conflicting values and aspirations for academic achievement that vary across social and ethnic groups). 3. Public or private recognition (carries extreme positive/ negative implications for the student dependent upon cultural values linked to social or ethnic background). Intended celebration can simply be a source for devastating humiliation.

There is always potential for experiential drift or conflict between teachers' expectations and theories of children's behaviour and codes of conduct in the home, in the neighbourhood and yet more strikingly elsewhere in the school community.

The opening and maintaining of access points to the school community and managing pupil or student behaviour in an increasingly complex, diverse school population are fraught with uncertainty and dilemma. In terms of the multiple identities reflected in the diverse social, ethnic and cultural backgrounds of pupils in the community, the fundamental question facing school leaders is often whether, on the one hand, to emphasize assimilation of diversity and difference in an English cultural identity in the school milieu, or on the other, to create a new cultural identity based upon multicultural values for the school community.

Creating and sustaining an inclusive community can presumably only be accomplished by pursuing the latter policy. Yet it cannot function in a separated way from the local community and more generally even national society. It is easy to imagine how a series of bi-cultural compromises and uneasy accommodations will, in all likelihood, characterize an interaction of each of these policy options as widening participation in a school community generates additional dilemmas, contradictions and tensions in managing school behaviour. The simplest of examples conveying the heat and intensity to be found in cultural collision remains the management of dress code, school uniform and the recent debate across Europe on the wearing of the *hijab* and more controversially, the *burka*.

Managing inclusion, diversity and PSE

Any attempt to incorporate diversity in the PSE curriculum reveals a similar set of issues surrounding personal and social differences. In an important review of diversity and citizenship education for the mainstream school curriculum in England (DfES, 2007), several key findings suggest a way forward in the development of teaching diversity and citizenship in the school curriculum. These themes include teaching topics and leadership actions to implement both in school and for national agencies:

- *Pupil voice* – enabling pupil participation and engagement in school using forums, school councils, pupil questionnaires or other ways of promoting discussions around identity, values and belonging.

- *School leadership* – should include understanding an education for diversity in relation to the curriculum, school ethos, pupil voice and the community.

- *Education for diversity in the formal curriculum* – an auditing of the existing provision for teaching citizenship and diversity in the school curriculum (the QCA publication *Respect for All* is recommended as a useful tool).

- *Harnessing the local context* – building active links between and across communities, with education for diversity as a focus. This should include planning for extended school provision, in which schools should seek to make contact with as wide a range of diverse community groups as possible, including supplementary schools.

- *Professional learning* – local authorities should be encouraged to develop Advanced Skills Teachers (ASTs) with a specific brief of education for diversity. This should be disseminated across the authority as part of outreach work. Schools should be encouraged to use the flexibilities in the teaching and learning responsibility points of a teachers' pay structure to promote excellence in education for diversity within school.

- *Accountability and school improvement* – the DfES and Ofsted should ensure that schools and inspectors have a clear understanding of the new duty on schools to promote community cohesion, of its implications for schools' provision, and of schools' accountability through inspection.

- *Citizenship, identity, values and diversity in the extended curriculum* – headteachers and senior management should prioritize whole-curriculum planning across a school and develop ways of linking citizenship education effectively with other subjects, together with the school ethos and the community.

The review body finally recommended further government action as to which organization or organizations should develop the help and support schools need in advancing the education for diversity agenda. In this process, full account needs to be taken of the importance of support for education in diversity being fully complementary to the wider context of support provided to schools and local authorities.

Managing diversity in an inclusive community

The most profound and enduring effect of schooling is the experience of community and the combining effect of culture, milieu and ethos. The psychology of self, both in terms of social identity and self reference, is hugely influenced by the organizational fabric and cultural climate of a community. In an inclusive learning community, the core concept of an institution must be a belief in the transformative function of learning. It is this function, situated in the school curriculum (formal and informal learning), that is a requirement for the effective learning community/organization if children and young people are to develop a notion of citizenship as both inclusive and relevant to each individual in the same community.

The report on diversity and citizenship education (DfES, 2007: 8) states that

> … it is crucial that issues of identity and diversity are addressed explicitly – but getting the pedagogical approach right will be critical: the *process* of dialogue and communication must be central to pedagogical strategies for Citizenship.

The teaching of citizenship should inherit many of the principles espoused in the model of inclusive leadership and integrative management throughout this book.

An inclusive ethic will therefore include moving beyond the recent either/ or debate surrounding an inclusive or special education provision, to one of an extended schools community. This alternative represents a fourth wave or strand of thinking around the question of managing diversity in an inclusive learning community. It is a perspective linked to the idea of a fourth strand proposed in the Citizenship Review and accepts that children and young people will only develop a secure notion of citizenship as inclusive, if they are engaged in explicitly dealing with issues of identity and diversity. This principle applies to all children irrespective of individual or social differ- ence. This should be understood to include disability, learning difficulties, personal problems, cultural group or ethnicity, gender and race. The crucial questions of access to the curriculum, voice and participation in the learning community will be addressed in the next chapter as part of consideration of assessment, differential pedagogy and personalized education – building blocks in the construction of an inclusive school curriculum.

9

Managing Learning Differences and a Differential Pedagogy

In this chapter the question of how to manage a developing knowledge of learning differences is explored. An implication of recent trends in approaches to teaching and learning in the inclusive setting is that the school workforce, in a learning community of the future, will need to continue to develop a differential pedagogy. Such an approach might well offer a way of moving beyond ability-based conceptions of education and needs-led, deficit-orientated forms of assessment in SEN provision. The key issues and themes central to the professional learning required in making these developments and for working with rather than denying individual differences in the classroom include thinking around:

- The nature of personal learning differences and differential psychology.
- The uses and place of assessment in the learning community.
- Developing a differential pedagogy for diversity in the classroom.
- Developing a curriculum process for 'learning how to learn' – involving meta-cognitive strategies and routines.
- Developing *praxis* as a curriculum process – with continuing practitioner enquiry and professional learning in the area of a differential and inclusive pedagogy.

UNDERSTANDING PERSONAL DIFFERENCES AND LEARNING

I suspect the greatest motivation for wanting to teach is to make a difference in the life of a student. The reward, buzz or magic of teaching is found in producing change and turning thinking and feelings into knowledge, insight and understanding, thereby channelling endeavour and activity and inspiring accomplishment and success. It is, on the face of it, something like the alchemist's quest to transform base metal into gold. A vital catalyst, however, and essential element if this whole process is to occur in an inclusive setting, is belief in the potential capacity for learning and the importance of meeting individual differences in the classroom. With respect to the first, Hart et al. (2004) explain how a seismic shift must take place in the twentieth century educational mind-set of fixed ability teaching for this to happen. An argument is presented for replacing the structuring device of differentiation by ability with an inclusive pedagogy curricula grounded in the core idea of teaching learning as transformability.

A second perspective is given by Howard Gardner, who (at the 1997 Seventh International Conference on Thinking), argued that in the not too distant future people will look back to the end of the millennium and laugh at the 'uniform school'. He suggested, wryly, that they would be greatly amused by the idea that educationists actually believed they could teach the same things to all children at the same time and in the same way. To believe that the 'uniform school' can provide efficient or effective education, he concluded, was to endorse educational failure! Teaching, then, might be described as working with individual learning differences to facilitate change associated with the alchemy of a transformative power – learning. At a professional level, this includes knowing more about learning to learn and learning leadership, and reflects the generation and acquisition of both personal and collective knowledge described by Aristotle as *praxis*.

The focus in this chapter is on *praxis* for managing diversity and difference as it refers to the experienced curriculum, learning, teaching and pedagogy. It is in other words about how we all think about teaching and develop it as a practice. Teachers aiming to achieve an inclusive approach in the classroom face the constant challenge of balancing the learning needs and differences of one child with those of many children, and within this approach, establishing a positive and effective learning experience for all. In the not too distant past, meeting such individual differences in the classroom was called 'differentiation', but more recently is referred to as 'ability matched teaching and learning', or 'targeted setting'. What is missing, however, is an understanding and development of learning capacity and what I would describe as 'authentic differentiation'. Making a difference, in this respect, relies upon an awareness of personal or differential psychology, and its implications for the teacher, learner and learning in the classroom (see Reid, 2005). It requires a sharply drawn focus upon learning and the learner as the participating subject in the process of assessment and is primarily concerned with understanding how the learner learns most effectively. Importantly, it has as its aims powerful learning, self-knowledge and the enabling of capacity for independent learning.

Recent developments in the psychology of individual differences

Two relatively recent developments in the field of personal psychology have hugely impacted upon the work of mainstream education. The first is the theory of Multiple Intelligences (MI), as developed by Howard Gardner (1993). The second is the theory of style differences in cognition and learning, focusing in particular upon the individual engaging with the process of learning (Rayner, 2001).

1. *MI* – in Gardner's most recent classification of MI there are eight distinct intelligences indicating skills and competence in each aspect of a person's profile of intelligence (see Table 9.1, page 176). Gardner believes that intelligences are modifiable and can be enhanced. An individual is born with all intelligences but some hardly develop, others develop moderately and others are more strongly developed. Benefits for the classroom identified by advocates of MI include:

- Perceiving intelligence and intellectual ability broadly and working with the idea that many young people who perform poorly on traditional tests are turned on to learning when classroom experiences incorporate artistic, athletic, and musical activities.

- An MI friendly classroom providing opportunities for authentic learning based on learners' needs, interests and talents. Students become more active, involved learners.

- Learners able to demonstrate and share their strengths in building up less developed capability. Building strengths gives a student the motivation to be a 'specialist'. This can in turn lead to increased self-esteem.

In Gardner's view, learning is a social and psychological process. In the MI approach, learners begin to understand how they are intelligent. When students understand the balance of their own MI they begin to:

- manage their own learning;

- value their individual strengths.

Teachers aware of MI begin to think more creatively about potential for learning and enabling learners to begin to learn about how to learn.

   Knowing which students have the potential for strong interpersonal intelligence, for example, will help create opportunities where that strength can be fostered in other learners as well as in the individual. Applying the knowledge of MI reflects a belief in capability rather than fixed traits, and learning capacity rather than competence.

2. *Style differences in learning performance* – The psychological construct of style in cognition and learning describes an individual's thinking and learning as a specific set of preferences, functions and behaviour. A person's cognitive style refers to the typical way in which they absorb, represent and process information.

   The model of cognitive style as described by Riding and Rayner (1998) proposes a structure of cognitive style made up of two dimensions: the first deals with the way information is visually or verbally represented in an

Table 9.1 The structure of MI

Linguistic	Listening, writing, reading, problem-solving related to language.
Logical-Mathematical	Logic and mathematical concepts, sequence, order, space and time.
Spatial	Visual and spatial manipulation, mechanics, systems and visual memory.
Bodily-Kinaesthetic	Touch, movement, physical expression, physical co-ordination and action-orientated memory.
Musical	Aural awareness, sensitivity to patterns, structure, pitch, tone and effect of sounds, sense of rhythm, musical expression.
Interpersonal	Integrates other forms of intelligence in the social setting, social relationships, empathy, sympathy, team-building.
Intrapersonal	Integrates other forms of intelligence in the development of self-perception and self-knowledge including self-concept, self-reference, personal values and belief.
Naturalist	Ability to recognize and categorize plants, animals and other objects in nature.
Existential	Sensitivity and capacity to tackle deep questions about human existence, such as the meaning of life, why do we die, and how did we get here.

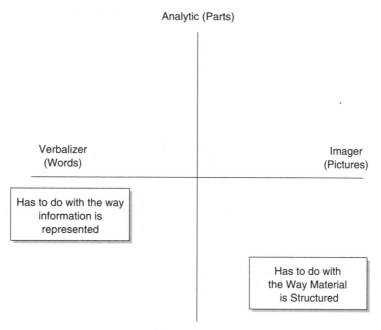

Figure 9.1   The Structure of a Person's Cognitive Style

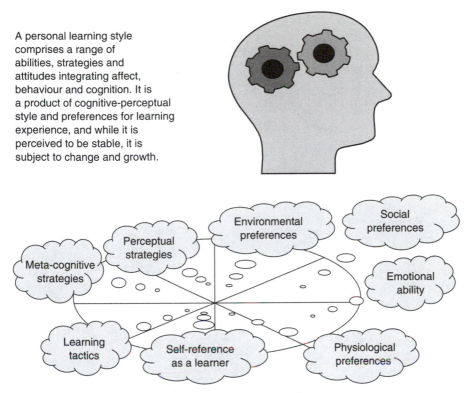

A personal learning style comprises a range of abilities, strategies and attitudes integrating affect, behaviour and cognition. It is a product of cognitive-perceptual style and preferences for learning experience, and while it is perceived to be stable, it is subject to change and growth.

Figure 9.2.   The Structure of a Person's Learning Style

individual's act of thinking; the second with the way the individual processes information, reflecting a continuum of perceiving information in holistic chunking to an analytic splitting into separate segments of information (see Figure 9.1). A useful critical review is to be found in Riding and Rayner (1998) and Rayner (2001). A personal learning style is defined by Rayner (2000) as a combination of cognitive style and learning strategies together with a range of preferences in a personal approach to the learning task. There are also many combinations of types of learning, forms of knowledge and assessment models developed for particular kinds of learning, as described by Reid (2005). A well known example is the theory of experiential learning and the 'Inventory of Learning Styles' aimed at further and vocational education (Kolb, 1999).

3. *Style in a learning performance* – Reid (2005: 32) offers a useful visual representation of this inter-relationship between individual characteristics, SEN, learning and style differences which I have adapted (see Figure 9.3).

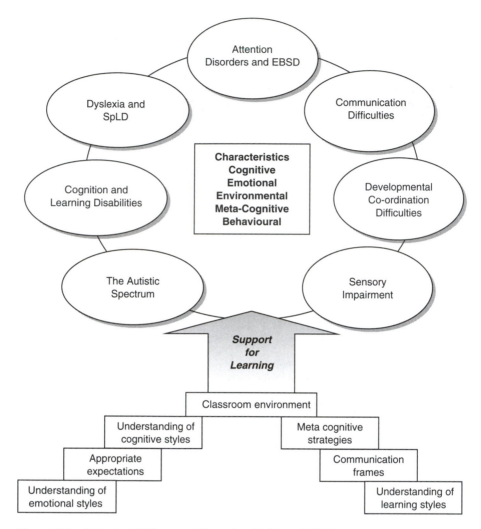

Figure 9.3   Learning Differences, Learning Styles and SEN
(Adapted From Reid, 2005)

A structure for the personal psychology of a learning performance related to understanding the function of styles of learning in the classroom is described in Figure 9.4.

These figures present a model of learning performance. This explanation can be used to link interacting aspects of personal psychology in an individual's performance – whether it is applied to a one-off specific task or a long-running

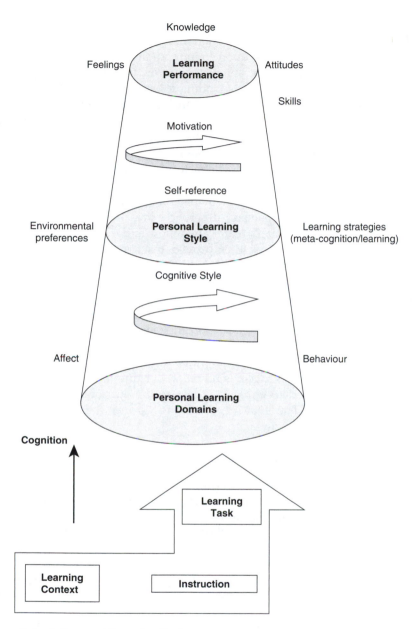

Figure 9.4   A Personal Learning Performance

series of instructional episodes – and is intended to fit with the wider notion
of an assessment-based pedagogy (see Reid, 2005).

   Aspects of an individual's learning performance are more generally made
up of an interaction of factors in their personal psychology and these

continuously occur within the learning context. This is where the interplay of teaching and learning occurs as a mix and inter-section of the personal and the social, involving and impacting upon an individual's expression of affect, cognition and ultimately behaviour. Interestingly, we can only ever really be sure of any of this by observing and responding to behaviour. Nonetheless, when teaching, while we work directly with the surface features of performance that reflect skills, attitudes, motivation and knowledge, we intuitively and constantly work too with a beneath-the-surface psychology of personal style, including the diverse range of learning preferences, orientation to study and a bio-physical response to environmental factors in the classroom. I suspect anyone who has taught will recognize the reality of many spinning plates being juggled in the busy-ness of classroom management, reflecting the rich range of diversity, individuality and personal differences in a class.

The argument here is that a greater awareness and deliberateness in a differences-led approach will yield improved teacher–student relations and performance in learning and teaching. While this approach to learning has not been without its critics (for example, Coffield et al., 2004), and many, including myself, would not wish to propose that learning is entirely and only about learning differences and abilities, it is the case that increasing knowledge about learning diversity and inclusion is frequently embedded in a study of the psychology of individual differences (Jonassen and Grabowski, 1993) and learning styles (Prashnig, 1998; Reid, 2005).

The important question to ask is how a better understanding of learning styles might be applied to enhance access to the curriculum and support educational equity? The DEMOS Working Group led by Hargreaves (DEMOS, 2005: 4) advises us that:

> Many teachers have begun to use learning styles as part of their repertoire of teaching strategies, not because they have become a fad or fashion, but because they offer a way of helping to personalize learning. As the agenda for personalizing learning develops – and there is every sign that teachers are responding to the idea with energy and creativity – the need for a better evidence base for recent developments and innovations on learning is of paramount importance. (DEMOS, 2005: 12)

Exploiting learning styles as a teaching device and utilizing the theory means developing a broad-based approach to the ideas of a process curriculum and differential pedagogy. Cheminais (2002: 1) provides a useful summary of this notion of individual differences in an approach to SEN provision, inclusion and school improvement. She writes that effective and successful teachers and inclusive schools will:

• show respect for pupils' individual learning styles and differences;

• be responsive to pupils' different learning styles;

• use different levels of tasks and activities;

- utilize a range of teaching strategies;

- teach thinking skills across the curriculum.

Style-led assessment should be seen as one way of providing data about the learner learning, thereby contributing to a wider range of formative assessment for learning. Assessing style differences is directed at a psychology of self located beneath the surface of a learning performance. The implications here are arguably for further developing new forms of understanding about the nature and use of assessment and differential psychology in the curriculum and pedagogy (see Jonassen and Grabowski, 1993). The idea that concern for learning to learn and developing a differential pedagogy for managing diversity in the curriculum is an important aspect of SEN provision is considered next, in an examination of how recent developments in assessment for learning should be combined with an assessment of learners and learning, creating opportunities for new levels of engagement for participants in the learning community.

ASSESSMENT IN THE LEARNING COMMUNITY

There is a multiple set of purposes and types of assessment relevant in the education setting. The purpose of particular assessments may vary but the function of collecting data remains the same, with assessment providing the basis of informed educational management, teaching or care interventions, thereby helping individuals with their difficulties and ensuring that teaching builds on what has been learned. The chief purposes of assessment in the learning community include:

- For learning – generating formative data that help to identify the next steps needed to make progress.

- Of learning – generating summative data that are concerned with judgements based on grades and ranks and with public accountability.

- Of the learner – providing insight into pupils' learning preferences, social, emotional and learning behaviour, and learning dispositions (strengths and weaknesses).

- For teaching and pedagogy – providing formative feedback on performance and professional knowledge for learning and *praxis*.

- For the learning community – providing information based upon comparative data and added value (practice-based evidence), facilitating strategic leadership and change management involving problem-posing and decision-making processes (generating testimony and new knowledge for the development of policy and provision).

- Of the organization and community – providing data for accountability and standards related audits.

Traditionally, assessment in managing SEN provision in the English school system has been used for the formal identification of children experiencing difficulty and the distribution of resources and placement. The SEN Code of Practice in England is geared to this, and is part of an administrative system more extensively supported by forms of multi-disciplinary appraisal aimed at producing a profile of the individual and completion of the SEN statement. The recent ECM initiative has introduced a number of changes into the wider assessment apparatus, and in particular, the proposed common assessment framework. Ideally, a Common Assesment Framework (CAF) for the identification of at-risk children will hopefully reinforce attempts to develop inter-agency working in a unified children's service. The purposes of this assessment, however, remain principally linked to needs analysis, to inform referrals and to guide broad-based intervention. The final use of this type of traditional Multi Disciplinary Assesment (MDA) assessment – usually seen as the responsibility of the SENCo in a mainstream school in England – is to provide data for an IEP and as a basis for the identification, monitoring and reviewing of annual provision for an identified child with SEN (for example, children are recorded on the school's SEN register following the guidance laid down in the SEN Code of Practice). The system is cumbersome and the aim of using assessment data (usually in the form of the IEP) is not always effectively transferred to the classroom context.

Recent developments in assessment for instruction, learning and teaching have been aimed at improving the relevance and validity of data for learning and teaching in the classroom. These include for example both formative and summative functions in the following types of assessment:

- *Learning Process/Class-based Assessment* – as an interactive collaboration in seeking and interpreting evidence for use by learners and their teachers to inform the learning process. This includes assessment for learning as developed by the Assessment Reform Group (see www.assessment-reform-group.org.uk).

- *Authentic Assessment* – in which students are asked to perform real-world tasks that demonstrate meaningful application of essential knowledge and skills. This is related to the model of problem-based learning.

- *Synoptic Assessment* – tests and exams constructed to ensure a focus upon the candidates' understanding of epistemic connections between the different elements of a subject.

- *Learner Assessment* – identifies preferences, strengths and weaknesses in the learner's learning performance aimed at enabling matched instructional design or increasing versatility in the learner's approach to the learning task.

- *Dynamic Assessment* – an interactive approach to conducting assessments within the domains of psychology, speech/language, or education, that focus on the ability of the learner to respond to intervention.

With the increasingly complex use of ICT to store, analyze and communicate data, it is vitally important that the school as a learning organization has a clearly stated policy for the networked collection and operation of assessment. The purposes and scope of assessment should be clearly defined and serve the common function of informing and enhancing intervention in learning and teaching. Formative assessment is clearly very demanding. It is, however, impossible to imagine learning and teaching without assessment occurring, albeit this can be informal as well as formal in nature. Important implications for managing assessment policy include, firstly, realizing that changes in classroom practice, for example, are central and not marginal to its effectiveness, so the accomplishment of formative assessment will mean making changes in pedagogy (Black and Wiliam, 2001). Secondly, effectively managing diversity and difference in the classroom will require handling more not less information, as well as additional variation in the design and application of instruction, learning and teaching. Thirdly, the operation of assessment for accountability is an opportunity for enhancing the access, participation and engagement of different member groups of the community in support for learning.

Using assessment for enabling engagement in the learning community

There is a motivating and empowering effect that can be released in the use of assessment, involving the participation and engagement of the individual in the process of acquiring new knowledge. It is this process that works so powerfully in the popularity of self-help literature with its inevitable quiz, questionnaire and prescription for new goals, better results and achievement. The same process can be managed to enable a similar effect in the learning community. It is one reason, albeit not the only reason, for directly involving the individual learner in the process of assessment for learning. The following aspects of managing assessment for accountability and diversity are important reference points in seeking to secure access and equity in the SEN impact areas identified at Level 1 in the MISE model for school organization. These points of reference are:

- enabling and listening to pupil voice in assessment for learning;
- ensuring parent dialogue in the school development cycle;
- enhancing school–home partnerships;
- informing inter-professional and multi-agency partnerships;
- engaging with voluntary interest groups in the local community.

New developments in extending and incorporating children's voice in assessment for learning are well documented (Black and Wiliam, 2001).

There are four good reasons for spending time and resources on developing this participation to ensure assessment reflects the following principles:

- A moral function serving to realize the principles related to human rights, social justice and equity in education.

- A legal function serving to meet the statutory and non-statutory guidance for purposes of accountability (for example, featured in the methods used to gather pupil perspectives in the Ofsted school inspection procedure).

- A pedagogic function serving to increase understanding of individual perceptions, enhance involvement in the learning task and inform target-setting and strategy.

- An educative function encouraging the learning experience and independent engagement in the life of the learning community (for example, peer-centred activities described in Chapter 8 such as mediation and counselling).

To manage this deeper approach to assessment is not easy. There are issues of bias and reliability inherent in this approach that while equally applicable to all assessment, can make listening to the child's voice and interpreting the collected data particularly challenging. For example, these assessments might include problems with:

- Response bias created by an inequality of power in the relationship between teacher and pupil.

- Observer bias on the part of the assessor (pre-conceptions and beliefs interfere with data recording).

- Ephemeral content in the response (reflecting rapidly changing perceptions, beliefs and attitudes in the child).

- Cultural bias in the response (reflecting beliefs, attitudes and values inhibiting open exchange).

- Capability and response limitations (characterized by individual differences such as SEN, disability or language).

There is a growing interest in further developing this work for a range of children and educational settings, and particularly for those identified with SEN or disability (Lewis and Porter, 2006). There are a number of pressing issues identified by these researchers relating to ethical and conceptual integrity, emphasizing again the need for careful management of the collection, interpretation and communication of information. One useful case example of the approach is an account of action research reported by Jelly et al. (2000). The project involved pupils in a special school directly contributing to assessment informing:

- the school assessment and review cycle;

- teaching thinking skills across the curriculum;

- involving pupils in institutional development.

The project outcomes included increased levels of pupil motivation and self-confidence, and enhancement of the school ethos promoting inclusion.

A similar approach can be applied to parents and other members of the learning community. Some useful case studies reported by Carnie (2006) describe how a number of schools, by setting up parent forums or councils as learning groups, integrated assessment and school improvement as well as other opportunities for stakeholders to participate in the school as a learning community, contributing to strategic management and development. For the purposes of accountability and, at the same time, involving stakeholder groups in the learning community, there were repeated attempts by the English government to increase direct parental involvement in the governance and management of the school (see www.parentscentre.gov.uk).

Current approaches reflect an emphasis upon the parent as a client, user and consumer of professional services provided by the school. This, however, is then complicated by long-standing research evidence in education affirming the role of parents as auxiliary partners in an extension of learning in the home and neighbourhood (Desforges, 2003). While this particular research tradition does not generally describe parental role, or its significance, in terms of a consumer–provider relationship, it is clear that positive steps taken to encourage parent and partner participation in processes of assessment and evaluation offer a potential for both organizational learning and an understanding of diversity and difference in the community. Management of this partnership, however, because of the previously described and sometimes conflicting ambiguities in the role and status of the parent, is not easy. Further, it is made no easier by government policy prescriptions that generally appear to presume an interest and readiness on the part of all parents in wishing to play a fuller part in school life, as well as professionals' preparedness to effectively manage this process. Again – this is not always the case.

A DIFFERENTIAL PEDAGOGY FOR DIVERSITY
AND DIFFERENCE

The implications for pedagogy in developing the kind of approaches so far described in this chapter have in passing been inferred but not explored in any depth. There is no doubt that such implications are profound. One response is to pursue a transformation of schools and a remodelling of 'new' teacher professionalism as currently being attempted by the government in England and Wales. This in turn reflects a vision of education for the year

2020 (DfES, 2006) and the current 'big idea' of personalized education (DfES, 2004e). (These will be considered more closely in Chapter 10.) An alternative proposition, however, to this current policy of prescriptive workforce remodelling is to adopt an 'organic metaphor' rather than the 'engineering metaphor' apparently underpinning the remodelling policy, and further develop schools as learning organizations and knowledge-based communities. An emphasis should be laid on developing growth and learning rather than knowledge transmission, knowledge as an economic asset or capital and systemic reconstruction of teaching entirely embedded in Information Communication Technology (ICT).

This approach conceptualizes learning as a transformative rather than a transformational process. It requires involvement of the learner and the empowerment of an active *praxis* as well as the teacher's belief in the mutability of learning capacity in the individual. It rejects the fixed ability notion of learning traditionally associated with selective education. It also raises the question of how a teacher develops their pedagogy for a better fit with an inclusive classroom. *Pedagogy* is the practical trade craft of teaching. It includes, for example, a wide range of variables such as the sequencing of lessons, grouping arrangements, promotion of particular attitudes, the selection and organization of lesson content and presentational style in the classroom. An answer to the following three questions might hopefully lead to a better understanding of the idea of focusing upon individual difference as a basis for developing an inclusive pedagogy.

1. How have teachers set about managing diversity in the classroom? Advocates for an inclusive education often insist upon an inclusive policy without an understanding of the pedagogic approaches that teachers can use to operationalize the policy. Nind and Wearmouth (2005) lament a shortage of evidence on teaching approaches for the inclusive classroom. The school effectiveness literature contains several examples of research into differentiated or adaptive instruction. One useful example is the work of Wang (1990) in which core features of adaptive instruction are identified as:

- Instruction based on the assessed capabilities of each learner.
- Each learner able to progress at their own pace.
- Periodic evaluation of a learner's progress by their teacher.
- Learners acquire increasing responsibility for their own learning.
- Alternative learning activities are made available.
- Learners have opportunities for choice/decision making.
- Learners assist one another.

This description is not greatly different to Zemelman's (1998) checklist of features to be found in effective inclusive schools in the USA. Nind and

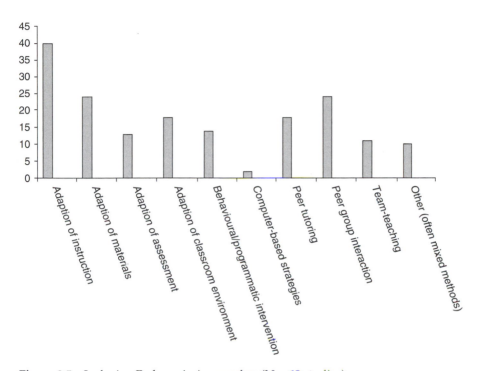

Figure 9.5   Inclusive Pedagogic Approaches (N = 68 studies)
Source: adapted from Nind and Wearmouth, 2005

Wearmouth (2005), in a systematic review of 68 studies, identify three key principles for an inclusive pedagogy: setting suitable learning challenges, responding to pupils' diverse learning needs and overcoming potential barriers to learning and assessment for individuals and groups of learners. These principles (listed in Figure 9.5) have produced a range of pedagogic strategies that have been shown to lead to positive outcomes in the areas of academic attainment, social involvement and improved behaviour. Figure 9.5 illustrates the distribution of these strategies, revealing that adaptation of materials is the most extensively applied response to diversity in the classroom. The full range of strategies includes:

- Adaptation of instruction
- Adaptation of materials
- Adaptation of assessment
- Computer-based strategies
- Adaptation of classroom environment
- Behaviour/programmatic intervention
- Peer tutoring

- Peer group interaction

- Team teaching

- Other (often mixed methods)

Nind and Wearmouth suggest that the most promising pedagogic strategy identified in their own research for the inclusive classroom setting is the use of peer group interactive work. They describe how teachers using peer group interactive approaches work on (basic) skills in an holistic way, embedded in classroom activity and subject knowledge, succeed in catering for a rich range of diversity in the class group. This is in contrast to the isolated skills development associated with traditional remedial pro-grammes for special needs. The use of peers also has the benefit of making social skills development and learning behaviour meaningful and relevant. They conclude that it is also important to combine attention to (subject-specific) adaptation of teaching and curriculum materials with attention to community participation, social grouping and roles within the learning group. The implication here is that all learners, including teachers as learn-ers, are engaged in an active agency. These notions of professional learning and a practical knowledge associated with pedagogy bring us back to the importance of developing *praxis*, and as Nind and Wearmouth argue, the importance of teachers as reflective practitioners and school itself as a site of reflective practice.

2. Is there such a thing as a distinctive SEN pedagogy?   Norwich and Lewis (2001) drawing upon a systematic review to address this question found con-siderable evidence that teachers attempt to differentiate their teaching according to perceptions of broad pupil ability. They found little evidence to support the idea of teachers adapting or developing an SEN specific peda-gogy. They suggest the existence of a 'high density' teaching approach that is comprised of a sliding rule or continuum of common 'pedagogic strate-gies'. Their review found a trend in research accounts signalling a movement away from ideas of a special needs-specific pedagogy toward an under-standing of pedagogy in terms of a 'general differences' composition. The implication of all of this, Norwich and Lewis argue, is the possibility of a case for exploring a relationship between individual differences, and devel-oping a differential rather than SEN specific pedagogy for inclusive educa-tion. They state that, for example:

> More pedagogically relevant groups may be identified in terms of learning process, such as learning styles ... than in terms of the general definitions (for example, MLD, SpLD). (Norwich and Lewis, 2001: 325)

The integration of differences and needs in developing new forms of assessment-led pedagogy is also represented in Figure 9.4 and further developed in work by Reid (2005). The proposition is that learners with different styles may benefit from specialized or personalized pedagogic strategies. This is of considerable significance for the development of a differential or inclusive pedagogy.

3. Is there scope for developing a differential pedagogy?   There are several examples of a deep commitment to the idea of a differential pedagogy linked to the field of learning styles and individual differences (Dunn and Griggs, 2003; Reid, 2005). The extent, however, to which the idea of an individualized approach to education has been explored, debated and rejected over the past fifty years or more points to the paramount importance of a social dimension in learning and education (Coffield et al., 2004). It is also an indication that teachers will invariably resist a prescriptive catch-all in developing modes of pedagogy. Tomlinson (1999: 108) makes the very important point that:

> Differentiating instruction is not an instructional strategy or a teaching model. It's a way of thinking about teaching and learning that advocates beginning where individuals are rather than with a prescribed plan of action, which ignores student readiness, interest, and learning profile. It is a way of thinking that challenges how educators typically envision assessment, teaching, learning, classroom roles, use of time, and curriculum.

The DEMOS Working Group acting as a think tank for the government in England, led by Hargreaves (DEMOS, 2005: 4), make a similar point in response to the question of what is learning, and state that:

> … learning theory does not provide a simple recipe for designing effective learning environments, but there are implications about the design of learning environments. These are characterized as learner-centred, knowledge-centred, assessment-centred and community-centred. (DEMOS, 2005: 12).

This is exactly the kind of approach I would propose – developing a best-fit pedagogy for managing diversity in the classroom. The extent to which an awareness of learning style or the self as a learner is currently considered and managed within the educational context raises key questions for the design of instruction and pedagogy, including a consideration:

- For the school of an assessment-based approach to learning and teaching.

- For the subject and pastoral leaders of differentiation within the learning process of the curriculum.

- For teachers of the development of a differential pedagogy.

- For the learner engagement with 'learning how to learn', meta-cognitive strategies and routines within and across the curriculum.

- For the school workforce with continuing practitioner enquiry and professional development in the area of differential and inclusive pedagogy.

Exploiting learning styles as a teaching device and utilizing individual differences theory actually mean developing a broad-based approach to the ideas of a process curriculum and differential pedagogy. It is not about simply lifting an assessment measure off the shelf, completing it, and labelling learners as XYZ. The scope for a differential pedagogy informing ways in which teaching is developed to manage diversity and difference in the classroom is crucially one that should be grounded in exploring rather than a levelling down of individual differences and diversity.

One seductive feature in a constructivist approach to learning and pedagogy is a rejection of labelling and a 'removal' of the dangers of any form of limiting categorization being applied to the learner. In differential psychology, categories persist as a form of theory, and it should be noted that their value should not be reductive, or their use for restricting practice, but rather as a way of enabling greater levels of personal engagement in the learning process. This involves, at one level, the hypothesis of enhancing learning performance by matching personal strengths and preferences to instructional design and forms of pedagogy. Importantly, however, on a second wider level, it involves developing new ways of exploiting personal differences in learning and teaching to facilitate rounded educational growth in a process of personal, social, emotional and intellectual development. This aspiration is very close to the holistic education espoused in the ECM initiative. The idea of adopting an individual differences approach to help in moving beyond the worn-out either/or policy debate of special or inclusive provision, with a focus upon a personalized education providing for all pupils and their learning differences, is considered in the next chapter.

10

Managing Differences, 2020 Vision and a Personalized Education

This chapter begins by looking at a vision of education in England by the year 2020 as described in a recent report published by the DfES (2006). Many of the ideas in this report do reflect key themes developed throughout this book. These, for example, include some but not all of the following key concepts for developing the management of inclusion and special education (MISE):

- An inclusion imperative as a referential basis for managing diversity and differences in the school setting.

- Reaffirming as cardinal principles in an *education for all* the need to remain focused upon issues surrounding the mix of equity, empathy, efficiency and efficacy in provision.

- Awareness of relevant knowledge contexts and the networking of knowledge creation, transfer, management and acquisition.

- The notion of learning differences in an assessment-led pedagogy that brings a renewed focus upon the individual as a learner and as a member of the wider learning community.

- A continuing focus on the impact areas that represent the surface provision of MISE (access with responsibility, participation, engagement and voice).

- Commitment to learning leadership as a distributed and distributing form of professional learning informing an integrative management of the learning community.

- The ultimate need to always ensure a blended combination of strategic and operational management in a cycle of development that reflects the systemic framework of a learning organization.

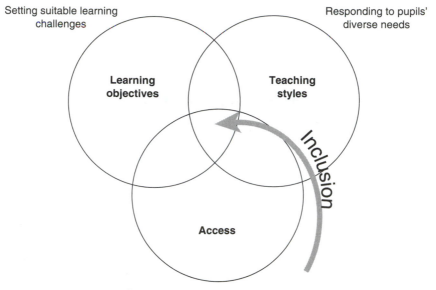

Figure 10.1   Personalizing the Learning Process (Source: DfES, 2006: 49)

THE 2020 VISION

The *2020 Vision* report (DfES, 2006) identifies personalized education as the core basis of a modernized schooling in England in 2020. It talks of the need to design a new school experience and a concomitant need for a new kind of learning-centred and professional leader heavily involved in managing change. This task is defined as leadership and innovation, and it contributes to the idea of a national strategy for a systemic renewal, in which learning and teaching should be transformed and applied to the complex processes of knowledge creation, capture and transfer. The report presents a strategic restructuring of education in England aimed at realizing a participatory consumerism presented as personalizing learning by 2020.

In many respects it is hard to argue with many of the aspects contained in this report. It is a little like trying to argue against the common sense view that choice or change, by definition, are a good thing and intellectualism is a bad thing. Indeed, for some writers, personalized education is synonymous with inclusion (Cheminais, 2006: 44). Cheminais refers to the representation of this idea in guidance published by the DfES (2004e) and illustrated in Figure 10.1. In the move toward personalizing education, schools are urged to begin by acknowledging that giving every single child the chance to be the best they can be, whatever their talent or background, is not compromising standards. This implies a move away from a single measure of academic excellence.

Personalized learning, the government guidance tells us, means high quality teaching that is responsive to the different ways students achieve their best. It means schools should:

- Be flexible enough to allow for a variety of learning and teaching approaches and greater diversity in the size and age mix of pupil groupings.

- Be familiar and welcoming to parents and the wider community, inviting and encouraging them into school.

- Emphasize participation and collaboration, through being open, safe and inviting.

- Support interaction, knowledge sharing and learning amongst teachers and support staff.

- Use technology – both within and outside classrooms – to enhance learning.

The focus upon the individual as a learner is an opportunity to develop a more inclusive approach to learning and teaching in which every child will matter or no child is to be left behind. However, the notions of larger classes, distant or remote learning and one-stop children's services for sale in what might feasibly be described as the brave new world of a learning hypermarket (academy), infer a widening agenda accommodating other competing interests at work in re-engineering the school system. There is, therefore, a rationale underpinning this 2020 vision which merits careful scrutiny. Hartley (2006), for example, is not wrong in pointing out the contradiction of several competing social and utilitarian forms of ethic at play behind the related policy imperative for excellence and enjoyment underpinning the National Primary Strategy in England (learning and teaching in the primary years). There is a similar contradiction at play in the personalizing of education, as a provider–consumer public service ethic extols the success of selling economic and social capital as an asset for the life-long learner/worker of tomorrow. There is perhaps a need to be cautious and discerning in a response to the unfolding new policy imperative to 'enjoy the excellence of a personalized future'. It is tempting to liken it to the declaration of a benign interrogator that there are ways to make us smile. Discussion in the rest of this chapter attempts to adopt a cautious appraisal of the personalizing agenda and offers a way forward for the management of inclusive and special education.

PERSONALIZED EDUCATION

As previously acknowledged, it is hard to argue against the logic of many of the ideas associated with the initiative for personalizing education. An approach that is described in Figure 10.2 at face value represents a reasonable structure for school development and an inclusive education for all.

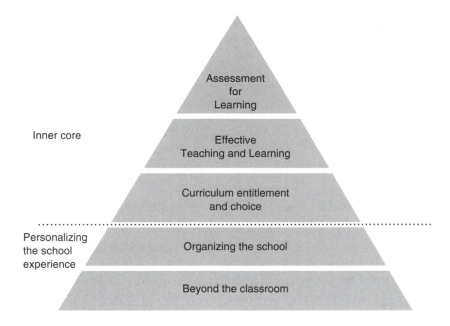

Figure 10.2   Personalizing Education: Modernizing Reform

DfES guidance (www.standards.dfes.gov.uk/personalisedlearning/) explains that creating these conditions for learning involves:

- Using the benefits of workforce remodelling to build a whole school team to better support the learning of each pupil and increase the planning, preparation and assessment (PPA) time for teachers.

- Utilizing ICT effectively.

- Creating a clear and consistent policy on 'behaviour for learning' to provide an environment in which all students feel safe and secure and can flourish as individuals.

There is, however, slippage in an inclusive friendly aspect to the policy as detail is gradually worked out and some fundamental values and ideas begin to surface in the policy agenda. The personalizing policy agenda originally aims at building multiple and flexible pathways for life-long learning in a 'learning networked transmission system' as an underpinning medium for modernizing reform. This is progressively revealed in references to e-literacy and reliance upon technology, and more importantly still, a commercialized commodification of education (DfES, 2004d).

The purposes of education that serve a humanistic or social function in a civilized society are virtually ignored. There is also a glossing over of issues related to SEN or other difficulties associated with vulnerability and disaffection as it is subsumed in a consumer's charter for customized fit in an access arrangement to be purchased by the consumer. Consequently, the following contradictory features of personalized provision reveal a sub-text and central thrust in policy intention smothering concerns for the human aspects of inclusion or the paradox of difference with the concept of an entrepreneurial citizenship. Thus, the recipe for personalization includes:

- ensuring young people are given the means and the motivation to become independent, e-literate, fulfilled, life-long learners;

- recognizing an ethnically and socially diverse society in which the gaps in achievement and prospects for people from different social and ethnic backgrounds will not be allowed to persist;

- developing far greater access to, and reliance on, technology as a means of conducting daily interactions and transactions;

- serving a knowledge-based national economy supporting a capacity to compete in global markets by offering products and services of high quality, reflecting a need for and value in complex pathways through education and training.

The seminal document positioning the personalizing education initiative in a wider context of public service reform is a pamphlet produced for DEMOS entitled *Personalisation Through Participation: A New Script for Public Services* (Leadbetter, 2004). The key concepts in this argument include re-casting learners in education as self-interested consumers and co-producers of their own learning. The key arbiter in this argument is 'customer satisfaction'. Leadbetter (2004: 25) explains how it is to be hoped that personalized education might serve as a modernizing catalyst and trigger ' ... waves of reform, leading from incremental innovations to existing public services but eventually leading to more radical solutions that combine better public services with more capacity for self-organising solutions in society?' The critical implication for service providers is that a script is prepared involving the client and their own professional role in the performance of a public service. In many ways this resembles the Patients' Charter in the English NHS system and offers the student a Learner's Charter.

Such scripts, initially framed by government, are intended to encourage participation and demand on the part of the consumer which will ensure quality and high standards in provision. There is a sense here, however, that reinforcing the value of consumption is fraught with the dangers of perverse incentive and the idea that production and consumption must by their very nature exponentially expand. There is no place in this scheme for values such as trust, loyalty, commitment, balance or in any stretch of the imagination, the solidarity or security of belonging (see Sennett, 1998). The analogy that springs to mind is one of the retail trade that produced the throw away coffee cup, with its disposable convenience, inferring a resource that is simply finite and certainly of limited value. The question remains, should education, knowledge and learning reflect these self-same values in a consumer driven ethic? Moreover, will such a consumer ethic extinguish any nurturing of a human or spiritual aspect to learning? Or must it continue to create the losers necessary for competition and selectivity to work?

In spite of these questions and contradictory aspects to the personalizing education agenda, it is to be hoped that developing more flexible approaches to learning and pedagogy might well reinforce an opportunity for the growth of an inclusive learning community. There is much in the emerging programme that can help improve present provision. The pressure to convert this growth into the equivalent of factory farming with the aim to produce more and better staple produce, however, will need careful scrutiny, if the school workforce is to maintain a commitment to education for all in an inclusively exclusive community rather than dealing only in skills training and knowledge delivery for those who can afford it.

MANAGING THE DIFFERENCES

A priority for those responsible for influencing and implementing educational policy is, arguably, to critically examine and exploit those aspects of government reform that will serve to ensure good education. This is in breach of the received wisdom at the heart of much of the current government drive toward a centralized school workforce, prescribed technical know-how for the educational technician and education as a knowledge-transmission system. In a very real sense it seems as if this policy and its implementation is intent on laying to rest a traditional notion of professional vocation and any sense of belief in a humanistic commitment to teaching, learning and education. In terms of making sense of this policy context for managing special and inclusive education, it is very clear that Simkin's emerging view of the educational leader is central to a continuing process of dealing with work and more increasingly, policy that is characterized by uncertainty, dilemma and contradiction (see Table 4.1, page 83), or my own model of inclusive leadership (see Figure 5.1, page 98). In a very real way, interpreting policy and managing practice are about mediating and navigating a series of cross-currents in differences swirling around the ever increasingly complex mix of diversity in the learning community.

For the purposes of inclusive leadership and an integrative management, three key perspectives do offer alternative, but yet importantly, perhaps, complementary prospects for establishing a way forward in developing SEN provision. Each carries some of the ideas contained in the personalizing education initiative but also contains fundamental differences in thinking and points to the importance of a re-conceptualization of a professional ethic and educational endeavour.

1. *A social justice perspective* – presumes school leaders will share a philosophy of inclusion and the reorganization of a school into a learning community. In this perspective leadership must be largely construed as co-agency

involving active membership of a community. A focus is drawn to the values and culture that must characterize this community, of which the most relevant will be a commitment to collaboration, reflection and empowerment. Inclusive leaders will need to ensure that the child, family, and the local community are positioned at the centre of the educational process as participating members of the learning community. The implications of a social justice perspective are that the educational endeavour should generate a *praxis* and empowerment reflected in personal and collective contributions to the learning community. This is particularly important when we consider issues related to social differences such as gender, ethnicity and disability. The ideas of participation and access are also repeated in the developing model of a personalized but diverse education.

2. *A differential perspective* – presumes a re-casting of education to incorporate a traditional special educational concern for the individual. It calls for a blending of the transformative power of learning with conceptions of individual potential, differences, capabilities and capacity for learning. The leadership focus in this perspective is more closely drawn to the processes of learning, teaching and pedagogy. It is an approach that requires a notion of distributing leadership and encourages a deeper awareness of both social and personal differences in the classroom and wider school community. To some extent, the implications of this approach are to re-examine and re-orientate a distribution of resources to support the idea of optimal provision for the individual. The ECM agenda in England reflects some of the ideas and aspirations that go with this idea of optimal focus and a 'wrap-around' provision for the individual child (see Farrell, 2004). Again, the idea of the learning guide or mentor for every pupil or student in an English school described in the personalizing education agenda reflects a similar idea.

3. *A knowledge management perspective* – presumes the restructuring of education to facilitate new ideas about how knowledge is created, acquired and exploited in society. It treats knowledge as a commodity and learning as capital to be used in the purchase and networked delivery of this commodity. A useful example of this approach is the booklet produced by Microsoft entitled *My Learning, My Way*, in which ICT media and the networking of distributed knowledge are presented as an emerging pedagogy (Lloyd, 2003). The approach is made up of the following principles:

- Extending the boundaries of teaching beyond the classroom using ICT.
- Developing awareness of multiple intelligences using ICT as a tool for differentiated instruction.
- Extending curriculum choice and access as part of the personalizing education agenda.
- Building connected learning communities via ICT, enabling knowledge and information transmission.

The underlying rationale for educational leadership in this perspective is technical and casts teachers in the role of broker and consultant, fulfilling a gate-keeping role in directing learners to access points in a network of knowledge. Justification for this approach is the endemic nature of change in contemporary society and the need to develop process skills in preparation for consuming and producing new knowledge. It is clear that this perspective has heavily influenced the central thrust behind the government's modernizing policy for education and ideas for personalizing learning.

All three perspectives are ultimately useful only when they are located in a learning context. Each of these perspectives contributes to the management of learning. The value of an integrative management of diversity and difference is that elements of all three perspectives can be adopted while preserving first principles of the professional's ethic in any educational endeavour. These principles in an integrated approach remain the qualities of success identified in the MISE model and are equity, empathy, efficiency and efficacy (see Chapter 3). Each must remain central to any re-shaping of the learning community. Each must inform the policy protocols and performance domains that exist and may be redeveloped in the same way. At the end of the day, it is quite crucial that the professional makes sense of their own role, policy and practices. In doing this they are acting as career-long learners who create and maintain their own *praxis*, which in this context should be directed at ensuring the impact areas of the MISE model are realized. Each of these areas will necessarily draw upon the three key perspectives previously summarized here and link to the government policy of personalizing education.

LOOKING BACK TO THE FUTURE: A WAY FORWARD

I began this book by admitting to feeling daunted by the task of writing about the idea of managing special and inclusive education. The area of work is so inclusive, complex, heavily contested and at present subject to change, that it is in every sense not work for the faint-hearted. I am aware too that there is much that I have not focused upon here. Management involves the handling of people and resources that necessarily invokes difficult decisions, grievances, complaints, prejudices, and vitriol. The cliché that you can 'never please all the people all of the time' springs to mind but at the same time as the fact that 'you never stop learning as a leader and a manager'. In this sense, a key theme throughout this book is that reflexive practice and developing a professional *praxis* are part of shaping an individual practitioner's pedagogy. It does, in turn, hopefully lay the foundation for teaching that can release a transformative power in learning associated with an inclusive leadership and differential pedagogy. It would be wrong, however, to presume that any emphasis upon the individual or personal as a leader contributing to the notion of a learning organization is to imply any

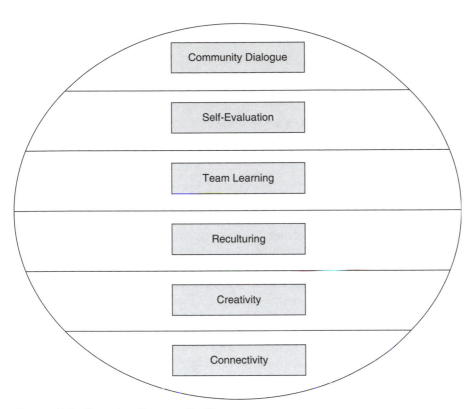

Figure 10.3   Learning Community Processes

neglect of the importance of social and cultural factors in the effective management of educational provision.

A second key theme in this book is the reality of a symbiotic relationship that characterizes learning and teaching, teacher and learner, or the personal and social aspects of the human condition. Relationships matter in education – forming a social compact – as the foundation of the wider learning community. In this respect, culture, ethics and milieu will always combine to form an important fabric with which to dress any infrastructure constructed for the purpose of education. The management of a learning community, nonetheless, necessitates 'putting the learner' at the heart of the organization in a way described by Stoll et al. (2003). It also requires a readiness to foster independence, mutuality and respect in a community that will offer support and security for the learner and integrating distinctive processes associated with developing the learning community (see Figure 10.3).

This leads to a third key theme in this book. It is important to always retain a focus on the function of any process, structure or agency as leadership and management ultimately are about making something worthwhile happen. It is equally important, however, that this approach retains an integrating principle that continuously revisits purpose and combines both a strategic and operational dimension in work related to organizing the community. The fuel for this work is resource. The glue that holds it together is time. This principle can be easily observed in any place and time by asking the critical questions: why, when and for whom? It is also part of this same process to include a consideration of resources and capacity in this same work.

The value of the learning community processes as explored by Stoll et al. (2003) is the close scrutiny of both of these in a tagging of time as part of work. Finding time, using time wisely, and linking time to priorities are central parts of exercising leadership and good management. It is set to become increasingly important as traditional boundaries and site-based location in the work-place context continue to disappear. Value for money is likely at some point to be joined by value for time as a prime indicator in resource management and accountability.

In a final but related way, time also plays a part in the reflexive process of professional and organizational learning. The clear and present danger in the fast enveloping knowledge society is saturation and overload created by a constant flow of useless junk, trivia and endless vistas offered by information technology. It is reminiscent of the paradox of choice – too little is as bad as too much, resulting in distress and breakdown. Giving time to continue learning as a professional and as a manager is essential but never without competing priorities and has to be an exercise in deliberate time management. It should ideally lead to reflection (looking back) in order to plan (looking forward) for the future. I hope reading this book is a justified use of time. Thank you for reading it. I hope you may well return to it time and again as you develop your own *praxis* in managing special and inclusive education. I would also like to invite you to email me at s.g.rayner@ bham.ac.uk if you should be interested in a conversation about developing any of the ideas I have shared in writing this book.

References

Abdelnoor, A. (1999) *Preventing Exclusions*. Oxford: Heinemann.

Adair, J. (1988) *Effective Leadership*. London: Pan.

Adams, J., Swain, J. and Clark, J. (2000) 'What's So Special? Teachers' models and their realisation in practice in segregated schools', *Disability Society*, 15 (2): 233–45.

Ainscow, M. (ed.) (1991) *Effective Schools for All*. London: David Fulton.

Ainscow, M. (2006) 'From Special Education to Effective Schools For All: A review of progress so far', in L. Florian (ed.), *The Sage Handbook of Special Education*. London: Sage.

Ainscow, M., Farrell P. and Tweddle, D. (2000) 'Developing Policies for Inclusive Education: A study of the role of education authorities', *International Journal of Inclusive Education*, 4 (3): 211–29.

Ainscow, M., Hargreaves, D.H. and Hopkins, D. (1995) 'Mapping the Process of Change in Schools: The development of six new research techniques', *Evaluation and Research in Education*, 9 (2): 75–89.

Allan, J. and Brown, S. (2001) 'Special Schools and Inclusion', *Educational Review*, 53 (2): 199–207.

Anning, A., Cottrell, D., Frost, N., Green, J. and Robinson, M. (2006) *Developing Multiprofessional Teamwork for Integrated Children's Services*. Maidenhead: OUP/McGraw-Hill Education.

Armstrong, D. (2005) 'Voice, Rituals and Transitions: What is inclusive education really about?', paper presented to the International Special Education Congress, 1–4 August, Glasgow.

Atkinson, M. and Hornby, G. (2002) *Mental Health Handbook for Schools*. London: RoutledgeFalmer.

Atkinson, M., Wilkin, A., Stott, A., Doherty, P. and Kinder, K. (2002) *Multi-agency Working: A Detailed Study*. LGA Research Report 26. Slough: NFER.

Audit Commission (2002) *Statutory Assessment and Statements of SEN: In Need of Review?* (June). London: Audit Commission.

Audit Commission and Ofsted (2002) *LEA Strategy for the Inclusion of Pupils with Special Educational Needs*. London: HMI 737.

Avissar, G., Reiter, S. and Leyser, Y. (2003) 'Principals' Views and Practices Regarding Inclusion: The case of Israeli elementary school principals', *European Journal of Special Needs Education*, 18 (3): 355–69.

Avramadis, E. and Norwich, B. (2002) 'Teachers' Attitudes Towards Integration/Inclusion: A review of the literature', *European Journal of Special Needs Education*, 17 (2): 129–47.

Baker, D. and Bovair, K. (eds) (1989) *Making the Special School Ordinary*. London: David Fulton.

Ball, S.J. (2003) 'The Teacher's Soul and the Terrors of Performativity', *Journal of Education Policy*, 18 (2): 215–28.

Ballard, K. (1995) 'Inclusion, Paradigms, Power and Participation', in C. Clark, A. Dyson and A. Millward (eds), *Towards Inclusive Schools?* London: David Fulton. pp. 1–14.

Bayliss, P. (1997) 'Models of Complexity: Theory-driven intervention practices', in C. Clark, A. Dyson and A. Millward (eds), *Theorising Special Education*. London: Routledge. pp. 61–78.

Benjamin, H. (1939) 'Foreword', in J.A. Peddlewell (ed.), *The Saber-tooth Curriculum*. New York: McGraw-Hill Inclusion.

Bennet, A. and Tomblin, M.S. (2006) 'A Learning Network Framework for Modern Organizations', *The Journal of Information and Knowledge Management Systems*, 3 (3): 289–303.

Bernard, M.E. (1997) *You Can Do It!: How to Boost Your Child's Achievement in School*. New York: Warner.

Bernstein, R.J. (1983) *Beyond Objectivism and Relativism*. Oxford: Blackwell.

Best, R., Lang, P., Lodge, C. and Watkins, C. (1995) *Pastoral Care and Personal-Social Education*. London: Cassell.

Black, P. and Wiliam, D. (2001) *Assessment and Classroom Learning*. London: School of Education, King's College, London.

Bolman, L. and Deal, T. (1984) *Modern Approaches to Understanding and Managing Organisations*. San Fancisco, CA: Jossey-Bass.

Booth, T. (2000) 'Inclusion and Exclusion Policy in England: Who controls the agenda?', in F. Armstrong, D. Armstrong and L. Barton (eds), *Inclusive Education: Policy, Contexts and Comparative Perspectives*. London: David Fulton. pp. 78–98.

Booth, T. and Ainscow, M. (2002) *Index for Inclusion: Developing Learning and Participation in Schools* (2nd Edition). Bristol: Centre for Studies in Inclusive Education.

Bottery, M. (2003) 'The Management and Mismanagement of Trust', *Educational Management and Administration*, 31 (3): 245–61.

Bottery, M. and Wright, N. (2000) 'The Directed Profession: Teachers and the state in the third millennium', *Journal of In-Service Education*, 26 (3): 475–87.

Brennan, W.K. (1983) 'The Future Development of Special Schools?', *Secondary Education Journal*, 13 (2): 24–6.

Bryant, M.T. (2003) 'Cross-cultural Perspectives on School Leadership: Themes from North American interviews', in N. Bennett, M. Crawford and M. Cartwright (eds), *Effective Educational Leadership*. London: Paul Chapman. pp. 216–28.

Burnett, N. (2003) *Special Leadership? What are the implications for the leadership of special schools of potential changes to the special school system?* Nottingham: NCSL.

Burnett, N. (2005) *Leadership and SEN: Meeting the Challenge in Special and Mainstream Settings*. London: David Fulton.

Bush, T. and Bell, L. (eds) (2002) *The Principles and Practice of Educational Management*. London: Sage.

Bush, T. and Glover, D. (2003) *School Leadership: Concepts and Evidence*. Nottingham: NCSL.

Caldwell, B.J. (2004) 'A Strategic View of Efforts to Lead the Transformation of Schools', *School Leadership and Management*, 24 (1): 81–99.

Carnie, F. (2006) *Setting up Parent Councils: Case studies*. Bristol: Human Scale Education.

Carpenter, B., Ashdown, R. and Bovair, K. (1996) *Enabling Access: Effective Teaching and Learning for Pupils with Special Educational Needs*. London: David Fulton.

Cheminais, R. (2002) *Inclusion and School Improvement*. London: David Fulton.

Cheminais, R. (2004) 'Inclusive Schools and Classrooms', *SENCO Update*, May, 6–7.

Cheminais, R. (2005) *Every Child Matters: A New Role for SENCOs*. London: David Fulton.

Cheminais, R. (2006) *Every Child Matters*. London: David Fulton.

Cheng, T.C. (2002) 'Leadership and Strategy', in T. Bush and L. Bell (eds), *The Principles and Practice of Educational Management*. London: Sage. pp. 51–69.

Clark, C., Dyson, A. and Millward, A. (1995) *Toward Inclusive Schools.* London: David Fulton.

Clark, C., Dyson, A., Millward, A. and Skidmore, D. (1997) *New Directions in Special Needs: Innovations in Mainstream Schools.* London: Cassell.

Clough, P. (ed.) (1998) *Managing Inclusive Education.* London: Paul Chapman.

Clough, P. and Corbett, J. (2000) *Theories of Inclusive Education.* London: Paul Chapman.

Coffield, F.C., Moseley, D.V.M., Hall, E. and Ecclestone, K. (2004) *Learning Styles and Pedagogy in Post-16 Learning: Findings of a Systematic and Critical Review of Learning Styles Models.* London: Learning and Skills Research Centre.

Cole, B.A. (2005) 'Mission Impossible? Special educational needs, inclusion and the re-conceptualization of the role of the SENCO in England and Wales', *European Journal of Special Needs Education,* 20 (3): 287–307.

Cole, T. (1989) *Apart or A Part? Integration and the Growth of British Special Education.* Milton Keynes: Open University Press.

Cole, T., Visser, J. and Upton, G. (1998) *Effective Schooling for Pupils with Emotional and Behavioural Difficulties.* London: David Fulton.

Collarbone, P. (2005) 'Touching Tomorrow: Remodelling in English schools', *The Australian Economic Review,* 38 (1): 75–82.

Cook, T., Swain, J. and French, S. (2001) 'Voices from Segregated Schooling: Towards an inclusive education system', *Disability and Society,* 16 (2): 293–310.

Cowie, H. and Sharp, S. (1996) *Peer Counselling in Schools.* London: David Fulton.

Cowne, E. (2003) *Developing Inclusive Practice: The SENCO's Role in Managing Change.* London: David Fulton.

Cremin, H. and Thomas, G. (2005) 'Maintaining Underclasses via Contrastive Judgement: Can inclusive education ever happen?', *British Journal of Educational Studies,* 53 (4): 431–46.

Croll, P. and Moses, D. (1998) 'Pragmatism, Ideology and Educational Change: The case of special educational needs', *British Journal of Educational Studies,* 46 (1): 11–25.

Croll, P. and Moses, D. (2000) 'Ideologies and Utopias: Education professionals' views of inclusion', *European Journal of Special Needs Education,* 15 (1): 1–12.

Cunningham, C., Glenn, S., Lorenz, S., Cuckle, P. and Shepperdson, B. (1998) 'Trends and Outcomes in Educational Placements for Children with Down Syndrome', *European Journal of Special Needs Education,* 13 (3): 225–37.

Daniels, H. and Garner, P. (2000) 'Introduction' (to the paperback edition), in H. Daniels and P. Garner (eds), *Inclusive Education: Supporting Inclusion in Education Systems.* London: Kogan Page.

Daniels, H., Creese, A. and Norwich, N. (2000) 'Supporting Collaborative Problem-Solving in Schools', in H. Daniels (ed.), *Special Education Reformed.* London: Falmer.

Daniels, H., Visser, J., Cole, T. and de Reybekill, N. (1998) *Emotional and Behavioural Difficulties in Mainstream Schools.* Research Report RR90. London: DfEE.

Davies, B. (2004) 'Developing the Strategically Focused School', *School Leadership and Management,* 24 (1): 1–27.

De Shazer, S. (1988) *Clues: Investigating Solutions in Brief Therapy.* New York: Norton.

Decker, S., Kirby, S., Greenwood, A. and Moore, D. (eds) (1999) *Taking Children Seriously: Applications of Counseling and Therapy in Education.* London: Cassell.

Deming, W.E. (1986) *Out of the Crisis.* Massachusetts: MIT Center of Engineering Studies.

DEMOS (2005) *About Learning: The Report of the Working Group.* London: DEMOS (www.demos.co.uk).

DES (1976) *The Education Act 1996.* London: DES.

DES (1978) *Report of the Committee of Enquiry into the Education of Handicapped Children and Young People (The Warnock Report).* London: HMSO.

DES (1981) *The Education Act 1981*. London: DfES.

DES (1988) *The Education Reform Act*. London: DES.

Desforges, C. (2003) *The Impact of Parental Involvement, Parental Support and Family Education on Pupil Achievement and Adjustment*, DfES Research Report 433. Nottingham: DfES.

DfE (1993a) *Good Management in Small Schools*. London: DfES.

DfE (1993b) *The Education Act 1993*. London: DfEE.

DfE (1994) *Code of Practice on the Identification and Assessment of Special Educational Needs*. London: HMSO.

DfEE (1996) *The Education Act 1996*. London: DfEE.

DfEE (1997) *Excellence for All Children*. London: The Stationery Office.

DfEE (1997a) *Excellence In Schools*. London: DfEE.

DfEE (1998a) *Teachers Meeting the Challenge of Change*. London: DfEE.

DfEE (1998b) *Meeting Special Educational Needs: A Programme of Action*. London: DfEE.

DfEE (1999) *Social Inclusion: Pupil Support, Circular 10/99*. London: Department for Education and Employment/Home Office/Department of Health.

DfES (2001a) *Schools Achieving Success*. London: DfES.

DfES (2001b) *The Code of Practice for Special Educational Needs*. Nottingham: DfES.

DfES (2001c) *Statistics of Education: Schools in England 2001*. London: The Stationery Office.

DfES (2001d) *The SEN and Disability Act 2001*. London: DfES.

DfES (2002a) *The Distribution of Resources to Support Inclusion* (Draft Guidance). www.dfes.gov.uk/sen/documents/SENFUND22JUNE.htm

DfES (2002b) *Time for Standards: Reforming the School Workforce*. London: DfES.

DfES (2003a) *SEN Toolkit*. London: HMSO.

DfES (2003b) *Data Collection by Type of Special Educational Need*. London: HMSO.

DfES (2003c) *The Report of the Special Schools Working Group*. Annesley, Nottingham: DfES.

DfES (2003d) *Every Child Matters*. London: DfES.

DfES (2004a) *Removing Barriers to Achievement: The government's strategy for SEN*. Nottingham: DfES.

DfES (2004b) *Raising Standards and Tackling Workload, Implementing the National Agreement, January 2004*, London: DfES.

DfES (2004c) *The Management of SEN Expenditure (LEA/0149/2004)*. London: DfES.

DfES (2004d) *A National Conversation about Personalised Learning*. Nottingham: DfES.

DfES (2004e) *Excellence and Enjoyment: Learning and Teaching in the Primary Years: Creating a learning culture*. London: DfES.

DfES (2005a) *Time for Standards: Transforming the School Workforce*. Nottingham: DfES.

DfES (2005b) *Children's Workforce Strategy: A Strategy to Build a World-Class Workforce for Children and Young People*. Nottingham: DfES.

DfES (2005c) *The Implementation Review Annual Report 2004–5: Reducing Bureaucracy in Schools – Progress Made, Challenges Ahead* (www.dfes.gov.uk/iru).

DfES (2006) *'20/20 Vision: Report of the Teaching and Learning in 2020 Review Group'*. Nottingham: DfES.

DfES (2007) *Diversity and Citizenship Curriculum Review*. Nottingham: DfES.

DfES/Ofsted (2004) *A New Relationship with Schools: Improving Performance through School Self-Evaluation*. London: DfES/Ofsted.

DfES/Ofsted (2005) *A New Relationship with Schools: Next Steps*. London: DfES/Ofsted.

Dimmock, C. and Walker, A. (2004) 'A New Approach to Strategic Leadership: Learning-centredness, connectivity and cultural context in school design', *School Leadership and Management*, 24 (1): 39–56.

DOH (1989) *The Children Act 1989*. London: HMSO.

DOH (2004) *The Children Act 2004*. London: HMSO.

Draper, I. (2005) 'Why Reform the Workforce? Effectively remodelling the school workforce requires a broader perspective than educational imperatives alone can provide', *Managing Schools Today*, 14 (3): 48–53.

Dunn, R. and Griggs, S. (2003) *Synthesis of the Dunn and Dunn Learning Styles Research: Who, what, when, where and so what. Dunn and Dunn learning styles model and its theoretical cornerstone*. New York: St John's University.

Dyson, A. and Millward, A. (2000) *Schools and Special Needs: Issues of Innovation and Inclusion*. London: Paul Chapman.

Elliot, J. (2004) 'Making Evidence-based Practice Educational', in G. Thomas and R. Pring (eds), *Evidence-Based Practice in Education*. Maidenhead: Open University Press. pp. 164–86.

Engestrom, Y. and Middleton, D. (eds) (1996) *Cognition and Communication at Work*. Cambridge: Cambridge University Press.

Evans, J. and Lunt, J. (2002) 'Inclusive Education: Are there limits?', *European Journal of Special Needs Education*, 17 (1): 1–14.

Farrell, M. (2004) *Special Educational Needs: A Resource for Practitioners*. London: David Fulton.

Farrell, P. (2001) 'Special Education in the Last Twenty Years: Have things really got better?', *British Journal of Special Education*, 28 (1): 3–9.

Fidler, B. (1996) *Strategic Planning for School Improvement*. London: Pitman.

Florian, M. (1998) 'Inclusive Practice: What, why and how?', in T. Tilstone, L. Florian and R. Rose (eds), *Promoting Inclusive Practice*. London: Routledge. pp. 13–26.

Florian, M. (2006) 'Re-imagining Special Education', in L. Florian (ed.), *The Sage Handbook of Special Education*. London: Sage. pp. 7–20.

Fogell, J. and Long, R. (1997) *Emotional and Behavioural Difficulties*. Tamworth: NASEN.

Foster, W. (1989) 'Towards a Critical Practice of Leadership', in J. Smyth (ed.), *Critical Perspectives on Educational Leadership*. London: Falmer.

Freire, P. (1972) *Pedagogy of the Oppressed*. London: Penguin.

Fuchs, D. and Fuchs, L.S. (1994) 'Inclusive Schools Movement and the Radicalisation of Special Educational Reform', *Exceptional Children*, 60 (4): 294–309.

Fulcher, G. (1989) *Disabling Policies? A Comparative Approach to Education Policy and Disability*. London: Falmer.

Fullan, M. (1991) *The New Meaning of Educational Change*. New York: Teachers College Press.

Fullan, M. (1993) *Change Forces*. London: Falmer.

Fullan, M. (2002) 'Moral Purpose Writ Large', *The Administrator, The School Administrator Web Edition*, September, 1–6.

Fullan, M. (2003) *The Moral Imperative of School of Leadership*. Paul Chapman.

Fullan, M., Cuttress, C. and Kilcher, A. (2005) 'Forces for Leaders of Change', *Journal of Staff Development*, 26 (4): 54–64.

Gallagher, J.J. (2006) *Driving Change in Special Education*. Baltimore, ML: Paul H. Brookes.

Gardner, H. (1993) *Multiple Intelligences: The Theory in Practice*. New York: Basic.

Gersch, I.S. and Gersch, A. (2003) *Resolving Disagreement in Special Educational Needs*. London: RoutledgeFalmer.

Gerschel, L. (2005a) 'The Special Educational Needs Coordinator's Role in Managing Teaching Assistants: The Greenwich perspective', *Support for Learning*, 20 (2): 69–76.

Gerschel, L. (2005b) 'Connecting the Disconnected: Exploring issues of gender, "race" and SEN within an inclusive context', in K. Topping and S. Maloney (eds), The *RoutledgeFalmer Reader in Inclusive Education*. Abingdon: RoutledgeFalmer pp. 95–110.

Gibson, S. and Blandford, S. (2005) *Managing Special Educational Needs*. London: Paul Chapman.

Glatter, R. (1997) 'Context and Capability in Educational Management', *Educational Management and Administration*, 25 (2): 181–92.

Glatter, R. and Kydd, L. (2003) 'Best Practice', *Educational Practice and Management*, 31 (3): 231–43.

Grace, G. (1995) *School Leadership: Beyond Education Management*. London: Falmer.

Greenhalgh, P. (1994) *Emotional Growth and Learning*. London: Routledge.

Grimley, M., Morris, S., Rayner, S. and Riding, R. (2004) 'Supporting School Improvement: The development of a scale for assessing pupils' emotional and behavioural development', *Assessment in Education*, 11 (3): 273–300.

Gronn, P. (1999) 'Substituting for Leadership: The neglected role of the leadership couple', *Leadership Quarterly*, 10 (1): 41–62.

Gronn, P. (2000) 'Distributed Properties – A New Architecture for Leadership', *Educational Management Administration and Leadership*, 28 (3): 317–38.

Gronn, P. (2002) 'Distributed Leadership as a Unit of Analysis', *The Leadership Quarterly*, 13: 423–51.

Grossman, H. (2004) *Classroom Behaviour Management for Diverse and Inclusive Schools*. Oxford: Rowman and Littlefield.

Grundy, S. (1987) *Curriculum: Product or Praxis*? London: RoutledgeFalmer.

Gulliford, R. (1971) *Special Educational Needs*. London: Routledge and Kegan Paul.

Gunter, H.M. (1997) *Rethinking Education: The Consequences of Jurassic Management*. London: Cassell.

Gunter, H.M. (2001) *Leaders and Leadership in Education*. London: Paul Chapman.

Gunter, H.M. (2003) 'Teachers as Educational Leaders', in M. Brundrett, N. Burton and R. Smith (eds), *Leadership in Education*. London: Paul Chapman. pp. 118–31.

Gunter, H.M. (2005) *Leading Teachers*. London: Continuum.

Gunter, H.M. and Rayner, S.G. (2006) 'Modernizing the School Workforce in England: Challenging transformation and leadership?', *Leadership*, 3 (1): 47–64.

Gunter, H.M. and Ribbins, P. (2002) 'Leadership Studies in Education: Towards a map of the field', *Educational Management, Administration and Leadership*, 30 (4): 387–416.

Halsey, K., Gulliver, C., Johnson, A., Martin, K. and Kinder, K. (2005) *Evaluation of Behaviour and Education Support Teams (NFER)*. DfES Research Report RR706. Nottingham: DfES.

Hargreaves, A. and Fink, D. (2006) *Sustainable Leadership*. San Francisco, CA: Jossey-Bass.

Harris, A. (2005) 'Distributed Leadership and Headship: A paradoxical relationship?', *School Leadership and Management*, 25 (3): 213–15.

Hart, S., Dixon, A., Drummond, M.J. and McIntyre, D. (2004) *Learning Without Limits*. Maidenhead: Open University Press.

Hartle, F. (2005) *Shaping up to the Future: A Guide to Roles, Structures and Career Development in Secondary Schools*. Nottingham: National College for School Leadership.

Hartley, D. (2006) 'Excellence and Enjoyment: The logic of a "contradiction"', *British Journal of Educational Studies*, 54 (1): 3–14.

Heung, V. (2006) 'Can the Introduction of an Inclusion Index Move a System Forward?', *International Journal of Inclusive Education*, 10 (4–5): 309–22.

HMI (1989) *Personal and Social Education from 5–16, Curriculum Matters 14*. London: HMSO/DES.

Hopkins, D. (2001) *School Improvement For Real*. Lewes: Falmer.

Hornby, G. (1999) 'Inclusion or Delusion: Can one size fit all?', *Support for Learning*, 14 (4): 152–57.

Hornby, G. (2001) 'Promoting Responsible Inclusion: Quality education for all', in T. O'Brien (ed.), *Enabling Inclusion: Blue Skies . . . Dark Clouds?* London: The Stationery Office. pp. 3–19.

House of Commons (HOC) (2006) *The SEN Select Committee Report, HC478–1* (Special Educational Needs, Third Report of Session 2005–06, Volume I). London: The Stationery Office.

ILEA (1985) *Educational Opportunities for All (The Fish Report)*. London: ILEA.

Istance, D. (2002) *Work on Schooling for Tomorrow: Trends, Themes and Scenarios to Inform Leadership Issues*. Nottingham: NCSL.

Jelly, M., Fuller, A. and Byers, R. (2000) *Involving Pupils in Practice: Promoting Partnerships with Pupils with Special Educational Needs*. London: David Fulton.

Jonassen, D.H. and Grabowski, B.L. (1993) *Handbook of Individual Difference, Learning and Instruction*. Hillsdale, NJ: Lawrence Erlbaum.

Kearney, A. and Kane, R. (2006) 'Inclusive Education Policy in New Zealand: Reality or ruse?', *International Journal of Inclusive Education*, 10 (2–3): 201–19.

Kenning, S. (2002) *The Intelligent Gaze: Leadership, Lead Learners and Individual Growth – A Reflective Enquiry. A practitioner enquiry report*. Nottingham: National College for School Leadership.

King, G. (1999) *Counselling Skills for Teachers*. Buckingham: Open University Press.

Kolb, D.A. (1999) *The Kolb Learning Style Inventory, Version 3*. Boston, MA: Hay Group.

Kugelmass, J.W. (2003) *Inclusive Leadership: Leadership for Inclusion*. Nottingham: NCSL.

Lacey, P. (2001) *Support Partnerships – Collaboration in Action*. London: David Fulton.

Lambert, L. (2003) 'Leadership Redefined: An evocative context for teacher leadership', *School Leadership and Management*, 23 (4): 421–30.

Law, S. and Glover, D. (2000) *Educational Leadership and Learning*. Buckingham: Open University Press.

Lawrence, J., Steed, D. and Young, P. (1984) *Disruptive Children: Disruptive Schools?* London: Croom Helm.

Leadbetter, C. (2004) *Personalisation Through Participation: A New Script For Public Services*. London: DEMOS.

Leithwood, K. (1994) 'Leadership for School Restructuring', *Educational Administration Quarterly*, 30 (4): 498–518.

Leithwood, K., Jantzi, D. and Steinbach, R. (1999) 'Leadership and Other Conditions which Foster Organizational Learning in Schools', in K. Leithwood and K. Louis (eds), *Organizational Learning in Schools*. New York: Lisse, Swets and Zeitlinger. pp. 67–92.

Lewis, A. and Porter, J. (2006) 'Research and Pupil Voice', in L. Florian (ed.), *The Sage Handbook of Special Education*. London: Sage.

Little, J.W. (2003) 'Constructions of Teacher Leadership in Three Periods of Policy and Reform Activism', *School Leadership and Management*, 23 (4): 401–19.

Lloyd, M. (2003) *My Learning, My Way: Realising Learning Potential*. London: Microsoft.

Lodge, C. (1995) 'School Management for Pastoral Care and PSE', in R. Best, P. Lang, C. Hodge and C. Watkins (eds), *Pastoral Care and Personal-Social Education: Entitlement and Provision*. London: Cassell. pp. 21–36.

Lorenz, S. (2002) *First Steps in Inclusion*. London: David Fulton.

Lucietto, S. (ed.) (2003) *Children as Learning Citizens: A European Project. A report on good pedagogical practice for learners' success at school*. Provincia Autonoma di Trento, Italy: Iprase del Trentino.

Luft, J. (1970) *Group Processes: An Introduction to Group Dynamics* (2nd Edition). Palo Alto, CA: National Press Books.

MacBeath, J. (2005) 'Leadership as Distributed: A matter of practice', *School Leadership and Management*, 25 (4): 349–66.

MacBeath, J., Galton, M., Steward, S., MacBeath, A. and Page, C. (2006) *The Costs of Inclusion*. Cambridge: University of Cambridge, Faculty of Education.

MacGilchrist, B., Myers, K. and Reed, J. (1997) *The Intelligent School*. London: Paul Chapman.

Maines, B. and Robinson, G. (1992) *The No Blame Approach*. Bristol: Lame Duck.

Male, D. (1996a) 'Who Goes to SLD schools?', *Journal of Applied Research in Intellectual Disabilities*, 9 (4): 307–23.

Male, D. (1996b) 'Who goes to MLD schools?', *British Journal of Special Education*, 23 (1): 35–41.

Marchant, C. (1993) 'Guilty until Proved Innocent', *Community Care*, 4 March.

Mertens, D.M. and McLaughlin, J.A. (2004) *Research and Evaluation Methods in Special Education*. Thousand Oaks, CA: Corwin.

Metcalfe, L. (1998) *Solution Focused Group Therapy*. New York: Norton.

Mosley, J. (1993) *Turn Your School Round*. Cambridge: LDA.

Murphy, J. and Hallinger, P. (1992) 'The Principalship in an Era of Transformation', *Journal of Educational Administration*, 30 (3): 77–88.

National Association of Special Educational Needs (NASEN) (1999) *Inclusion Policy Document*. Stafford: NASEN.

National Governors Association (NGA) (2006) *Extended Schools – A Guide for Governors* 1, Birmingham: National Governors' Association.

National Union of Teachers (NUT) (2006) *NUT Briefing: Pupils with Special Educational Needs – June 2006*, 1–17. London: NUT.

Neuman, M. and Simmons, W. (2000) 'Leadership for Student Learning', *Phi Delta Kappan*, September, 9–13.

Newman, J. (2001) 'Beyond the New Public Management? Modernizing public services', in J. Clarke, S. Gewirtz and E. McLaughlin (eds), *New Managerialism New Welfare?* London: Open University/Sage.

Nind, M. and Wearmouth, J. (2005) *Pedagogical Approaches that Effectively Include Children with Special Educational Needs in Mainstream Classrooms: A Systematic Literature Review*. Paper presented to the International Special Education Congress, University of Strathclyde, 1–4 August.

No Child Left Behind Act of 2001, PL 107–110. 115 Stat. 1425. Education Publications Center, U.S. Department of Education, P.O. Box 1398, Jessup, MD 20794–1398.

Norwich, B. (1990) *Reappraising Special Needs Education*. London: Cassell Education.

Norwich, B. (1993) 'Ideological Dilemmas in Special Needs Education: Practitioner's views', *Oxford Review of Education*, 19 (4): 527–46.

Norwich, B. (2000) 'Inclusion in Education: From Concepts, Values and Critique to Practice', in H. Daniels (ed.), *Special Education Re-formed: Beyond Rhetoric*. London and New York: Falmer. pp. 5–30.

Norwich, B. (2006) 'Categories of Special Educational Needs', in L. Florian (ed.), *The Sage Handbook of Special Education*. London: Sage. pp. 55–66.

Norwich, B. and Lewis, A. (2001) 'Mapping a Pedagogy for Special Educational Needs', *British Educational Research Journal*, 27 (3): 313–29.

O'Brien, T. (2001) *Enabling Inclusion: Blue Skies, Dark Clouds*. London: The Stationery Office.

OECD (2000) *Special Needs Education: Statistics and Indicators*. Paris: OECD.

Ofsted (2000) *Evaluating Educational Inclusion*. London: Ofsted.

Ofsted (2004) *Special Educational Needs and Disability: Towards Inclusive Schools*. London: Ofsted.

Ogawa, R. and Bossert, S. (1995) 'Leadership as an Organizational Quality', *Educational Administration Quarterly*, 31 (2): 224–43.

O'Hanlon, C. (ed.) (1995) *Inclusive Education in Europe*. London: Fulton.

Oliver, M. (1998) *Disabled People and Social Policy*. London: Longman.

Piggot-Irvine, E. (2006) 'Sustaining Excellence in Experienced Principals? Critique of a professional learning community approach', *International Electronic Journal For Leadership in Learning*, 10 (16).

Pijl, S.J. and Meijor, C.J.W. (1991) 'Does Integration Count for Much? An analysis of the practices of integration in eight countries', *European Journal of Special Needs Education*, 3: 63–73.

Porter, J. and Lacey, P. (2002) *The Role of Special Schools: A Review of the Literature*. Unpublished paper, Birmingham University, School of Education.

Prashnig, B. (1998) *The Power of Diversity: New Ways of Learning and Teaching*. Auckland, NZ: David Bateman.

PricewaterhouseCoopers (2007) *Independent Study into School Leadership: The Main Report*. Nottingham: DfES.

Puonti, A. (2004) *Learning to Work Together: Collaboration Between Authorities in Economic-Crime Investigation*. PhD thesis: University of Helsinki, Department of Education, Center for Activity Theory and Developmental Work Research. Helsinki: University of Helsinki.

Qualifications and Curriculum Authority (QCA) (2001) *Supporting School Improvement: Emotional and Behavioural Development*. London: QCA.

Rayner, S.G. (1994) 'Restructuring Reform: Choice and change in special education', *British Journal of Special Education*, 21 (4): 169–73.

Rayner, S.G. (1999) 'A Case History of Provision for Pupils with Emotional and Behaviour Difficulties', in J. Visser and S.G. Rayner (eds), *Emotional and Behaviour Difficulties: A Course Reader*. Stafford: QED. pp. 16–41.

Rayner, S.G. (2000) 'Re-Constructing Style Differences in Thinking and Learning: Profiling learning performance', in R.J. Riding and S. Rayner (eds), *International Perspectives in Individual Differences: New Developments in Learning/Cognitive Style*. Stamford, CT: Ablex. pp. 115–80.

Rayner, S.G. (2001) 'Cognitive Style and Learning Styles', in N.J. Smelser and P.B. Baltes (eds), *International Encyclopaedia of the Social and Behavioural Sciences*. Oxford: Elsevier. pp. 2171–75.

Rayner, S.G. and Gunter, H.M. (2005a) 'Rethinking Leadership: Perspectives on remodelling practice', *Educational Review*, 57 (2): 1–11.

Rayner, S.G. and Gunter, H.M. (2005b) *The Entrepreneurial Role in School Leadership: Lessons from Transforming the School Workforce Project in England*. Paper presented at AERA Conference, Montreal.

Rayner, S.G. and Ribbins, P. (1999) *Headteachers and Leadership in Special Education*. London: Cassell.

Rayner, S., Gunter, H., Thomas, H., Butt, G. and Lance, A. (2005) 'Transforming the School Workforce: Remodelling experiences in the special school', *Management in Education*, 19 (5): 22–8.

Reid, G. (2005) *Learning Styles and Inclusion*. London: Paul Chapman.

Ribbins, P. and Gunter, H. (2002) 'Mapping Leadership Studies in Education: Towards a typology of knowledge domains', *Educational Management, Administration and Leadership*, 30 (4): 359–86.

Riding, R.J. and Rayner, S.G. (1998) *Cognitive Styles and Learning Strategies*. London: David Fulton.

Riehl, C.J. (2000) 'The Principal's Role in Creating Inclusive Schools for Diverse Students: A review of normative, empirical, and critical literature on the practice of educational administration', *Review of Educational Research*, 70 (1): 55–81.

Robinson, G. and Maines, B. (1997) *Crying for Help: The No Blame Approach to Bullying.* Bristol: Lucky Duck.

Robson, M. (1997) 'Developing Pupil Counselling and Peer Support', in D. Tattum and G. Herbert (eds), *Bullying: Home, School and Community.* London: David Fulton. pp. 88–98.

Rogers, C.R. (1983) *Freedom to Learn for the 80s.* London: Merrill.

Rogers, W.A. (1990) *You Know The Fair Rule.* London: Pitman.

Rosenholtz, S. (1989) *Teacher's Workplace: The Social Organization of Schools.* White Plain, NY: Longman.

Rouse, M. and McLaughlin, M.J. (2006) 'Changing Perspectives of Special Education in the Evolving Context of Educational Reform', in L. Florian (ed.), *The Sage Handbook of Special Education.* London: Sage. pp. 85–106.

Sallis, E. and Jones, G. (2002) *Knowledge Management in Education.* London: Kogan.

Sayer, J. (1983) 'A Comprehensive School for All', in A. Booth and B. Potts (eds), *Integrating Special Education.* Oxford: Blackwell.

Schafner, C.B. and Buswell, B.E. (1996) 'Ten Critical Elements for Creating Inclusive and Effective School Communities', in S. Stainback and W. Stainback (eds), *Inclusion: A Guide for Educators.* Baltimore, ML: Paul H. Brookes. pp. 49–66.

Schein, E. (1985) *Organisational Culture and Leadership.* San Francisco, CA: Jossey-Bass Wiley.

Schon, D. (1983) *The Reflective Practitioner: How Professionals Think in Action.* London: Maurice Temple Smith.

Schostak, J.F. (1983) *Maladjusted Schooling: Deviance, Social Control and Individuality in Secondary Schooling.* London: Falmer.

Senge, P.M. (1993) *The Fifth Discipline: The Art and Practice of the Learning Organisation.* London: Century.

Sennett, R. (1998) *The Corrosion of Character: The Personal Consequences of Work in the New Capitalism.* New York: Norton.

Sergiovanni, T.J. (1991) *The Principalship: A Reflective Practice Perspective.* Needham Heights, MA: Allyn and Bacon.

Shaw, L. (1999) *Follow-Up Papers: An Inclusive Approach to Difficult Behaviour.* Bristol: Centre for Study for Inclusive Education.

Simkins, T. (2005) 'Leadership in Education: "What Works" or "What Makes Sense"?', *Educational Management Administration and Leadership,* 33 (1): 9–26.

Skrtic, T.M. (1991) *Behind Special Education: A Critical Analysis of Professional Culture and School Organization.* Denver, CO: Love.

Slee, R. (1998) 'High Reliability Organizations and Liability Students – The Politics of Recognition', in R. Slee, G. Weiner and S. Tomlinson (eds), *School Effectiveness for Whom? Challenges to the School Effectiveness and School Improvement Movement.* London: Falmer. pp. 101–114.

Slee, R. (2000) 'Policies and Practices? Inclusive education and its effects on schooling', in H. Daniels and P. Garner (eds), *Inclusive Education: Supporting Inclusion in Education Systems.* London: Kogan Page. pp. 194–206.

Spillane, J.P., Halverson, R. and Diamond, J.B. (2001) 'Investigating School Leadership Practice: A Distributed Perspective': Research News and Comment. *Educational Researcher,* 23–8.

Stacey, H. (1996) 'Mediation into School Does Go!', *Pastoral Care in Education,* 14 (2): 7–9.

Stainback, S. and Stainback, W. (eds) (1996) *Inclusion: A Guide for Educators.* Baltimore, ML: Paul H. Brookes.

Stenhouse, L. (1975) *An Introduction to Curriculum Research and Development.* London: Heinemann.

Stoll, L., Fink, D. and Earl, L. (2003) *It's About Learning (and It's About Time): What's In It For School?* London: RoutledgeFalmer.

Swann, W. (1982) *Psychology and Special Education.* Unit E241. Milton Keynes: Open University Press.

Sytsma, S.E. (2006) 'It's About Time: Productive Pedagogues and Professional Learning Communities', *International Electronic Journal For Leadership in Learning,* 10, 12. (http://www.ucalgary.ca/~iejll)

Tallis, R. (2006) 'Targets Have Failed the NHS', *The Times,* COMMENT, p. 18, 10 August.

Tangen, T. (2005) 'Promoting Inclusive Education in Secondary School in Norway: A national programme for teacher development', *European Journal of Special Needs Education,* 20 (1): 57–70.

TDA (2005) Remodelling Tools. London: TDA Development. Accessed 12 December 2006, www.remodelling.org/remodelling/managingchange/tools.aspx.

The Times (1993) 'Unions Warn Teachers over Threat of False Abuse Claims', 29 January.

Thomas, G. (1997) 'Inclusive schools for an inclusive society', *British Journal of Special Education,* 24 (3): 103–7.

Thomas, G. and Vaughan, M. (2004) *Inclusive Education: Readings and Reflections.* Maidenhead: Open University Press.

Thomas, H., Butt, G., Fielding, A., Foster, J., Gunter, H., Lance, A., Pilkington, R., Potts, E., Powers, S., Rayner, S., Rutherford, D., Selwood, I. and Szwed, C. (2004) *The Evaluation of the Transforming the School Workforce Pathfinder Project.* Research Report 541. London: DfES.

Tilstone, T., Florian, L. and Rose, R. (eds) (1998) *Promoting Inclusive Practice.* London: Routledge.

Timperley, H.S. (2005) 'Distributed Leadership: Developing theory from practice', *Journal of Curriculum Studies,* 37 (4): 395–420.

Tomlinson, C.A. (1999) *Differentiated Classrooms: Responding to the Needs of All Learners.* Alexandria, VA: Association for Supervision and Curriculum Development.

Tomlinson, S. (1982) *A Sociology of Special Education.* London: Routledge and Kegan Paul.

Topping, K. and Maloney, S. (eds) (2005) *The RoutledgeFalmer Reader in Inclusive Education.* London: RoutledgeFalmer.

Turton, A. and Rayner, S. (forthcoming) 'Behaviour Intervention for a Student with Tourette's Syndrome (using peers as a support)', *Emotional and Behavioural Difficulties.*

Usher, R. and Bryant, I. (1989) *Adult Education as Theory, Practice and Research.* London: Routledge.

van Loon, J. (2006) 'Network', *Theory, Culture and Society,* 23 (2–3): 307–22.

Walker, A. and Walker, C. (eds) (1997) *Britain Divided: The Growth of Social Exclusion in the 1980s and 1990s.* London: CPAG.

Walters, B. (1994) *Management for Special Needs.* London: Cassell.

Wang, M.C. (1990) 'Learning characteristics of students with special needs and the provision of effective schooling', in M.C. Wang, C. Reynolds and H.J. Walberg (eds), *Special Education Research and Practice: Synthesis of Findings.* Oxford: Pergamon.

Warmington, P., Daniels, H., Edwards, A., Brown, S., Leadbetter, J., Martin, D. and Middleton, D. (2004) 'Interagency Collaboration: A review of the literature'. University of Bath: Learning in and for Interagency Working Project.

Warnock, M. (2005) *Special Educational Needs: A New Look.* London: Philosophy of Education Society of Great Britain.

Watkins, C. and Wagner, P. (2000) *Improving School Behaviour.* London: Paul Chapman.

Wenger, E. (1998) *Communities of Practice: Learning, Meaning and Identity.* Cambridge: Cambridge University Press.

West-Burnham, J. (1997) *Managing Quality in Schools* (2nd Edition). London: Financial Times.

Whiteley, P. (1993) 'Staff Concerned About Rise in Allegations', *Community Care,* 18 February.

Whittaker, M. (2004) 'School Leadership: Clued Up On Special Needs', *Times Educational Supplement,* 10 September, p. 31.

Wolger, J. (2005) 'The Tide has Turned: A case study of one inner city LEA moving towards inclusion', in K. Topping and S. Maloney (eds), *The RoutledgeFalmer Reader in Inclusive Education.* Abingdon: RoutledgeFalmer. pp. 205–218.

Zaretsky, L. (2005) *Inclusive Models Require Inclusive Theories.* Lecture, AERA Annual Conference, Montreal.

Zemelman, S. (1998) *Best Practice: New Standards for Teaching and Learning in America's Schools.* London: Heinemann.

Index